Feminism's Queer Temporalities

D1740451

Despite feminism's uneven movements, it has been predominantly understood through metaphors of generations or waves. *Feminism's Queer Temporalities* builds on critiques of the limitations of this linear model to explore alternative ways of imagining feminism's timing. It finds in feminism's literary and cultural archive narratives of temporality that might now be diagnosed as queer, where queer designates modes of being historical that exceed the linear and the generational.

Few theorists have looked to popular feminist figures, literature, and culture to theorize feminism's timing. Through methodologically creative readings, McBean explores non-generational, anti-linear, and asynchronous time in the figure of Antigone, Marge Piercy's *Woman on the Edge of Time*, the film *Ladies and Gentlemen, the Fabulous Stains*, Valerie Solanas and *SCUM Manifesto*, and Alison Bechdel's *Fun Home*.

The first to substantially bring together the ways in which time has come to matter in both feminist and queer disciplines, this book will appeal to students and scholars of feminist, queer and gender studies, cultural studies and literary studies.

Sam McBean is Lecturer in Modern and Contemporary American Literature at Queen Mary University of London. She has published on contemporary literature, new media, queer theory, and feminist theory in journals including *Feminist Review, Camera Obscura*, and the *Journal of Lesbian Studies*.

Transformations: Thinking Through Feminism
Edited by:

Maureen McNeil, Institute of Women's Studies, Lancaster University
Lynne Pearce, Department of English, Lancaster University

Other books in the series include:

Feminism's Queer Temporalities

Sam McBean

Routledge
Taylor & Francis Group

LONDON AND NEW YORK

First published 2016
by Routledge
2 Park Square, Milton Park, Abingdon, Oxon OX14 4RN

and by Routledge
711 Third Avenue, New York, NY 10017

First issued in paperback 2017

Routledge is an imprint of the Taylor & Francis Group, an informa business

British Library Cataloguing in Publication Data
A catalogue record for this book is available from the British Library

Library of Congress Cataloging in Publication Data
McBean, Sam.
Feminism's queer temporalities / Sam McBean.
pages cm. -- (Transformations : thinking through feminism)
Includes bibliographical references.
1. Feminist theory. 2. Feminist literature. 3. Feminism and mass media.
4. Queer theory. I. Title.
HQ1190.M384 2015
305.42--dc23
2015002395

ISBN 13: 978-1-138-48500-6 (pbk)
ISBN 13: 978-1-138-79365-1 (hbk)

Typeset in Times New Roman
by Taylor & Francis Books

Contents

List of figures

Acknowledgements

I want to take the time here to acknowledge the multiple people whose support, generosity, and friendship influenced not only the arguments in the book but fundamentally gave me the courage to make these arguments. The research for this book began when I was a PhD student in the English and Humanities Department at Birkbeck, University of London. First thanks need to go to my thesis supervisor, Heike Bauer. Thank you for always encouraging me to be two steps ahead of where I thought I was capable of being. I want to also thank the postgraduate community at Birkbeck for never making doing a PhD feel like a lonely pursuit. I had the particular privilege to work alongside some of the smartest people I know, Zara Dinnen, Bianca Leggett, and Holly Pester. I cannot imagine an academic life that does not include our never-ending email chains and as many brunches as we can stomach. I want to thank as well all of the participants in the Feminist Reading Group at the Institute of English Studies, and particular thanks go to Elsa Richardson for being an amazing co-organizer. This has been and continues to be one of my favourite spaces to test ideas, get things wrong, and revel in how fun feminism can be. It has been a vital space that pulls me out of my solitary pursuits and reminds me of the collective potential of academic feminism.

I want to thank the numerous individuals who, whether by reading early versions of this work or by just being there, were integral to this book's completion, including: Kate Atkinson, Simon Avery, Gianfranco Bettocchi, Jeanette Chua, Ellie Gore, Carly Guest, Victoria Hesford, Rahim Jamal, Lydia Malmedie, Ania Ostrowska, and Jessica Southgate. Special thanks go to Jackie Stacey for her intellectual rigour and her ongoing support as well as to Jane Elliott for her encouragement, her generosity, and her laugh. Sadie Wearing has been an ongoing source of support as a dissertation supervisor, then as a colleague, and now, as a friend.

I feel incredibly lucky to be able to be included in the *Transformations* series alongside preeminent scholars in the field. Lynne Pearce and Maureen McNeil have shown such faith in this project from the beginning and have been absolutely incredible to work with. Emily Briggs from Routledge has been a joy of an editor and the whole production team made the process much smoother than I could have imagined.

My students continue to remind me of the pleasures of learning and I want to thank them for giving me reasons to both put my research aside and keep at it. Special thanks go to the students on '21st Century Feminist Fiction and the World in Crisis' at Birkbeck, who worked through questions of feminism and crisis with me and particularly inspired my reading of Sarah Hall's *The Carhullan Army* in Chapter 2. I want to thank as well all the students I got to work with on the InterGender 'Queer Temporalities' course at the University of Gothenburg, who helped me think about the potentials and limitations of queer temporality theory.

Thanks also need to go to the friends who have never read a word of my writing and who exist outside of what sometimes feels like an academic vacuum. Thank you for the nights out, the dancing, and for reminding me that work is not everything – sometimes not even that important. I want to especially thank Lizzie Botfield, Joe Cohen, Jen Lexmond, Bridie Mahon, Sharon Shaw, Lydia Stober, and Zoe Palmer.

My parents, Pat and James, supported me through my first degree and had faith that a BA in Women's Studies might turn into some kind of future. I want to thank them for giving me the confidence to speak my mind. I want to thank as well my sister, Mandy, who is too far away yet whose own academic pursuits mean we can both share in the joys and trials of academic life. I want to thank her for trusting me with her work and for being on this journey alongside me.

Lastly, I thank Kate Graham for constantly distracting me with pictures of cats, bunnies, cats, drag queens, and cats. I do not want to ever have to navigate any of this without you.

I am grateful for the permission to include revised forms of previously published work. Parts of Chapter 1 were first published as 'Dragging Antigone: Feminist Revisions of Citizenship', in *Beyond Citizenship: Feminism and the Transformation of Belonging*, ed. Sasha Roseneil (Basingstoke and New York: Palgrave Macmillan, 2013); an earlier version of Chapter 2 first appeared as 'Feminism and Futurity: Revisiting Marge Piercy's *Woman on the Edge of Time*', *Feminist Review*, 107 (2014), 37–56; and a version of Chapter 5 appeared as 'Seeing in Alison Bechdel's *Fun Home*', *Camera Obscura: Feminism, Culture and Media Studies*, 28.3_84 (2013), 103–23.

Introduction

As an undergraduate at McGill University, I took the philosophy course, 'Introduction to Feminist Theory'.[1] It was my first module in feminism and I still remember the joy in having found it listed in my course handbook. As an introductory module, it deftly proceeded through liberal feminism, radical feminism, black feminism, the sex wars, and ended with postmodernism. This particular narrative of feminism is probably not surprising. Structured as such, the course moved through feminism's history, building a picture of not only key debates in feminism but also feminism's progress through time. Yet, despite this seemingly linear model that might seem to guarantee the present as having "moved on" from the past, the professor worked within this dominant frame to complicate its narrative effects. A skilled arguer, the professor would teach each class in staunch defense of whatever theorist was up for discussion that day. She would outline the theorists' presumptions, arguments, and supporting points, walking us through the logic of the work. Moreover, any questions or challenges posed of the text by the class would be carefully responded to approximating the particular thinker's reasoning and arguments. While this perhaps does not seem that unusual, the professor's refusal to step outside of each week's argument made the lessons incredibly striking. There was never a moment in which we were given a perspective, from the present, of how we were supposed to secure a final meaning for the theorist or argument in question.

Each class thus refused to deal with a particular text or idea as something that could be said to be over. This method of teaching, this immersion in particular feminist theoretical ideas, created an experience of feminism's timing that was not bound by the very markers through which it was structured. In other words, the course did not, in fact, allow any easy experience of progress or linear movement through feminism's history. Each week I struggled, and I imagine that many of my classmates struggled as well, to find a way to concretize feminist history and situate myself in relation to it. I wanted to know which perspective survived, which proved to be right, and where exactly we were in the feminist present. Yet, the persistent encouragement to identify with each week's argument troubled these desires. While each week seemed to move forward in feminist time, this move through time was anything but an easy move on. In considering each week's theoretical frame-work as still worthy of being accounted for, grappled with, and defended, the course created in me feelings of attachment to what are often understood as past moments. The course, while seemingly structured by a developmental model of feminism, refused to approach an archive of feminist thinking as settled, with its meaning secured, and closed off from the present. Through the professor's insistence each week on identifying with and defending specific theorists' arguments, the course traced through a history of feminist thought without making each week instrumental to the present – its emphasis on identification with various "pasts" in fact disrupted any easy understanding of the present. In some ways the course's structure reflected Sara Ahmed's arguments that an ethical relationship to feminism's histories *'takes time'*, where encountering feminism's multiplicities involves being open to an encounter with the past as that which still has life in the present.[2]

I think back now to this formative course in my feminist education as not only a lesson in the foundational frames or texts of feminist philosophy or feminism's academic history, but also as a lesson in feminism's timing. By "feminism's timing", I refer not to the entirety of feminism's decidedly uneven and disparate political and academic histories, but rather the way in which these multiplicities are experienced, understood, and managed. In particular, it was a lesson in what Robyn Wiegman describes as the difficulties of being 'in time' with feminism.[3] This difficulty arises, as Wiegman explains it, from the fact that feminism is 'a political and intellectual project that is itself his-torically transforming and transformative, and whose transformations are neither produced by nor wholly disengaged from the historical and psychic temporalities of the subjects who act in feminism's name'.[4] Feminism, in other words, does not cohere into a singular discourse, is not reducible to our own lifetimes or the lifetimes of any particular feminists, and its past cannot be solely understood as the grounds for the present.

Yet, despite this, feminism's time is overwhelmingly organized by and understood through one model, the generational. As Judith Roof explains, it is generations and their associated metaphors that have become the means 'by which feminist critics define feminist movements'[5] and Wiegman similarly agrees that the generational model of feminism has become the 'predominant model'.[6] This model, as Wiegman suggests, imagines feminism as linked to 'progressive understandings of time and indebted to reproduction as its implicit epistemology'.[7] The potentially limiting effects of this model became particu-larly apparent at the turn of the millennium, where it enabled a number of declarations of feminism's end. Around the turn of the twenty-first century, Lynne Segal expressed fears that feminism was losing its radical edge,[8] Susan Gubar declared that feminism was suffering from 'critical anorexia',[9] Cathryn Bailey stated that younger feminisms had failed to 'join their shovels to the backlash forces that would bury the history and significance of feminism',[10] and Martha Nussbaum worried that feminism had retreated from its presumably more effective 'old-style feminist politics'.[11] These images of anorexic, waning feminists digging their own graves (and those of other women) rely on the presumption that feminism moves linearly through time – so that the present is failed because it has failed to properly take up the causes, politics, theories, and energies of the past.[12] In other words, in their diagnoses of contemporary feminism's failure as a turn away from the tools, politics, and demands of the past, utterances of feminism's death rely on an understanding of feminism's timing that depends on a linear model of progress. This millennial moment made visible the dangers of the generational model and its potential for spinning feminism into a crisis, tying contemporary feminism to a particular relationship to an imagined better past that was perceived as having been lost in the present.

I begin this book then with the premise that how we think time matters. How we encounter, experience, or manage feminism's time, following Wiegman, 'has great bearing on the way we not only inhabit feminism as a contemporary politics but produce scholarship that speaks to the political desire for social change and futurity that we imbue with its name'.[13] As I hope my story about the 'Introduction to Feminist Theory' course illustrates, I am interested precisely in encountering feminism's unruly temporalities, in complicating the linear and the generational. If, overwhelmingly, feminism's timing has been managed as linear and generational, "queer" has recently come to represent an opposition to this "straight" model of time. Judith Halberstam, for instance, imagines how heterosexual life courses proscribe 'hetero temporalities', temporalities which queer bodies run askew of.[14] Elizabeth Freeman considers how queer temporalities pit themselves against the dominant order of time as 'seamless, unified, and forward moving', and instead 'are points of resistance to this temporal order that, in turn, propose other possibilities for living in relation to indeterminately past, present, and future others'.[15] Indeed, Lee Edelman's polemic *No Future* identifies as queer a refusal to accede to the 'telos of the social order' which privileges 'a fantasy of the future' through the figure of the Child.[16] These queer thinkers have thus opened up a number of ways of exploring the limitations of progressive and generational modes of time. I draw in this book on these queer theorists of temporality as a way to enable alternative connections and modes of being historical that exceed the linear and the generational. This book is interested in precisely narrating feminism's timing in queerer ways. Yet, I perform my own queerly temporal move by resisting imagining queer as the corrective to feminism. Rather than suggesting that feminism's timing needs to be "queered", I argue that what might now be recognizable as "queer temporalities" are located within feminism's literary and cultural archive.

Despite the dominance of narratives of feminism's timing as generational, it is my contention that queerer temporalities can easily be located. They can be read not in an obscure archive or experimental forms, but through the lens of the popular. These popular feminist texts, named as such for their repeated surfacing as sites for feminist creative output and critical attention, reveal models of feminism's timing as, drawing on recent queer theorizing, decidedly queer. I focus in particular on a theoretical, literary, and cultural archive which starts with feminism's entrance into Western academia – the decade of the 1970s – and continues into the early twenty-first century. I look in particular at myth, the utopian novel, riot grrrl subcultural production, and manifestos, with a fifth chapter turning to stake a feminist claim on a graphic narrative which has become canonized in and by queer theory. Despite the overwhelming narration of feminism's timing as linear, I explore in this book an archive which reveals a history of feminist conceptualizing of time as less linear and less generational. This exploration of an archive of what I will describe as feminism's queer temporalities, aims to contribute to thinking outside of the generational model in feminism by arguing that such models are readily available in feminism's own recent literary and cultural archive.

To situate this book's interventions, I start by considering how time has come to matter in both feminism and queer theory. While these bodies of thought have, for the most part, as Victoria Hesford argues, 'left each untouched and unnoticed by the other', I challenge this separation by including feminist literary and cultural production in queer temporality's archive.[17] I start by considering the feminist critiques of linear, generational models to build my argument for the necessity of encountering feminism's timing in more complex ways. I then consider recent work which follows on from these critiques to engage with feminism's archive outside of the proscriptive limitations of dominant models. This is followed by a consideration of time in queer theory. Tracing through queer theory's challenge to the linear and the generational, I argue that a queer commitment to temporality must challenge the notion that queer is a move "on" from feminism. Finally, I will outline in more depth this book's investment in its chosen archive, considering how a focus on time might open up new entry-points into feminism's recent archive – entry-points that side-step the generational model of feminism, resisting what Wiegman describes as 'stabilizing temporal formulations'.[18] Much like my first module in feminist theory performed for me the complexity of feminism's timing even as it proceeded through a generational narrative, this book uncovers models of temporality that are both contained within yet also exceed the already known.

Feminism and temporality

Elizabeth Grosz argues that 'concepts of time are relevant to and underlie many of the central projects of feminist theory'.[19] As Grosz outlines, key sites of feminist enquiry (including representation, subjectivity, identity, and sexuality), as well as debates over transformation and politics, 'all make assumptions about the relevance of history, the place of the present, and the forward-moving impetus directing us to the future'.[20] She explains that despite this, 'temporality is very rarely the direct object of analysis'.[21] As I have already suggested, I am particularly interested in a turn of the millennium context in which discussions of feminism's future placed time as an increasingly direct object of feminist analysis. However, I want to be clear that feminist theorizing of time both pre-exists and develops in different ways alongside this work. For instance, much earlier than the millennial crisis rhetoric, Julia Kristeva foregrounded the importance of temporality to feminist projects in 'Women's Time'.[22] Kristeva uses temporality to frame the question of whether women should fight to be included in or resist patriarchal structures: 'to situate the problematic of women in Europe within an inquiry on time: that time which the feminist movement both inherits and modifies'.[23] Kristeva argues that female subjectivity is traditionally linked to the timing of the domestic and the reproductive. This repetitive, cyclical time is, according to Kristeva, in opposition to the linear temporalities of history. Moreover, female subjectivity is not just the opposite of, but antagonistic to, 'time as project, teleology, linear and prospective unfolding; time as departure, progression, and arrival – in other words, the time of history'.[24] Kristeva goes on to narrate a history of feminist struggle as a relationship to time – so that feminism might be defined as either wanting to 'aspire to gain a place in linear time as the time of project and history' or to 'situate itself outside the linear time of identities'.[25] Through narrating the realm of culture and history as linear, progressive and the domestic or the private as circular, Kristeva imagines debates over inclusion or difference as a struggle with time.

Explorations of the gendering of time have continued to be a site of feminist concern, often framed through the question of national time. The field has been shaped and defined in part by the influential work of Inderpal Grewal and Caren Kaplan, Anne McClintock, and Chandra Mohanty.[26] McClintock, for instance, argues that in colonial discourse, women are represented as the 'atavistic and authentic body of national tradition (inert, backward-looking and natural) embodying nationalism's conservative principle of continuity', and men come to be the 'progressive agent of national modernity (forward thrusting, potent and historic) embodying nationalism's progressive or revolutionary principle of discontinuity'.[27] In McClintock's argument, colonial discourse both relies upon and propagates conceptions of temporality that position women on the side of tradition and men on the side of progress. As an outgrowth of these colonial discourses, recent uses of gender equality as a marker of development have necessitated further feminist interventions. Rosi Braidotti describes how the 'alleged "clash of civilizations" is postulated and fought out on women's bodies as bearers of authentic ethnic identity and as indicators of the stage of development of their respective civilisation fault-lines'.[28] Gender equality has become an important measure of a nation's development, so that feminism and feminist aims are now used to measure a country or culture's progress. This model too frequently functions, as Clare Hemmings explains, as a 'central mechanism for securing rather than challenging global inequality in the name of freedom'.[29]

This history of feminist critiques of the gendering of time and its national and transnational implications have inspired this book's concern for challenging generational models of time, as it is notions of progress that enable the production of value-coded concepts of development. Yet, this book's particular interest in the theme of temporality in feminism is situated more specifically in the wake of the abundance of narratives of feminism's progress that clustered around the turn of the century. Across numerous conferences, edited collections, and special issues of journals, feminism as an academic field was being assessed at the close of the millennium, often not particularly favourably.[30] While many of the stated aims were to assess feminism as a field, what became first apparent was that these narratives made a number of presumptions about feminism's timing.[31] As Hemmings convincingly demonstrates in *Why Stories Matter*, there is an overwhelming dominance in stories of feminism's recent history of one linear, decade-dividing temporality. While Hemmings points out that a number of different stories seem to circulate about contemporary feminism, she argues that the temporal structure of divided decades persists throughout and radically limits how feminism's complex history can be thought.[32] Moreover, as Wiegman has argued, millennial diagnoses of loss make certain presumptions not only about a "better" past but about the "correct" relationship that the present should have to this past. Wiegman argues that when feminism is claimed as having failed, 'failure is defined by measuring the present according to the ethos, intentions, and critical dimensions of a purportedly more active feminist past'.[33] In narratives of failure, the present is imagined as having failed to fulfil the political desires of the past – a presumption that the present is best understood as the future of the past. Over the following pages, I consider the critiques of generational models of time that came out of these turn-of-the-millennium conversations.[34]

In the first instance, this singular narrative obscures feminism's multiple histories and presents as well as creates Oedipal-like relations in the present. Kimberly Springer demonstrates for instance that the wave model 'perpetuates the exclusion of women of color from women's movement history and feminist theorizing'.[35] Springer argues, for example, that the wave model's description of the first and second waves ignores the role that race-based movements played as 'precursors, or windows of political opportunity, for gender activism'.[36] Moreover, transnational feminists, including Aili Mari Tripp, critique the wave model's Western centrism. Despite the common perception that the West spreads ideas about women's emancipation around the globe, feminism has moved in far more complicated ways and often in parallel, so that in different contexts, feminism has 'often had quite independent trajectories and sources of movement'.[37] Along with privileging a particular version of feminism, the wave model has also been accused of creating Oedipal-like relations, so that 'rebellious daughters' create their feminism at a distance from their feminist '(fore)mothers'.[38] Roof describes the way that generation is not an innocent model, as the reproductive familial narrative assumes a chronological time in which the past is presumed to directly inflect what comes later. This model of relating in time, argues Roof, 'reflects and exacerbates Oedipal relations and rivalries among women, relies on a patriarchal understanding of history and a linear, cause-effect narrative, and imports ideologies of property'.[39] This model affects the kinds of relationships that feminists can have with each other, creating, as Halberstam argues, 'women's studies professors who think of their students as "daughters"' and 'next wave feminists who see earlier activists as dowdy and antiquated mothers'.[40] In generational logic, difference is primarily attributed to generational thinking over and above political differences, and as Lisa Marie Hogeland argues, this psychologizes relationships between feminists and 'works to mask real political differences – fundamental differences in our visions of feminism's tasks and accomplishments'.[41]

Moreover, the generational model limits the kinds of futures that feminism might imagine. As Roof argues, generational narratives are written with the future in mind so that narratives of generational change:

> inscribe a past and a pattern of generational change as a way of trying to control the future, a future that will be sufficiently attentive to the past to go in the direction imagined by the past, fulfilling the past through precisely the reproductive dream that generations import in the first place.[42]

Halberstam similarly argues that the Oedipal dramas that so frequently accompany generational models of time 'snuff out the potential future of new knowledge formations'.[43] This vexed relationship to futurity is an effect of linear, generational narratives of feminist time which presume generational inheritance is the primary means through which feminism reproduces itself. As Wiegman points out, these narratives rely on and propagate an understanding of feminism's political time as one of continuity, so that narratives of feminism's failed present rely on an impoverished definition of feminism in requiring that feminism be 'self-identical' through time.[44]

Narratives that imagine feminism as moving linearly through time are also proscriptive about what feminism's proper objects of study should be. They frequently link progress or loss with ideas about the "correct" or "incorrect" objects of study or analysis. For instance, as Lisa Adkins demonstrates, the generational narratives of feminism's death that I refer to at the beginning of this introduction contain assumptions about feminism's relationship to the concept, woman. Adkins argues that millennial narratives of feminism's 'passing' not only rely on linear, generational time, but 'also operative in these accounts are hidden claims and assumptions regarding what the proper objects of feminism are, and should be, and the relationship of these objects to feminist subjectivity and feminist consciousness'.[45] When a younger generation of feminists are accused of not properly inheriting feminism, this is inextricable from pronouncements about what feminist criticism and feminist activism should look like. Adkins argues that feminists who do not reflect upon the material reality of woman as a knowable socio-empirical object and instead 'engage in critiques of earlier forms of feminism, or who have been engaged in abstract theoretical projects focusing on the inclusions and exclusions of identity, are castigated for their lack of politics and their failure to pass on'.[46] Narratives of feminism's passing thus presume a clear distinction between feminism as subject and its objects of study, binding models of feminism's timing to feminism's proper object of study. In other words, there is a disciplining that accompanies generational narratives so that they do more than close off feminism's history and relationship to time – they also limit and prescribe feminism as a field.[47]

As I have suggested already, what these criticisms of feminism's timing have made apparent is the need to challenge the disciplining effects of linear, generational narratives. Indeed, in response, a number of feminists have explored alternative conceptions of temporality. These alternative imaginings of feminism's timing resist imposing an already known future while also engage in complicated ways with the past as an ongoing site of contestation. Grosz is perhaps a leading voice here for her theorization of time's dynamism.[48] Rather than consider the linear predictability of generational narratives, Grosz aims to instantiate a concept of open futurity. She argues that feminist theory needs an account of time that can draw on the resources of the past yet 'which do[es] not tie us to the past in any definitive way or with any particular orientation and which provide[s] for us the very resources by which to supercede the past and the present – the very project of radical politics'.[49] If generational narratives seemingly dictate in advance what the future will look like, Grosz theorizes a concept of futurity that might not be determined by the past. In opposition to the disciplining of feminism's futurity, Grosz considers a future that is invested in 'the power of the leap, by which the actual emerges and produces itself from its virtual resources, that generates the surprise of the new'.[50]

While Grosz's work seemingly privileges the possibility of the new, there has also been an insistence that feminism's future depends, paradoxically, on resisting an orientation toward the future that would leave the past behind. Jane Elliott frames this as an argument for risking the 'genuine untimely' – suggesting that feminism might do well to resist the rhetoric of the new.[51] She argues that 'the production of the new as a signal intellectual value can be used to dismiss uncomfortable insights, which don't have to be disproved as long as they can be made to seem passé'.[52] This is an argument for a more nuanced and thus ethical relationship to the feminist past attainable only through a critical awareness of the ways that the past might not be over. Ahmed defines feminism as necessarily future-oriented, 'a politics that not only calls into question the way in which the world is organized in the present, but also seeks to transform how the world is organized and engender new ways and forms of living'.[53] However, she argues against a privileging of the future as 'the time of and for otherness' and instead suggests that 'it is through attending to the multiplicity of the pasts that are never simply *behind* us, through the traces they leave in the encounters we have in the present, that we can open up the promise of the "not yet"'.[54] In other words, Ahmed considers how our encounters in the present are never simply an encounter that is present.

While Ahmed's theorization of time comes from an ethics of encountering the other, Hemmings explores an approach to feminism's time through a practice of recitation.[55] This, for Hemmings, is a way of intervening into dominant narratives to uncover the other possible narratives that might exist. As her example, Hemmings takes Judith Butler's book *Gender Trouble*, which she argues is a key turning point in narratives of feminism in time. Traditionally narrated both as the book which precipitates queer and the first to challenge feminism's foundational category, "woman", the book has become a touchstone for a moment that is equally described as one of progress and one of loss. In her reading of the book, Hemmings returns to consider the effects of Butler's alignment with a male theoretical legacy and aims to recite Butler to different effect. Focused in particular on the oft-pairing of Butler with Michel Foucault, Hemmings argues that this pairing emphasizes Butler as belonging to a queer poststructuralist history. Hemmings deftly shows how this citational pairing matters to how feminism's narrative proceeds, and explores how a stronger focus on Butler's relationship to Monique Wittig complicates dominant narratives of feminism's history (notably the erasure of lesbian materialism). Through reciting Wittig – experimenting with what happens when Wittig is substituted for Foucault – Hemmings aims to 'reveal a lesbian materialist history to feminist poststructuralism and to reference a more complex feminist past, present, and future than existing narratives usually allow'.[56] In other words, recitation enables, for Hemmings, an 'imagining of feminist subjects as inheritors of contradictory legacies that cannot be resolved by a return to a fabricated past free of contest'.[57]

Work such as this opens up the past as something that is necessarily unfinished. The present, in other words, cannot be said to follow on in any clear way from the past. For some, this is also about recognizing the ongoing way that the feminist past is produced in the present. This is part of the underlying logic of Hesford's consideration of the women's liberation movement in *Feeling Women's Liberation*. She argues that this historical period in American feminism has 'largely been read as evidence of specific and coherent theoretical and ideological standpoints'.[58] Hesford resists narrating the movement in this way, suggesting instead that the movement was far more complex and continues to be an unsettled narrative in the present. In her book, she returns to the women's liberation movement as not a settled past moment but instead a series of conflicting politics and rhetoric that exceed the dominant narratives that are told about it. Refusing to narrate the women's liberation movement, Hesford explores its 'eventfulness' to both trouble dominant narratives and also insist on its ongoing production in the present.[59] Through this resistance to seeing the movement as a finished product, Hesford gets at what a linear, narrative approach to the movement obscures – that it is 'unfinished and beyond the capacity of any one story or account to know or apprehend it in the present'.[60] This is a means of conceptualizing feminism's history outside of generational models and instead insists on it as an unsettled narrative.

This book contributes to theorizing feminism's timing in ways that might engage with its complexities. However, I attempt this not through philosophical models, a focus on citation practices, or by turning to a particular moment in feminism's history. Instead, this book turns to an archive of feminist literary and cultural production that coexists with feminism's induction into the Western academy in the 1970s and proceeds to the early twenty-first century. Despite creative engagements with feminism's recent past, more accountable narratives of its complexity, and philosophically-guided models of time's openness, what has remained underexplored is the possibilities contained in the temporalities of popular texts, figures, and genres. In other words, I explore how these temporalities challenge linear models of time. These alternative temporalities are obscured, I suggest, when feminism's archive is approached through a generational model – where the literary and cultural outputs of the past are situated within their particular (and presumedly) known history. Before exploring this methodology in more depth, I consider this book's claims to queerness. To explore why feminist thinking on time has thus far remained separate from queer work I consider the very different disciplinary concerns that undergird queer theorizing of temporality. Despite these different concerns, I argue for the importance of thinking these two disciplines together. Temporality is a charged site for considering the relationship between feminism and queer. This is precisely because queer is frequently understood as the discipline or politics that is situated after feminism. I propose conversely that the queerest of temporalities might require more sustained dialogue between feminism and queer, resisting the teleology that would map queer as that which supersedes feminism.

Queer temporalities

A queer turn to temporality is now predominantly marked by the 2007 special issue of *GLQ*, 'Queer Temporalities'.[61] Included in this issue are a number of articles by leading thinkers in the field, as well as a roundtable discussion which outlines the contributors' various approaches to the question of time in queer theory. It is worth noting, however, that similar to how feminism's work on temporality preceded the millennial crisis rhetoric and has evolved in a number of directions, there are significant problems which might be raised by beginning queer theory's temporality genealogy here. As Elizabeth Freeman insists in her introduction to *Time Binds*, time has always been a dominant concern in queer theory. Referencing the focus on the archive in Michel Foucault, the figure of the child in Eve Sedgwick, as well as Douglas Crimp's work on mourning and Cherríe Moraga's *Giving Up the Ghost*, Freeman argues that questions of time and the affects of historical enquiry have a long history in queer theory.[62] Moreover, as Edelman argues in the *GLQ* roundtable, framing the discussion as a recent "turn" makes presumptions about time's historical procession 'obedient to origins, intentions, and ends whose authority rules over all'.[63] This, as Ben Davies and Jana Funke point out, imagines that 'time is something that we are in the process of discovering as opposed to something that allows us to anticipate its discovery in the first place'.[64] Moreover, as I have argued elsewhere, such "turn" rhetoric not only potentially obscures histories of concerns with time in queer theory, but also, in its apparent inauguration of a new field, makes it difficult to consider links between queer theory and histories of postcolonial, critical race, and feminist work.[65]

In some ways, queer, formulated as a deconstructionist project, is inherently linked to a temporality of disruption. In *Tendencies*, Sedgwick uses queer to refer to 'the open mesh of possibilities, gaps, overlaps, dissonances and resonances, lapses and excesses of meaning when the constituent elements of anyone's gender, of anyone's sexuality aren't made (or *can't be* made) to signify monolithically'.[66] A queer approach is thus attentive to gaps and slippages; it is attuned to the failure of the norm – for Edelman, it 'can never define an identity; it can only ever disturb one'.[67] In this, queer is a radical project of resistance, acquiring meaning, as David Halperin explains, 'from its oppositional relation to the norm'.[68] This refusal to signify makes queer "work", as Carolyn Dinshaw explains, 'by contiguity and displacement, knocking signifiers loose, ungrounding bodies, making them strange'.[69] This makes queer a project that is always on the move, refusing to settle in meaning, and drawing its oppositional strength from this refusal. As Butler argues, queer's ability to be oppositional requires that it 'will have to remain that which is in the present, never fully owned, but always and only redeployed, twisted, queered from a prior usage and in the direction of urgent and expanding political purposes'.[70]

This conception of queerness as opposed to an identity, as a mode of becoming, has been translated differentially to argue that queer is definitively future-oriented as well as staunchly opposed to the future. For instance, in the work of Halberstam, queer subjects figure the possibility of temporalities that run opposed to the heteronormativity of reproductive time. Halberstam suggests that 'queer lives exploit some potential for a *difference in form* that lies dormant in queer collectivity not as an essential attribute of sexual otherness but as a possibility embedded in the break from heterosexual life narratives'.[71] In other words, queer lives open up other kinds of temporalities and suggest the possibility of different modes of living. Similarly, José Esteban Muñoz argues that queer is precisely what brings the future into being. For Muñoz, queer is 'a structuring and educated mode of desiring that allows us to see and feel beyond the quagmire of the present'.[72] In a utopian register, Muñoz explains that queerness 'is a longing that propels us onward, beyond romances of the negative and toiling in the present'.[73] However, queer's refusal to signify has also been imagined as a refusal of futurity. This position, which could be described as theorizing temporality through the antisocial strand of queer theory, has been vocalized most forcefully by Edelman in *No Future*.[74] Edelman takes up the characterization of queerness as backward or a bar to the future to argue that the queerest politics would not challenge this characterization but instead would resist the desire to be enfolded into the timing of the future.[75] Emphasizing that the governing temporality of normative politics is 'reproductive futurism', the queer, for Edelman, is outside of this dominant political narrative that privileges a 'viable political future' or the 'fantasy of meaning's eventual realization'. Instead, 'the queer comes to figure the bar to every realization of futurity, the resistance, internal to the social, to every social structure or form'.[76]

If a strand of recent work in feminism concerned with temporality has come in part as a response to millennial narratives of feminism's failed future, a dominant strand of queer temporality work responds to the notion that queer subjects do not have a past, or are without history. This traditional erasure of queer sexuality from history produces, as Dinshaw argues, 'a queer desire for history'.[77] Yet, as Valerie Rohy argues, gay and lesbian history has been disciplined by the imperative to resist ahistoricizing sexuality and desire – an imperative that seemingly denies the possibility of queer continuity or connections across time periods. In response to this, more recent queer historiography has experimented with creative methodologies that might, as Rohy describes her own approach, be attentive to historical specificity, but 'does not demand a defense of an authentic past against the violation of backwardness'.[78] This queer work has focused on contingent connections, bodily experiences of history, and an affective approach to the past that might make queer connections across time. For Dinshaw, the 'queerly historical' questions moments when the 'past touches the present'.[79] In Heather Love's *Feeling Backward*, this becomes a resistance to progress narratives of gay and lesbian history and instead an exploration of the affective hold that the damaged past retains on queer presents. This, for Love, is what is queer about historiography – a refusal to put the past to 'good use'.[80] Dana Luciano similarly describes as queer a historiography which asks 'what it means to think history as something other than a linear chronology, a public record of steady "progress" enabled and stabilized by the domestic-familial reproduction of successive generations'.[81]

While the rich explorations of time and history that have come out of queer thinking have enabled creative and affective engagements with the past and with the asynchronies of the present, its limitations have also been voiced. One critique, as outlined by Davies and Funke, is a focus on the exceptionality of queer time, imagined as oppositional to so-called straight time.[82] Perhaps this emphasis on oppositional temporality is one of the reasons that queer scholars who explore how gay and lesbian sexuality has become integral to the production of US exceptionalism are not traditionally enfolded into the "turn" to queer temporalities. For example, Jasbir K. Puar and Butler both consider how the asynchronous present becomes value-coded through sexuality.[83] Expanding on Lisa Duggan's 'homonormativity',[84] which names the ways in which lesbian and gay culture have become normalized under human rights discourse and neoliberalism, Puar explores how queerness 'colludes with U.S. exceptionalisms embedded in national foreign policy via the articulation and production of whiteness as a queer norm and the tacit acceptance of U.S. imperialist expansion'.[85] Puar thus considers how queerness might not be 'exclusively as dissenting, resistant, and alternative (all of which queerness importantly is and does)' and instead she 'underscores [queerness's] contingency and complicity with dominant formations'.[86] In the register of historiography, a further effect of this privileging of the oppositional queer has been outlined by Hesford, who suggests that '[t]he queer desire for history' be understood 'as a practice of producing loving attachments to what has often remained marginal or discarded in the writing of history'.[87] This desiring approach to the past, 'while capable of generating archives that can be world and community making in the present, tends to elide or downplay the implicatedness of any putatively queer history in cultural and social regimes of normalization'.[88] In other words, a desiring look back might not be able to account for that which is undesirable and less queer.[89]

Whether due to separate disciplinary concerns or to queer's privileging of a particular notion of opposition, queer and feminist work on theorizing temporality has remained remarkably separate. Notably, one of the few works that does bring together feminism with queer time is Freeman's. Sceptical of the deconstructive impulse of queer theory that would pit queerness as that which is always ahead, Freeman instead explores what it might mean to be 'warmed by the afterglow of the forgotten'.[90] Rather than considering queer as 'always ahead of existing social possibilities', she argues that queer might instead 'trail behind actual existing social possibilities: to be interested in the tail end of things, willing to be bathed in the fading light of whatever has been declared useless'.[91] This conception of queer enables her to consider how what is supposedly past has queer potential in its ability to disrupt the present tense – queerness here is about 'mining the present for signs of undetonated energy from past revolutions'.[92] The chapter of her book that deals in particular with feminism considers how contemporary subjects might drag the lesbian feminist past in ways that disrupt the coherence of the queer present in their articulation of 'a kind of *temporal* transitivity that does not leave feminism, femininity, or other "anachronisms" behind'.[93] Freeman thus considers how the relics of feminisms' unfinished past might productively drag on the queer present. However, as Hesford has convincingly shown, even Freeman ends by leaving behind the lesbian feminist. While beginning with an interest in the figure of the lesbian feminist, Freeman shifts her interest to the 'not-yet-identified', or the moment before women's liberation becomes a 'completed movement'.[94] It is precisely then the not-yet-lesbian-feminist, not the lesbian feminist, that Freeman settles on as the most disruptive to our historical categories and sense of the present. Hesford argues that this move, 'while opening up the pastness of the pre-women's movement moment to the queer present, enacts a further stabilization of *radical feminism* and *lesbian feminism*'.[95] Women's liberation becomes a moment that is skipped over.

Temporality, I suggest, is thus a charged frame for considering the relationship between feminism and queer. While queer theory historically emerged after feminism, there has been contestation about exactly how to understand feminism's historical antecedence. Queer theory's emergence is often seen as reactionary to the kinds of identity-based politics that feminism seemingly depends upon, potentially making feminism incompatible with queer – irrevocably in the past, stuck to identity politics. The ground for the emergence of queer as a conceptual tool is often seen as the gradually experienced insufficiency of identity categories to fully capture and critique actual social experience, so that queer theory is defined as antithetical to feminism as a supposed identity-based knowledge formation. Indeed, some have argued that the field-defining claims of queer have depended upon false characterizations of feminism as only focused on gender identity politics.[96] In opposition, there have been calls for more complex accounts of feminist theorizing of sexuality, as well as its anti-identitarian strands.[97] It is precisely the temporal tensions that exist in the relationship between feminism and queer that motivate this book's aims to bring into queer temporality theory a number of feminist literary and cultural texts. In other words, I argue that feminism's late twentieth- and early twenty-first-century archive contains a number of explorations of temporality which we might now label as queer. In this book's investment in bringing feminist and queer time together, I resist what Annamarie Jagose describes as 'the temporal disciplining of feminist from queer thought that stages them as the before and after of some narrative of critical advancement'.[98] This is to insist that feminism is more than queer theory's precursor and is instead its 'present-tense interlocutor'.[99]

The popular in feminism

This book responds both to recent calls for non-generational models of feminist time as well as to queer explorations of experiences and methodologies of untimeliness or asynchrony. I offer a number of readings of feminism's recent popular archive as a way to suggest that alternative, queer models of time are readily available in this archive, while simultaneously suggesting that this archive expands the remit of queer temporality. In both feminist and queer theorizing of time there has been a lack of consideration of feminist literary and cultural output. Thus far, as should be clear from my summarizing of the field, feminist work on time has overwhelmingly focused on institutionalization and more academic critiques. Most notable here are Hemmings' aforementioned mapping of citation practices and Wiegman's archive of thinking, including her most recent book *Object Lessons*.[100] On the other hand, queer work on temporality has tended to focus on avant-garde and experimental cultural forms and practices. For example, Freeman's work turns to contemporary experimental video art, Love's to an archive of modernist literature, and Muñoz's to performance art. Counter to these approaches in feminism and queer theory, this book aims to make claims about feminism's queer timing by turning to popular figures and texts in feminism.

First, a note on the popular in feminism. Historically, there has been scepticism in feminism toward the popular, where popular genres (and the women who consume them) have often been positioned as counter to feminist politics and feminist subjects, associated as they are with mass-mediated femininity. Canonical approaches to the popular in feminism, including Tania Modleski's *Loving With a Vengeance* and Janice Radway's *Reading the Romance*, have thus been motivated by a desire to both explain and critically understand its appeal.[101] These two books were some of the first to resist dismissing popular culture and instead take the pleasures of popular genres (soaps, Gothic novels, and romance novels) seriously. As Ien Ang explains it in relation to the romance genre, '[t]he enormous popularity of romantic fiction with women has always presented a problem for feminism'.[102] Understanding the problem of the popular continues in more recent work, including Lauren Berlant's ongoing work on sentimentality in American culture and specifically her study of "women's culture". Berlant argues that 'gender-marked texts of women's popular culture cultivate fantasies of vague belonging as an alleviation of what is hard to manage in the lived real – social antagonisms, exploitation, compromised intimacies, the attrition of life'.[103] In other words, Berlant considers what is offered by mass cultural genres, interested in how these genres produce a worldview in which 'people's interests are less in changing the world than in not being defeated by it, and meanwhile finding satisfaction in minor pleasures and major fantasies'.[104]

More recently, the turn to postfeminism as a critical concept, a popular sensibility, or a defining feature of contemporary media, has further complicated the popular in feminism. The lens of postfeminism has been a dominant way in which the contemporary mediascape has been both characterized and critically approached in feminist media and cultural studies. Notably, postfeminism is a term which aims to frame popular media's timing in relation to feminism. In other words, contemporary mass culture is overwhelmingly considered for its apparent positioning as after feminism – where postfeminist becomes a declaration of death and, predominantly, understood as an attack. For example, Yvonne Tasker and Diane Negra define postfeminism as a set of assumptions within popular media about the pastness of feminism.[105] Angela McRobbie similarly understands postfeminism as that which 'positively draws on and invokes feminism as that which can be taken into account, to suggest that equality is achieved, in order to install a whole repertoire of new meanings which emphasise that it is no longer needed, it is a spent force'.[106] This feminist history of considering the desires, attachments, and effects of popular culture as well as the more recent questions about feminism's undoing in the popular realm, makes a turn to the queer temporalities of the popular a perhaps strange move.

However, my interest is not so much in popular culture at large, but in exploring what is popular in feminism. By popular, I mean to highlight that the focus of this book is not on obscure cultural texts or experimental mediums. Refusals of linear narratives of time are not a niche subset of feminist literary and cultural production but are, I argue, central to those figures, texts, and genres which seem to have a hold on what might be described as feminism's imaginary. I am interested not so much in a particular narrative, a critical term, or a concept, but a number of texts, genres, and figures that I am suggesting are continued sites of interest and return in feminism. They all retain a certain stickiness – they continue to be objects of feminist interest, culture, and critical theory. This is to suggest that there are places that feminists continue to return to, perhaps suggesting that what is popular has not only political but possibly an affective value. Indeed, following Ahmed, we might suggest that an object circulates in feminism primarily because of its affective value, through the desires that become attached to what it might do. In this way, emotions circulate through the circulation of objects – '[s]uch objects become sticky, or saturated with affect, as sites of personal and social tension'.[107] I am interested in what sticks in feminism both out of an interest in the temporality of "being stuck" as well as for what kinds of temporalities these sites offer. Indeed, I am interested in what temporal concerns stick across a range of different popular genres, texts, and figures. This is a tracing of recurrent temporal forms, or perhaps resistances to certain temporalities, that exist across my case studies. In other words, it is possible to consider a questioning of linear temporality as a formal preoccupation across a number of popular sites in feminism. Despite the overwhelming dominance of generational models of telling feminism's time, the returns to these literary and cultural sites, sites which challenge singular notions of the present, settled understandings of the past, and knowable futures, evidence an ongoing investment in time otherwise conceived.

Across a range of different forms, I uncover a repeated investment in disrupting linear, generational time. Each of my case studies begins from an exploration of literary and cultural sites that have inspired continued return in feminism – myth, the utopian novel, riot grrrl, and manifestos. In each case, there is a wealth of feminist revision, academic attention, and cultural production around these sites. As a whole, I aim for a larger argument about what crosses these genres, historical periods, and mediums. All of the texts I have chosen are about time, meaning that each chapter is structured around a literary or cultural text that I read as itself intervening into linear time. In turning to this particular archive, I argue that assertions about the need for more complex modes of feminist timing need not only challenge the generational model through addressing its shortcomings or providing corrective readings, just as queer temporality need not only be found in an avant-garde archive of queer cultural production or theory. Feminist literary and cultural sites not only provide examples of the insufficiency of linear models of feminism's time but can also be read for the alternative, queer models that they sketch out. This, again, is distinct from suggesting that feminism's archive might be queered, and is instead an argument for the queer temporalities of feminism's archive. This is an integral distinction because whilst feminism's timing has predominantly been narrated through the linear or the generational, and queer has recently been theorized as precisely that which is counter to the generational and the linear, I resist this dichotomous relationship. I achieve this through exploring how my chosen case studies imagine temporality outside of or in resistance to the dominant, the linear, and the generational. In other words, this feminist archive speaks very clearly to contemporary queer theorizing of time.

This also similarly speaks to contemporary feminist desires to consider ways of approaching feminism's timing outside of the linear and the generational. Claire Colebrook argues for a kind of feminist timing that might resist approaching its archive through some idea of what the past was, but which 'reads each text again not according to the time within which it occurred but to a time it might enable'.[108] Reading feminist literary and cultural texts through what we think we might know about the time in which they were created keeps these texts at a distance from the present. Indeed, this strategy ensures that feminism's archive remains meaningful only in and to an imagined past. This book argues for turns to feminism's past which consider the possibility that these pasts might not be left for dead but might instead travel into various feminist presents. Critiques and challenges to the generational and wave models in feminism are by now well-rehearsed, yet the effects of these critiques for feminist literary and cultural theory require further exploration. This book considers what it means to resist generational approaches to texts – or indeed to presume that a text's meaning lies in what it can tell us about its particular moment. I argue throughout this book that the temporal possibilities of the literary and the cultural have yet to be foregrounded in explorations of time in feminism. I resist reading my chosen texts for what they reveal about a particular moment in feminism and, instead, I approach these texts for what kinds of temporalities they might open up for feminism.

The chapters

In each chapter I explore the popularity of a particular object in feminist theory, literature, and culture. This book starts with an exhaustive, but forever incomplete, tracking of Antigone through feminism. I argue that the continued return to the so-called mythic past of Antigone be read as a feminist practice of refusing to settle. Antigone has been one of the most popular mythic figures in feminism and the first chapter explores how Antigone's popularity might be an effect of the temporality that she offers various feminists. While the burial of her brother in defiance of the king's edict – traditionally read as Antigone speaking from the private against the public – has been an inspiration to many feminists, this chapter suggests that it is not this act but Antigone's timing that has made her such a key figure in feminist thinking. The chapter thus reads the persistence of Antigone in feminist theory, creating a transdisciplinary archive of feminist investment in unsettling the present. In this, I bring together feminist political theory, modernist fiction, French feminist theory, and queer theory to demonstrate that despite their very different historical moments, arguments, and formal writing strategies, Antigone remains a popular site for questioning the inevitability of the present through unsettling the past.

Chapter 2 turns to the feminist utopian novel and considers the critical implication of the genre's traditional framing as the fictional counterpart to 1970s feminist criticism. I suggest that the tendency to read 1970s feminist utopias through this historicizing frame has meant that certain temporal dimensions of the genre have been critically underexplored. Through focusing on a reading of Marge Piercy's canonical *Woman on the Edge of Time*, this chapter explores how the novel's conception of temporality in fact counters the dominant reading strategy that would house the text within its historical moment. I draw out a reading of the text that foregrounds the themes of mourning and loss as constitutive of the protagonist Connie's relationship with the future utopia. The emphasis on mourning and loss as productive of Connie's future challenges any simple distinctions between pasts and futures. As such, I suggest that the novel speaks to contemporary feminist concerns about the future as a lost tense in feminism and advances a model of futurity that develops out of rather than in opposition to past losses. Moreover, I also bring a queer reading to the novel's exploration of time travelling as a touching between two women, bridging a gap between the feminist 1970s and contemporary queer theory.

Chapter 3 takes as its focus riot grrrl subculture from the 1990s through a reading of the film *Ladies and Gentlemen, the Fabulous Stains*. Situating the chapter within a recent archive of contemporary remembrances of the riot grrrl movement, I suggest that such remembering offers a timely case study for considering what it means to turn back to recent feminist history. I consider how this turn back is often linked to contemporary subjects' own pasts – so that riot grrrl comes to have a causal effect on contemporary feminist speakers. I resist this "then" and "now" structure, and the linearity it implies, by focusing on what did not happen. Despite being enveloped into riot grrrl cultural history, *The Fabulous Stains* predates the subculture by at least a decade and narrates the fall of the all-girl band, The Stains. Through this film, I consider an approach to riot grrrl that foregrounds temporal rebellion, arguing that the film be read as a refusal of models of heterosexual narrative time which insist on growing up as being equivalent to growing into certain heterosexual norms. Finally, I offer a reading of female fandom that might see it as an alternative growth – a challenge to linear forward movement through time with community-building in the present.

In Chapter 4, I consider Valerie Solanas and her *SCUM Manifesto*. Similar to Piercy's *Woman on the Edge of Time*, Solanas' manifesto and Solanas as a figure have been overly-attached to a particular moment in feminist time, namely the radical feminist past. The chapter explores the popularity of Solanas as an iconic figure and argues that engagements with Solanas as a figure are frequently invested in either claiming her as the archetypal radical feminist or arguing that she exceeds the definitional boundaries of the historical moment of second wave feminism. Resistant to this approach, this chapter considers how Solanas might open up a model of queer feminist futurity. This chapter reframes Solanas' timing away from questions of historical absence or presence in second wave feminism through focusing instead on the timing of the manifesto. Attention to the generic form of the feminist manifesto moves Solanas outside of questions about historical periodization and productively renews engagements with the key questions of the manifesto itself – namely how to generate a future in the present.

The final chapter looks at a more contemporary text to consider claims to its queer temporalities. Centrally concerned with Alison Bechdel's *Fun Home*, I consider how the narrative has been overwhelmingly embraced in queer historiography and queer theory. However, despite (or perhaps because of) this popularity, there has been little work which considers the narrative's feminist debts. Drawing on the image/text relationship of graphic narratives, I argue that a focus on the visual in Bechdel's graphic narrative requires a feminist analysis. In other words, the queer historiographic quality of the novel cannot be separated from its emphasis on the partiality of vision as an embodied practice. Close readings of scenes in the novel highlight the importance of vision and produce an argument for the way that *Fun Home* must be read not only in relation to histories of graphic novels or queer historiography, but also feminist debates on the role of vision in the constitution of sexuality and knowledge production.

This book builds on recent critiques of generationality and linearity from both feminist and queer theory to explore alternative temporalities in feminism's literary and cultural archive. Moreover, I suggest that feminism's archive contributes to contemporary queer and feminist theorizing of time – so that these objects might be understood as theoretical arguments themselves, objects which contribute to challenging generational logic and exploring asynchrony, temporal displacement, open futurity, and unsettled relationships to the past. Freeman describes as her 'queerest commitment' the close reading of a small number of texts – 'the decision to unfold, slowly, a small number of imaginative texts rather than amass a weighty archive of or around texts, and to treat these texts and their formal work as theories of their own'.[109] This book, structured as a number of case studies, is limited in its chosen texts and relies on close reading. Yet, similar to Freeman, I consider how these texts might be read as theories of their own, theories which destabilize and disturb the dominant model of feminism's timing. By working across forms, time periods, and genres, this book builds an archive of feminist timing – one not limited to a particular moment, genre, or figure. This seemed imperative to me as a way to counter the dominance of the singular model of generational time. To counter the dominance of the singular narrative of feminism's timing as linear and generational, this book offers a number of queer narratives. Indeed, it is my aim to begin conversations which widen approaches to feminism's temporality, to create an archive of feminist literary and cultural production which imagines temporality's queerness. This book began because I wanted to find models of time that exceeded the generational – the pre-dominance of this narrative, for me, needed unsticking. It is my hope that through a focus on what sticks, what remains popular in feminism, this book might offer a number of new ways in to thinking about time and feminism, revealing feminism's queer temporalities.

Notes

1 I took the module in September 2003 and at the time it was taught by Professor Marguerite Deslauriers.
2 Sara Ahmed, 'This Other and Other Others', *Economy and Society*, 31.4 (2002), 558–72 (p. 559, emphasis in original).
3 Robyn Wiegman, 'On Being in Time with Feminism', *Modern Language Quarterly*, 65.1 (2004), 161–76 (p. 163).
4 Wiegman, 'On Being in Time', p. 163.
5 Judith Roof, 'Generational Difficulties; or, The Fear of a Barren History', in *Generations: Academic Feminists in Dialogue,* ed. Devoney Looser and E. Ann Kaplan (Minneapolis and London: University of Minnesota Press, 1997), pp. 69–87 (p. 70).
6 Robyn Wiegman, 'Feminism's Apocalyptic Futures', *National Women's Studies Association Journal*, 14.2 (2000), 805–25 (p. 811).
7 Wiegman, 'On Being in Time', p. 165.
8 Lynne Segal, 'Only Contradictions on Offer', *Women: A Cultural Review*, 11.1–2 (2000), 19–36.
9 Susan Gubar, 'What Ails Feminist Criticism?', *Critical Inquiry*, 24.4 (1998), 878–902 (p. 901).
10 Cathryn Bailey, 'Making Waves and Drawing Lines: The Politics of Defining the Vicissitudes of Feminism', *Hypatia*, 12.3 (1997), 17–28 (p. 27).
11 Martha Nussbaum, 'The Professor of Parody', *The New Republic*, 220.116 (1999), 37–45, (p. 38).
12 This argument is explored in some depth in Wiegman, 'Feminism's Apocalyptic Futures'; Lisa Adkins, 'Passing on Feminism: From Consciousness to Reflexivity?', *European Journal of Women's Studies*, 11.4 (2004), 427–44.
13 Wiegman, 'On Being in Time', p. 164.
14 Carolyn Dinshaw and others, 'Theorizing Queer Temporalities Roundtable', *GLQ: Journal of Lesbian and Gay Studies*, 13.2–3 (2007), p. 182.
15 Elizabeth Freeman, *Time Binds: Queer Temporalities, Queer Histories* (Durham, NC and London: Duke University Press, 2010), p. xxii.
16 Lee Edelman, *No Future: Queer Theory and the Death Drive* (Durham, NC and London: Duke University Press, 2004), p. 11.
17 Victoria Hesford, *Feeling Women's Liberation* (Durham, NC: Duke University Press, 2013), p. 6.
18 Wiegman, 'On Being in Time', p. 164.
19 Elizabeth Grosz, *Time Travels: Feminism, Nature, Power* (Durham, NC and London: Duke University Press, 2005), p. 1.
20 Ibid.
21 Ibid.
22 While an important foundational piece of feminist thinking on temporality, this work has been critiqued for its linkage of female subjectivity with the maternal. See, for instance, Judith Butler, *Gender Trouble* (New York and London: Routledge, 1990), pp. 79–92; Gerardine Meaney, *(Un)Like Subjects: Women, Theory, Fiction* (New York: Routledge, 1993); Jacqueline Rose, 'Julia Kristeva – Take

Two', in *Ethics, Politics, and Difference in Julia Kristeva's Writing*, ed. Kelly Oliver (New York: Routledge, 1993), pp. 179–83.

23 Julia Kristeva, 'Women's Time', *Signs: Journal of Women in Culture and Society*, 7.1 (1981), 13–35 (p. 15).

24 Ibid., p. 17.

25 Ibid., p. 18; p. 19.

26 Inderpal Grewal and Caren Kaplan, eds, *Scattered Hegemonies: Postmodernity and Transnational Feminist Practices* (Minneapolis and London: University of Minnesota Press, 1994); Anne McClintock, *Imperial Leather: Race, Gender, and Sexuality in the Colonial Contest* (New York and London: Routledge, 1995); Chandra Talpade Mohanty, *Feminism Without Borders: Decolonizing Theory, Practicing Solidarity* (Durham, NC and London: Duke University Press, 2003). See also Victoria Hesford and Lisa Diedrich, eds, *Feminist Time Against Nation Time: Gender, Politics, and the Nation-State in an Age of Permanent War* (London and Plymouth: Lexington Books, 2008); Betty Joseph, 'Gendering Time in Globalization: The Belatedness of the Other Woman and Jamaica Kincaid's *Lucy*', *Tulsa Studies in Women's Literature*, 21.1 (2002), 67–83.

27 McClintock, pp. 358–59.

28 Rosi Braidotti, 'Learning from the Future', *Australian Feminist Studies*, 24.59 (2009), 3–9 (p. 6).

29 Clare Hemmings, *Why Stories Matter: The Political Grammar of Feminist Theory* (Durham, NC and London: Duke University Press), p. 11.

30 A number of key publications and responses include: Wendy Brown, 'The Impossibility of Women's Studies', *differences: A Journal of Feminist Cultural Studies*, 9.3 (1997), 79–101; Devoney Looser and E. Ann Kaplan (eds), *Generations: Academic Feminists in Dialogue* (Minneapolis: University of Minnesota Press, 1997); Segal, 'Only Contradictions on Offer'; Robyn Wiegman, 'Feminism, Institutionalism, and the Idiom of Failure', *differences: A Journal of Feminist Cultural Studies*, 11.3 (1999), 107–36; Robyn Wiegman, 'Academic Feminism Against Itself,' *NWSA Journal*, 14.2 (2002), 18–37; Robyn Wiegman (ed.), *Women's Studies on Its Own: A Next Wave Reader in Institutional Change* (Durham, NC: Duke University Press, 2003); *differences: A Journal of Feminist Cultural Studies*, Special Issue: Women's Studies on the Edge, 9.3 (1997).

31 See for instance the conversation between Susan Gubar and Robyn Wiegman: Gubar, 'What Ails Feminist Criticism?'; Susan Gubar, 'Notations in *Media Res*', *Critical Inquiry*, 25.5 (1999), 380–96; Robyn Wiegman, 'What Ails Feminist Criticism? A Second Opinion', *Critical Inquiry*, 25.2 (1999), 107–36. See also Adkins, 'Passing on Feminism'; Rebecca Coleman and Debra Ferreday (eds), Special Issue: Hope and Feminist Theory, *Journal for Cultural Research*, 14.4 (2010); Margaret Ferguson, 'Special Issue: Feminism in Time', *Modern Language Quarterly*, 65.1 (2004); Holly Laird (ed.), Special Issue: Feminism and Time, *Tulsa Studies in Women's Literature*, 21.1 (2002).

32 Hemmings, p. 5.

33 Wiegman, 'Feminism's Apocalyptic Futures', p. 807.

34 This is not to say that there have not been some arguments for the productivity of the concept of generations in feminism. For an exploration of the potential use of generational models, see Iris van der Tuin, '"Jumping Generations": On Second- and Third-Wave Feminist Epistemology', *Australian Feminist Studies*, 24.59 (2009), 17–31. Or, for a consideration of how generational antagonism might be productive in and for feminism, see Sianne Ngai, *Ugly Feelings* (Cambridge, MA: Harvard University Press, 2005), Chapter 3.

35 Kimberly Springer, 'Third Wave Black Feminism?', *Signs: Journal of Women in Culture and Society*, 27.4 (2002), 1059–82 (p. 1063).

36 Ibid., p. 1061.

37 Aili Mari Tripp, 'The Evolution of Transnational Feminisms: Consensus, Conflict, and New Dynamics', in *Global Feminism: Transnational Women's Activism, Organizing, and Human Rights*, ed. Myra Marx Ferree and Aili Mari Tripp (New York and London: New York University Press, 2006), pp. 51–75 (p. 52). See also Shu-Mei Shih, 'Towards an Ethics of Transnational Encounter, or "When" Does a "Chinese" Woman Become a "Feminist"?', *differences: A Journal of Feminist Cultural Studies*, 13.2 (2002), 90–126.

38 Astrid Henry, *Not My Mother's Sister: Generational Conflict and Third-Wave Feminism* (Bloomington: Indiana University Press, 2004).

39 Roof, 'Generational Difficulties', p. 71.

40 Judith Halberstam, *The Queer Art of Failure* (Durham, NC and London, Duke University Press, 2011), p. 124.

41 Lisa Marie Hogeland, 'Against Generational Thinking', *Women's Studies in Communication*, 24.1 (2001), 107–21 (p. 107).

42 Roof, 'Generational Difficulties', p. 83.

43 Halberstam, *The Queer Art of Failure*, p. 124.

44 Wiegman, 'Feminism's Apocalyptic Futures', p. 808.

45 Adkins, p. 431.

46 Ibid., p. 432.

47 A similar argument could be made about Martha Nussbaum's now famous diatribe against Judith Butler. See Nussbaum, 'The Professor of Parody'. See also the links made between feminism's objects of study and futurity in Wendy Brown, 'Women's Studies Unbound: Revolution, Mourning, Politics', *parallax*, 9.2 (2003), 3–16.

48 See Elizabeth Grosz, *Becomings: Explorations in Time, Memory, and Futures* (Ithaca, NY: Cornell University Press, 1999); *The Nick of Time: Politics, Evolution, and the Untimely* (Durham, NC: Duke University Press, 2004); *Time Travels*.

49 Elizabeth Grosz, 'Feminist Futures?', *Tulsa Studies in Women's Liberature*, 21.1 (2002), 13–20 (p. 18).

50 Ibid., p. 19. For an analysis that builds on Grosz's conception of time, see Rebecca Coleman, '"Things That Stay": Feminist Theory, Duration and the Future', *Time & Society*, 17.1 (2008), 85–102.

51 Jane Elliott, 'The Currency of Feminist Theory', *PMLA*, 121.5 (2006), 1697–1703 (p. 1701).

52 Ibid., p. 1700.

53 Ahmed, 'This Other and Other Others', pp. 558–59.

54 Ibid., p. 559 (emphasis in original).

55 Hemmings, p. 165.

56 Ibid., p. 194.

57 Ibid.

58 Hesford, *Feeling Women's Liberation*, p. 2.

59 Ibid., p. 14.

60 Ibid., pp. 210–11.

61 Elizabeth Freeman (ed.), 'Special Issue: Queer Temporalities', *GLQ: A Journal of Lesbian and Gay Studies*, 13.2–3 (2007).

62 Freeman, *Time Binds*, p. xiii.

63 Dinshaw and others, p. 180.

64 Ben Davies and Jana Funke (eds), *Sex, Gender and Time in Fiction and Culture* (Basingstoke: Palgrave Macmillan, 2011), p. 2.

65 Sam McBean, 'Review Article: Queer Temporalities', *Feminist Theory*, 14.1 (2013), 123–28.

66 Eve Sedgwick, *Tendencies* (Durham, NC and London: Duke University Press, 1993), p. 7 (emphasis in original).

67 Edelman, p. 17.

68 David M. Halperin, *Saint Foucault: Towards a Gay Hagiography* (Oxford: Oxford University Press, 1995), p. 62.

69 Carolyn Dinshaw, *Getting Medieval: Sexualities and Communities, Pre- and Postmodern* (Durham, NC and London: Duke University Press, 1999), p. 151.

70 Judith Butler, 'Critically Queer', *GLQ: A Journal of Lesbian and Gay Studies*, 1.1 (1993), 17–32 (p. 19).

71 Halberstam, *The Queer Art of Failure*, p. 70 (emphasis in original).

72 José Esteban Muñoz, *Cruising Utopia: The Then and There of Queer Futurity* (New York and London: New York University Press, 2009), p. 1.

73 Ibid.

74 Another key text in antisocial queer theory is Leo Bersani, *Homos* (Cambridge, MA: Harvard University Press, 1995). See also Robert L. Caserio and others, 'The Antisocial Thesis in Queer Theory', *PMLA*, 121.3 (2006), 819–28.

75 For an elaborated summary of queerness's linkage with concepts of backwardness or atavism, see Elizabeth Freeman, 'Introduction', *GLQ: A Journal of Lesbian and Gay Studies*, 13.2–3 (2007), 159–76 (pp. 161–62); Heather Love, *Feeling Backward: Loss and the Politics of Queer History* (Cambridge, MA and London: Harvard University Press, 2007), p. 6.

76 Edelman, p. 4.

77 Dinshaw and others, p. 178. See also Dinshaw, *Getting Medieval*. For another exploration of queer desires for historicity see Christopher Nealon, *Foundlings: Lesbian and Gay Historical Emotion Before Stonewall* (Durham, NC: Duke University Press, 2002).

78 Valerie Rohy, 'Ahistorical', *GLQ: A Journal of Lesbian and Gay Studies*, 12.1 (2006), 61–83 (p. 66).

79 Carolyn Dinshaw, 'Temporalities', in Paul Strohm (ed.), *Oxford Twenty-First-Century Approaches to Literature: Middle English* (Oxford: Oxford University Press, 2007), pp. 107–23 (p. 112).

80 Love, p. 4.

81 Dana Luciano, 'Nostalgia for an Age Yet to Come: *Velvet Goldmine*'s Queer Archive,' in E. L. McCallum and Mikko Tuhkanen (eds), *Queer Times, Queer Becomings* (Albany: SUNY Press), pp. 121–55 (p. 123).

82 Davies and Funke, p. 11.

83 Judith Butler, 'Sexual Politics, Torture, and Secular Time', *The British Journal of Sociology*, 59.1 (2008), 1–23; Jasbir K. Puar, *Terrorist Assemblages: Homo-nationalism in Queer Times* (Durham, NC: Duke University Press, 2007). See also Jin Haritaworn, Adi Kuntsman, and Silvia Posocco (eds), *Queer Necropolitics* (London: Routledge, 2014); Jin Haritaworn, 'Loyal Repetitions of the Nation: Gay Assilimation and the "War on Terror"', *DarkMatter*, 3 (2008).

84 Lisa Duggan, *The Twilight of Equality? Neoliberalism, Cultural Politics and the Attack on Democracy* (Boston: Beacon Press, 2003).

85 Jasbir K. Puar, 'Queer Times, Queer Assemblages', *Social Text*, 23.3–4 (2005), 121–39 (p. 123).

86 Puar, 'Queer Times', p. 122.

87 Hesford, *Feeling Women's Liberation*, p. 13.

88 Ibid.

89 For a consideration of the temporality of the lesbian, see Noreen Giffney, Michelle M. Sauer, and Diane Watt (eds), *The Lesbian Premodern* (New York: Palgrave Macmillan, 2011).

90 Elizabeth Freeman, 'Still After', *South Atlantic Quarterly*, 106.3 (2007), 495–500 (p. 498).

91 Freeman, *Time Binds*, p. xiii.

92 Ibid., p. xvi.

93 Ibid., p. 63 (emphasis in original).

94 Ibid., p. 83.
95 Hesford, *Feeling Women's Liberation*, p. 232 (emphasis in original).
96 Some of the key texts mapping the debates about the relationship between sexuality and gender or queer and feminism include Judith Butler, 'Against Proper Objects', *differences: A Journal of Feminist Cultural Studies*, 6.2–3 (1994), 1–26; Annamarie Jagose, 'Feminism's Queer Theory', *Feminism & Psychology*, 19 (2009), 157–74; Biddy Martin, 'Sexualities Without Genders and Other Queer Utopias', *Diacritics*, 24.2–3 (1994), 104–21; Gayle Rubin, 'Thinking Sex: Notes for a Radical Theory of the Politics of Sexuality', in *Pleasure and Danger: Exploring Female Sexuality*, ed. Carole Vance (Boston: Routledge, 1984), pp. 267–319.
97 See Butler, *Gender Trouble*; Halberstam, *The Queer Art of Failure*, p. 124; Denise Riley, *'Am I That Name?': Feminism and the Category of 'Women' in History* (Basingstoke: Macmillan, 1988).
98 Jagose, 'Feminism's Queer Theory', p. 160.
99 Ibid.
100 Robyn Wiegman, *Object Lessons* (Durham, NC and London: Duke University Press, 2012).
101 Tania Modleski, *Loving With a Vengeance: Mass-Produced Fantasies for Women* (Hamden, CT: Archon Books, 1982); Janice Radway, *Reading the Romance: Women, Patriarchy and Popular Literature* (London: Verso, 1987).
102 Ien Ang, 'Feminist Desire and Female Pleasure: On Janice Radway's *Reading the Romance: Women, Patriarchy and Popular Literature*', *Camera Obscura*, 6.1_16 (1988), 179–90 (p. 180).
103 Lauren Berlant, *The Female Complaint: The Unfinished Business of Sentimentality in American Culture* (Durham, NC: Duke University Press, 2008), p. 5.
104 Ibid., p. 27.
105 Yvonne Tasker and Diane Negra, *Interrogating Postfeminism: Gender and the Politics of Popular Culture* (Durham, NC: Duke University Press, 2007).
106 Angela McRobbie, *The Aftermath of Feminism: Gender, Culture and Social Change* (Los Angeles and London: Sage, 2009), p. 11.
107 Sara Ahmed, *The Cultural Politics of Emotion* (Edinburgh: Edinburgh University Press, 2004), p. 11.
108 Claire Colebrook, 'Stratigraphic Time, Women's Time', *Australian Feminist Studies*, 24.59 (2009), p. 13.
109 Freeman, *Time Binds*, p. xvii.

1 Dragging the not-yet

Archiving Antigone

Sophie Callé's *Take Care of Yourself* is a tornado of an exhibition that centres its eye on a break-up email Callé receives from a former lover.[1] Callé, not knowing how to reply, gathers 107 women, from 107 different professional backgrounds, to respond each in their own way to the email. Through the aid of the 107 women, Callé tries to fulfil her ex-lover G.'s request at the close of the email, to 'take care' of herself. The resulting exhibition is an expansive mixed media creation, comprised of simultaneously playing videos of singers, dancers, and comedians performing the email, and walls full of photographs of other professionals (such as a criminologist, Latinist, children's author) holding the letter next to or above their interpretation/reading/response. Some of the professionals comment and reflect merely on the email's form (as with the proofreader, who goes through the email with a red pen), some only on its content (as with the chess player), but most of the responses invariably reflect on a combination of both form and content (as with the schoolgirl, who endearingly comments on the difficulty of some of the language while also concluding sombrely with three simple words: 'It is sad.'). In the hands of the 107 women, the email is translated into, among other things: braille, a crossword puzzle, a piece of music, a short film, and a children's book. It is analysed by a mother, a historian, an ikebana master, a psychiatrist, and a judge, and performed by opera singers, a rapper, and a parrot. Callé gathers and collects witnesses to her failed relationship while also actively creating and pressing the possibility of documenting, understanding, and performing the pain of a failed love affair. The sheer amount of text that the piece contains, combined with the multiple perspectives contained in the gallery space, makes it almost impossible to experience everything in one visit alone. As one respondent puts it, Callé has formed a 'choir' around the email.

In part, Callé's piece reflects on the links between private lives and public cultures – between the privacy of her break-up and the larger public that she gathers around it to assist her in making it meaningful. Ann Cvetkovich argues that we might 'use accounts of affective experience to transform our sense of what constitutes a public sphere'.[2] In making public the kinds of mourning rituals that often occur in private after affairs end, Callé not only challenges distinctions between public and private, but also uses her private experience as the basis to form a public. Callé's break-up email serves as the centre of a collection of individual women's feelings about love, relationships, and heartbreak. The responses are not simply about the one specific email, but are products of and situated within a larger cultural context – the social meanings, feelings, and emotions that surround what it means to write or receive a break-up letter, or even what it means to be in the midst of the end of an affair. In asking women to respond from their professional backgrounds, Callé draws attention to the gendered nature of mourning while also insists on mourning as something of an expertise. The women's professional skills are called upon to assist Callé in her mourning, emphasizing mourning as work and blurring the lines between public and private advice.

One of the most striking responses in the whole show comes from the writer, Christine Angot, who is the respondent that describes the women Callé gathers as a choir. She is the only participant to directly challenge Callé, telling her that she will never get what she wants from all of these women. In her response to the email, she writes to Callé: 'You have nothing. You have a hole, you have a lack, that is all.' Evocatively, she ends her letter with the sentence: 'The choir you have formed around this letter is the choir of death.' Angot tells Callé that if she really loved G., she would not need the 107 women. My own initial response to the piece was to be similarly struck by what I initially saw as the failure of Callé's project to help her take care. Confronted with the piece in the gallery space, the email feels neither answered nor exhuasted – two of the aims that Callé lays out as being the impetus for reaching out to the 107 women. Neither the email nor the end of the relationship is made any clearer in the process of all the interpretations. Yet, to read the piece as a hole or a lack is, I believe, to miss the piece's most powerful point. *Take Care of Yourself* is not about finally providing meaning where there is a void, or explaining the object – indeed, the email itself becomes somewhat muted amongst the voices of the women. Rather than answering the email or exhausting it, the piece explores how this project is itself a futile one – there are always more answers and more interpretations. The project, in effect, makes the object more mobile. The email, in each of the translations, becomes something entirely different – by "sticking" with it, the object is also simultaneously "unstuck" from its one meaning.

I begin with this work of art not only because the theme of mourning resonates with this chapter's focus on Antigone, but also because the work explores what it means to get stuck with an object. While conventional wisdom advises that we move on after a break-up, Callé instead draws out this process and seemingly suggests that moving on might not mean moving away from an object, but conversely, cleaving to it. Callé's project takes one email and multiplies it to produce an overwhelming amount of text, interpretations, and emotions. Callé's piece does not so much explain the email (the ostensible aim of the project), as it produces more stories, more threads, and more desire. The resulting effect is that the death of her relationship is multiplied in meaning far beyond what G. writes to her. Rather than moving away from G.'s email, Callé stays ever closer to it, demonstrating that this might not just look like being stuck in or to the past but, instead, might create new kinds of openings. For Jacques Derrida, the archive is always turned towards the future, anticipating the kinds of documents and knowledge that will be needed in the future. The archive then is not only a recording of the past, but is also 'a token of the future'.[3] As Callé works to take care of herself, building an archive of documentation around the email, this gathering of knowledge and expertise not only or simply mourns her relationship by laying it to rest. Instead, this turn towards the dissolution of an affair to understand and perform its passing simultaneously creates and multiplies meaning, not consolidating the past but creating the possibility of new relationships, meanings, and even futures.

It is this interest in the possibilities of repetition, or of sticking with an object, that I bring to this chapter's focus on Antigone. One of the claims of this book is that alternatives to the dominant model of feminism's timing, as one of linearity, might be found by considering what is popular, or what sticks, in feminism. By considering the temporal quality of being stuck with a figure from the past, new temporalities might emerge. In Sophocles' *Antigone*, the title character, daughter of Oedipus, suffers condemnation at the hands of Creon, her uncle and king, for disobeying his edict.[4] In the wake of a war between her brothers Polyneices and Eteocles in which both are killed, Creon declares Polyneices a traitor and disallows anyone from performing funerary rites on his body. Antigone refuses to obey Creon's commands and secretly buries her brother twice, getting caught the second time by Creon's guards. Never denying her deed and speaking out against Creon's laws, Antigone is sentenced to a living burial. In the final moments of the play, Creon revokes her punishment, but it is too late for Antigone; she takes her own life, entombed and alone.

Similar to the choir that Callé forms around the break-up email, a choir too has formed around Antigone. To search through Antigone's presence in feminism is to find a figure who: stands in for the limits of kinship,[5] embodies maternal thinking,[6] inspires Virginia Woolf,[7] offers an alternative centre for psychoanalysis,[8] represents radical futurity,[9] and is an inspiration for women and girls.[10] So powerful is Antigone, that she has been described as the 'archetypal face' for women today to 'recognize their own reflection'.[11] Indeed, seemingly synonymous with resistance to state tyranny and patriarchy, Antigone does appear to be, as Katie Fleming argues, 'the feminist heroine *par excellence*'.[12] Fleming states that Antigone 'has transcended the restrictions of any particular incarnation and become truly, if not simply, iconic'.[13] The 'allure of Antigone' for feminists, as Fanny Söderbäck describes it, does indeed exceed that of any other mythic woman.[14] While there is seemingly no consensus on precisely why Antigone, above all other myths, has attracted so much feminist critical attention, what is clear is that Antigone has consistently represented and contained various feminist political desires. This chapter, while not aiming to answer the question of Antigone's allure definitively, explores how to read this consistent return. Through this, I out-line an approach to the past that refuses to bury it, refuses to move on, and instead considers the kinds of futures that might be enabled through being stuck with Antigone.

There has been scepticism about Antigone's value for contemporary feminist thinking, given her distance from the contemporary moment. However, drawing on Elizabeth Freeman's concept of 'temporal drag', I argue that returns to Antigone be read as attempts to disrupt the coherence of the pre-sent tense with the promise of the "not-yet".[15] Temporal drag provides a means of considering Antigone as a practice that disrupts any concept of cohesive feminist historical narratives of progress. The frequent backwards iterations of Antigone in feminism refuse to leave her be, to properly bury her, and instead, through consistently bringing her into various presents, insist on keeping the past a contested ground. While Antigone is traditionally explored for the way in which she dramatizes the collision between the public and the private (or state and kinship), this chapter situates her most enticing promise in and for feminism as an effect of her relationship to time. I first consider how to read this practice of turning back to Antigone before then tracing through Antigone in the writing of Woolf, Luce Irigaray, and Judith Butler. Antigone, I argue, offers an opportunity to conceptualize feminist relation-ships to the past as marked by the refusal to leave it for dead, a resistance to moving on.

Dragging on

From Sophocles' story of betrayal, love, punishment, war, gender, and power, an abundance of analyses and interpretations have appeared. As George Steiner explains, even an incomplete catalogue of the many interpretations, operas, plays, translations, and theoretical engagements with *Antigone* would number in the hundreds, showing 'no sign of any abatement'.[16] In the preface to his *Antigones*, Steiner argues that Sophocles' *Antigone* is 'one of the enduring and canonic acts in the history of our philosophic, literary, political consciousness'.[17] The many existing readings and adaptations of the myth suggest the significance of *Antigone* is such that, as Fleming suggests, 'it is arguable that (re)reading and rewriting this play are always already political actions'.[18] That Antigone has served as an object to which many divergent political, ethical, and representational desires have been attached goes without question. Moreover, that she has had a particular allure for feminist think-ing – an allure that seemingly transcends historical period – is similarly unquestionable. While I have no intention of cataloguing every utterance of her defiance, I do want to consider how to read the practice of returning to Antigone in feminism. Antigone challenges Creon's dictate that Polyneices shall not receive burial rites and Bonnie Honig thus argues that the play asks 'not whether to lament the dead but rather how to do so'.[19] Antigone and Creon disagree over how Polyneices shall be lamented and we might consider

Antigone as not arguing for the need to lament the dead but consider the play as being about precisely how to perform this act. This question of lamentation or putting to rest, moreover, can be translated to explore how the play asks what to do with what is supposedly past. Antigone's continued evocations through various feminist presents might be framed as an ongoing conversation over what to do with feminism(s) past.

Myth has been seen as ripe for feminist revision. From Monique Wittig's reworking of Homer in *Les Guérillères* to Angela Carter's revisions of classical myth in *The Passion of New Eve* or *The Magic Toyshop* to the deployment of the Radha-Krishna story from Hindu mythology in Deepa Mehta's *Fire*, feminists have frequently returned to rewrite classical mythology, finding ways to use these narratives to tell feminist stories.[20] As Amber Jacobs describes it, feminists can use myth in radical ways to challenge the structures which undergird social worlds – this writing 'can contribute to change at a symbolic level'.[21] Structural approaches to myth, such as Claude Lévi-Strauss's, suggest that myths reveal the building blocks of the social world.[22] If myths contain the underlying assumptions of the social world, a feminist project might challenge and reorganize myth as a way to reorganize the social world. Jacobs argues that a feminist rereading of myth and tragedy 'is a process of *undoing* the imaginary constructions of the dominant symbolic order and thus carries with it the demand that contemporary culture confront the phantasies that dominate and determine its social and political realities'.[23] In other words, if myths reveal something about a culture's underlying structure, a feminist challenge to the dominant social order might work with myth to expose the unspoken laws that govern societies. As Irigaray argues, 'it is very important to question the foundations of our symbolic order in mythology and in tragedy, because they deal with a landscape which installs itself in the imagination and then, all of a sudden becomes law'.[24] For Irigaray, to intervene at the level of the imaginary is an absolutely necessary political project as it is in the terrain of myth and tragedy that the social takes shape. In this view, fantasy and myth are integral to the naturalization of social norms and systems – the dominant social order is secured through mythology.

Yet, there is also something potentially counter-transformative in feminist revisions of myth. In turning to myth, feminists choose to work from within a given history. As Vanda Zajko and Miriam Leonard describe it, feminists working with myth 'revivify ancient narratives to arm contemporary struggles' rather than create new genealogies.[25] Zajko and Leonard explain that '[t]here is a tendency to overlook the strangeness of this choice'.[26] The strangeness that they refer to is the decision to work within a tradition that does not easily accommodate feminist speech. Moreover, this is not unrelated to the potential strangeness of working with narratives that are situated in the distant past. As Catherine A. Holland argues, feminist readings of Antigone raise 'a series of questions about the symbolic significance of the past within contemporary feminist political theory'.[27] Söderbäck, in her introduction to the edited volume *Feminist Readings of Antigone*, frames the dilemma as follows:

'Can a feminist politics that turns to this ancient heroine be progressive, or is it bound to romanticize the past?'[28] On the one hand, myth raises questions for feminism about genealogy, about what histories to claim or to intervene in. On the other, it also poses questions about what it means to turn back, about the use-value of the past for the present. The danger seems to be, as Söderbäck puts it, that turning to the past potentially means being stuck there. It is this question of whether it is possible to turn to the past without being bound to it, stuck in it, and thus held back in the present that I am interested in. Myth seems to be bound up in considerations of what it means to turn to the past – it seemingly always asks us to consider the relationship between past and present.

Indeed, with regards to Antigone, the practice of turning to her has often been read as being antagonistic to moving forwards. For instance, in Judith Roof's review of Butler's reading of Antigone in *Antigone's Claim*, she explores the repetitiveness of returns to Antigone. Casting Butler in the role of 'Antagone' and Hegel and Lacan in the roles of Creon, Roof writes her review as 'Antagone: A Play in Three Acts'. Roof argues that Butler's challenge to Hegel and Lacan's previous readings of Antigone might be staged as repeating Antigone's own defiance of Creon: 'Like Antigone, Antagone defies the father, then defies him again by speaking her crime. The drama replays again and again.'[29] Highlighting that returns to Antigone frequently involve the theorist taking the part of Antigone in defiance of those who would silence her, Roof argues that engagements are doomed to repeat Antigone's narrative: 'all who take her part perform her play'.[30] Drawing attention to tragedy as a repetitive form, Roof seems to suggest a certain futility in continuing to replay Antigone's narrative. In replaying and repeating the drama of speaking back to power, theorists can only ever be tangled in the same logic that Antigone herself plays out.

The argument that returns to Antigone cannot move feminism forward or open up radical futures is repeated by Holland. She objects to the way that a number of key feminist reiterations each find in Antigone's defiance 'the remnant of a lost past, a past that may serve as the ontological ground of feminist politics and thus inform and invigorate contemporary feminist practice'.[31] In Holland's reading, Antigone offers for feminism a past moment that contemporary feminists want to reinstate. Antigone comes to represent 'an almost prelapsarian moment of resistance'.[32] However, Holland suggests that this 'strategic reinstatement of the past does not serve feminism well, for it overcommits feminists to a backward-looking and reclamationist rather than a transformative imagination'.[33] In this argument, returns to Antigone that aim to reinstate her defiance in the present as a model of feminist politics cannot move feminism forwards. Instead, these turns to Antigone leave contemporary feminism stuck pining after a lost past. In differing ways, both Roof and Holland suggest that engagements with Antigone are varyingly caught in the language, the dilemma, or the form of the original in ways that cannot be transformative in the present.

While I agree with Holland that feminists frequently draw on what Holland describes as Antigone's so-called prelapsarian qualities and what I call her "not-yet temporality", we differ in the diagnosis that we want to bring to this strategy of reading. Through repetition, do we only get more of the same, the same drama replayed over and over, or might we see this repetition differently? It is in the separation between transformation and backwards-looking that I want to intervene. Rather than claim Antigone as ontological ground, we might consider the ways in which turns to Antigone do not use the past as a settled ground but insist on constantly keeping it mobile. To work with a myth is to answer to the potential possibilities and pitfalls of working with a text which is both historically past, yet also, as Zajko and Leonard put it, a 'constantly evolving point of reference'.[34] Rather than position Antigone as past, I suggest instead that iterations of Antigone do more than draw on the past, but engage with the continued life of this past in the present. Indeed, precisely by resisting to see her as past, feminists engage with the possibilities of the past as not that which must be left behind in transformative politics but the very site for future transformation. These questions reverberate with many of the concerns I raised in the introduction about challenges to generational models of progress within feminism. Presumptions about what is passed have political implications for what is continued to be engaged with in the present. The performing of Antigone, the positioning of contemporary women in her position, and the embodying of her defiance might signal not nostalgia for times past, but instead a temporality that refuses to let the past be past.

Rather than consider turns to the past as only ever repeating or consolidating the past's ontological status, Freeman suggests that iterations of the past might be framed as 'temporal drag'.[35] Adding a focus on the temporal to the concept of drag, Freeman interrogates the time presumed by Butler's concept of drag. In *Gender Trouble*, Butler argues that drag, as imitation, undoes the illusion of originary gender, so that the parody performed by a drag king is more than an imitation of maleness or masculinity, but a performance that undoes the fiction of essential gender identities.[36] In her analysis, Freeman explores the temporal connotations of this concept of drag. Namely, that queer performativity is always progressive, requiring and depending on repetitions that are transformative and oriented towards the future. Freeman argues that, in Butler's formulation of drag, '[r]epetitions with any backwards-looking force are merely "citational," and can only thereby consolidate the authority of a fantasized original'.[37] In other words, Freeman argues against turns to the past as only or necessarily acceding to its presumed authority. Freeman questions this privileging of the new and the effect it has on qualifying backwardness as always working in the name of the status quo.

Freeman begins her article with a surprise encounter she has with a student of hers who identifies as a lesbian, and wears 'Birkenstocks, wool socks, jeans, and a women's music T-shirt' and professes her love for potlucks.[38] In short, the student reminds Freeman of the feminist teachers that she had in college. This student disidentifies with what Freeman thinks of as the now of lesbian – i.e., queer, riot grrrl – and instead identifies with 'a set of social coordinates that exceeded her own historical moment'.[39] This cross-temporal identification exhibited by her student brings Freeman to consider how the so-called after-life of lesbian disrupts generational narratives that presume certain identities go out of fashion, so to speak. It is this identification with a moment that Freeman assumes is past that leads her to consider how this student might be engaged in a kind of temporal drag – where her iteration of the identity of "lesbian" is more than a parody of the 1970s stereotype.

The possibilities of temporal drag are worked out more thoroughly through a reading of Elisabeth Subrin's film *Shulie*, a shot-by-shot remake of a film from 1967 following the life of a then-unknown 22-year-old art student, Shulamith Firestone.[40] Similar to the way that Freeman's student identifies with the potluck lesbian, the film identifies with Firestone, a figurehead from the second wave, and suggests that this moment might not be entirely past. Freeman reads the film for the ways in which the dragging of the past disrupts the present, where *Shulie* emphasizes strange connections and dissonances between the past and present. Indeed, these moments of temporal disruption point to the lapses and failures in attempts to narrate a cohesive movement in feminism. Freeman considers how the past might be a threat to the political present, whereby backwards iterations may not consolidate a sense of continuity but instead puncture the present. The film returns to Firestone as 'not-yet-identified', and it is this particular iteration of a moment that is not yet past but also not entirely present that has the potential to disrupt.[41] Shulie in the film inhabits multiple identities that are "not-yet". She is not-yet adult woman, not-yet feminist, not-yet lesbian, not-yet author of *The Dialectic of Sex* and thus not-yet icon of the feminist second wave. In returning to a time before Firestone enters into feminist history, the film implicitly questions the moment of being written into history, opening up the possibility for alternative narratives, where the past might be conceptualized as an ongoing pressure in and on the present. This kind of dragging, Freeman suggests, is a queer performativity that aims not forward for transformation but backwards, to past moments and disavowed political histories. Freeman argues that *Shulie's* promise 'lies in what the language of feminist "waves" and queer "generations" sometimes effaces: the mutually disruptive energy of moments that are not yet past and yet are not entirely present either'.[42] Through suggesting that preserving collective melancholic identifications 'might propel us toward a barely-imagined future', Freeman shows that there is something transformative about backwards iterations.[43]

The collective practice of returning to Antigone in feminism pushes further Freeman's point. While she considers the kind of productive "left-overs" from feminism past, her objects of study are individual artworks – Subrin's *Shulie*, Allyson Mitchell's *Lady Sasquatch*, and Sharon Hayes' performance pieces, respectively. In each case, the artist in question look back to the so-called second wave of feminism – a particular historical moment – and drags what Freeman refers to as its 'undetonated energy' into the present.[44] As a group of contemporary artists, they perhaps signal a current interest in re-visiting the feminist 1970s. Yet, dragging Antigone as a practice has much deeper roots. Indeed, this practice is not only about a contemporary desire, but instead a tradition within feminism of interrupting various presents with the undetonated energy of Antigone. Freeman's theory enables readings of these "drag acts" that recognize the ways that they not only refer to a past as past but through backwards iteration they articulate ways that the past continues to have surprising, powerful, and unexpected life in the present. Moreover, I would suggest that as this practice is not confined to a contemporary moment but itself moves through decades, turns to Antigone are never simply turns to Antigone. Given Antigone's continuous dragging through decades of feminism, reiterations of her can never simply be about reinstating one past historical moment. Antigone might be said to contain numerous sites of undetonated energy – at every historical junction, she accrues additional meaning. Indeed, the practice of dragging her through time seems to me to be about more than her promise as a "not-yet" and, more clearly than Freeman's examples, about a feminist practice. The repeated backward iteration of Antigone is legible I believe as a persistent refusal of a feminist timing that would see the past as certain, knowable, and removed from the time of the present. In other words, the practice of dragging Antigone reveals a feminist timing that is anything but linear.

Antigone's timing

Before turning to recount a number of canonical feminist readings of Antigone, I want to suggest that Antigone is particularly ripe for these continued returns because she herself refuses to "settle" in time. From the moment she decides to bury her brother, Antigone's death is secured, with the rest of the play being a slow march to this already decided conclusion. After her death sentence has been pronounced by Creon, Antigone's sister Ismene asks, 'But how could I go on living without her?', and Creon responds, 'You are. She is already dead.'[45] In this pronouncement, Antigone is declared dead from the moment she decides to bury her brother, surviving this death to live on through the play only to meet her actual death after being buried alive. As Peggy Phelan argues in *Mourning Sex*, Antigone's story is inherently about the rippling effect of death, challenging the notion that death occurs once along a linear trajectory. Phelan explains that this multiplication of death extends beyond Antigone, where '[t]he characters in Sophocles' play discover that what is truly tragic about death is that they survive it, at least once, only to realize that having survived it once they will have to face it again'.[46] From the opening deaths of Antigone's brothers Eteocles and Polyneices, death is introduced as multiple, as twinned. Further, Antigone's death has rippling effects, causing further death in the play including those of both Haimon and Eurydice. These multiple deaths and their connection to each other leads Phelan to conclude that 'Sophocles' play is a meditation on the ways in which

Figure 1.1 Antigone crawling out of the television, *Antigone.* © Copyright 2006 David Hopkins and Tom Kurzanski. Published by Silent Devil. Reprinted by permission. All rights reserved.

dying reproduces and multiplies death'.[47] In this multiplication of death, the play refuses a linear temporality and Antigone in particular is denied a present – she is dead before the play even begins.

It is precisely the coherence of the present that the figure of Antigone disrupts. Antigone's timing is highlighted in a comic version of *Antigone* by David Hopkins and Tom Kurzanski, in which they make a connection between Antigone and the film *The Ring*.[48] The film follows Rachel Keller's (Naomi Watts) search to uncover the mystery of a cursed videotape – anyone who views the video dies seven days later. Rachel traces the origins of the videotape to the death of a young girl, Samara, who suffers a living burial at the bottom of a well. This, of course, echoes Antigone's own living burial in a cave. After discovering Samara's remains in the bottom of the well, Rachel has seemingly solved the mystery and laid Samara to rest, thus presumably stopping the curse of the videotape. In this logic, death haunts when it is somehow left incomplete – when its finality has not been secured. However, the deaths do not stop with Rachel's discovery of Samara's body and her uncovering of Samara's story. Rachel eventually ascertains that the only way to avoid the curse of the videotape is to duplicate it and show it to someone else. In other words, there is no way to end the curse of the videotape – there is no way to avoid death's multiplication. The timing of the film is encapsulated in the title, which references circularity over linearity, repetition over singularity. In the comic version, Antigone enters the story by emerging out of a television screen (Fig. 1.1). With her dark hair, crawling out of the screen towards her sister, Antigone's entrance alludes to perhaps the most chilling moment in *The Ring*, where the haunting ghost of Samara crawls out of a television screen with her dark hair across her face, towards her soon-to-be victim. This comparison, I suggest, highlights the importance of a resistance to linearity at work both in Antigone's story and in *The Ring*.

Moreover, Antigone not only resists a kind of linear timeline, she also refuses the singularity of meaning that Creon attempts to ascribe to Polyneices' death. Instead, she insists on the multiple and conflicting meanings of his death. Creon's edict that Polyneices will not be buried is an attempt to write a coherent history – clearly declaring a victor and a traitor. One brother was loyal and deserves a state funeral; the other was disloyal and shall not obtain funerary rites. Creon's edict demands that Polyneices' role in the battle be remembered as traitorous and it is precisely through denying him his funerary rites that this meaning will be secured. In other words, history will retain its coherency through the division of funerary rites. In this light, Antigone's betrayal of Creon's edict can be read not only as a challenge to the public realm in the interest of a private woman's familial duties, but instead as an action that would disrupt Creon's attempt to secure a cohesive historical narrative. Madelyn Detloff describes this as Antigone's 'refusal to forget as she is instructed'.[49] It is precisely Antigone's burial of her brother that will intervene in this history – writing into it the love of a sister for a brother. It will suggest her love for her brother coincides with her brother's position as traitor – denying the coherence that Creon's narrative requires. Her desire to bury him insists on the cotemporaneous existence of these narratives.

Through burying Polyneices, Antigone insists on the impossibility of securing his death with one, singular meaning. Antigone's timing is one of multiplicity and resistance to being settled; this is evident in her premature death, the multiple deaths that are contained in her story, and finally in her resistance to a singular narrative about her brother. In this model of time, death and life do not have a linear relationship to each other; death refuses to be final and occur but once, and meaning is instead always contested and multiplied. To return to Antigone is to turn to a figure who both has no coherent present and who challenges the coherence of the present with another narrative. It is precisely this characteristic that makes Antigone a particularly powerful figure for feminists to turn back to. Moreover, the "not-yet" status of Antigone is not only an effect of her original story but is continuously performed as she is dragged through time. The repeated turns to Antigone continue to perform Antigone's own resistance to settling meaning once and for all. The ongoing dragging of Antigone means that she does not just remain in feminism's past but moves through numerous sites of desire, accruing meaning as she travels. I want to turn now to considering a number of invocations of Antigone, considering how the "not-yet" potential of Antigone is evoked in disparate feminist presents. Through this archiving of Antigone's travels and refusals to settle in feminism, I aim to foreground both the way that Antigone offers to feminism a means of refusing the coherence of the present, and a reading of these evocations of Antigone as a collective feminist investment in temporal drag – exploring the past's possibilities for various present tenses.

Woolf's Antigone

As Sybil Oldfield outlines, Woolf's fascination with Antigone can be traced through her published and unpublished work: her fiction, political prose, and private diaries.[50] Oldfield catalogues the many ways in which Woolf read, reread, translated, and annotated *Antigone* during a period of almost twenty years. In 1924, Woolf's annotations contain the reflection: 'Antigone is the perfect type of heroic woman: unflinching and uncompromising.'[51] For Woolf, Antigone's representative status as both a daughter of patriarchy and a rebel of the state binds together, in Diana L. Swanson's words, 'the daughters' struggle against patriarchy with the struggle against fascism and reveals the two causes to be the same'.[52] In *The Years* and *Three Guineas*, Antigone represents and contests the damage that is suffered by the daughters of patriarchy as well as stands for the unique vision that might be accorded to them as an effect of their disadvantaged position.

In *Three Guineas*, Woolf, concerned with answering the question of how to prevent war, sets out to prove that the patriarchal domination of women provides the paradigm for the domination that causes war. In asserting that 'men's private tyrannies cause their public tyrannies', Woolf argues that the conditions of war emerge from the conditions of women's oppression.[53] She sees the position of the daughter as particularly relevant to thinking through the causes of war, as it is the daughters' 'bird's-eye view of the outside of things' which reveals the link between fascism and private life.[54] Antigone, as daughter to Oedipus and patriarchal daughter under Creon more generally, functions for Woolf, as Swanson argues, to bind 'the daughters' struggle against patriarchy with the struggle against fascism and reveals the two causes to be the same'.[55] Moreover, the outsider perspective of the daughter enables not only an analysis of domination but also might produce its strongest opposition. While Creon's laws represent the attachments and commitments that are bred into men involved in public life, Antigone refuses those laws, in favour of burying her brother. Quoting Antigone's most famous lines, Woolf demonstrates that Antigone embraces a different value system: 'Tis not my nature to join in hating, but in loving.'[56] Antigone is in a position then to not only diagnose the domination that leads to fascism, but also to present a different belief system that would oppose it.

Woolf drags Antigone into her present as a figure of political opposition – a genuine alternative to fascism as it is rooted in patriarchy. It is through enlivening Antigone's position that Woolf argues against the law. Dragging Antigone into her present, Woolf compares her dissent to the political actions of her contemporaries, arguing that they, in the same way as her, represent genuine opposition. In a footnote in *Three Guineas*, Woolf argues that 'Antigone herself could be transformed either into Mrs. Pankhurst, who broke a window and was imprisoned in Holloway; or into Frau Pommer'.[57] In this comparison to Emily Pankhurst, a leader of the British suffragette movement, and Frau Pommer, a Nazi dissenter, Antigone is unburied from her context and is made to speak through Woolf's contemporary political agitators. Indeed, these contemporary women become actors for whom Antigone's politics might be performed in the present. Woolf argues that Antigone's words of defiance could have been spoken by either of these two women, arguing too that Creon's words could easily have come from the mouth of Hitler or Mussolini.

The insistence on Antigone as representative of the other to Creon, the alternative to patriarchal fascism, is echoed in Antigone's appearance in *The Years*. Antigone is not a character in the text, but instead the Sophoclean text itself appears in Woolf's fictional history of the Pargiter family. The text appears twice, read by cousins Edward and Sara, respectively. In the 1880 segment of the book, Edward is described translating *Antigone* as part of his Oxford education. While translating, Edward fantasizes about his cousin Kitty, whom he sexualizes through Antigone. He brings Antigone into the present through comparing her to Kitty: 'There she stood among the marble and the asphodel, yet there she was among the Morris wallpapers and the cabinets […] She was both of them – Antigone and Kitty; here in the book; there in the room.'[58] The very act (the translation) that will inaugurate

Edward into the value system of education and gain him public esteem is thus intimately linked to his desire for Kitty through the figure of Antigone – in effect, he reads male desire into the text. Edward's desire to achieve greatness and esteem in the education system, a system that values the same competitiveness that Woolf argues leads to war, is also a desire to sexually possess Kitty.[59] In using Antigone as the figure through which Edward's desire for privilege and his desire for Kitty intersect, Woolf highlights Antigone, in *The Years* as she does in *Three Guineas,* as a figure who symbolizes the interconnection between domination and patriarchal privilege.

Yet, Woolf also sees in Antigone's outsider status the possibility for an alternative. Sara, the other reader of *Antigone* in *The Years*, experiences the text altogether differently than Edward. While Edward's translation is an attempt at precision and accuracy, an academic achievement to make his father proud, Sara's reading is playful and erratic. As Edward translates the text, he relishes when he manages to make phrases more exact, 'he must be precise', he thinks to himself, 'exact; even his little scribbled notes must be clear as print'.[60] Sara, on the other hand, 'skipped through the pages', reading a line here and there, collecting images, scenes, and words 'quickly, inaccurately'.[61] Sara's way of reading, characterized by this indifference to accuracy or even full comprehension of the story, is outside of the system of valorization and competition in which Edward's translation sits. Sara's engagement with *Antigone*, characterized by playfully selective reading, becomes even more performative when she positions herself in Antigone's story, as Antigone. As she finishes her reading of *Antigone*, Sara positions her body just as she imagines Antigone's body lay in the tomb, using her blankets to entomb her, with 'just room for her to lie straight out'.[62]

Sara reads *Antigone* in her room while a party carries on outside her window. Patricia Cramer points out that from this vantage point, outside of the mating rituals of heteropatriarchy, Sara mocks Edward's fantasies of Kitty and mimics love talk.[63] Sara's reading is entwined with her own comic critique of heteropatriarchy – it is a performative and playful identification with Antigone's outsider perspective. Sara's identificatory reading of *Antigone* becomes a way for Sara to mock heterosexual mating rituals as well as express her feelings of being trapped in the patriarchal home. Embracing her as an outsider, Sara identifies with Antigone's position outside of the values of dominant society as she herself is shut up in her room. While Edward's engagement with Sophocles' classic is entrenched in the value system of the university and patriarchal heterosexuality, Sara instead sees Antigone as a means for giving voice to her position as outsider. Her embodiment of Antigone in her tomb becomes a minor act of identification with being outside of dominant values. Through her appearance in both *Three Guineas* and *The Years*, Antigone upholds for Woolf the possibility of women, specifically the figure of the daughter, as offering an outsider's perspective on patriarchy's connection to fascism. For Woolf, Antigone embodies this specific outsider perspective – a perspective that, were it given adequate attention, could provide an alternative political centre, and resistance to state tyranny. Woolf drags Antigone through her work, investing her with the weight of her political desires. As the "not-yet" alternative Antigone represents the possibility of imagining a radical other to patriarchal fascist values.

Irigaray's Antigone

Decades after Woolf's writing, Antigone figures in Irigaray's psychoanalytic and deconstructionist feminist project. Antigone appears in *Speculum of the Other Woman* and *Thinking the Difference* as a figure that is misunderstood and misinterpreted. In *Thinking the Difference*, Irigaray draws on Hegel's insistence in *The Phenomenology of Spirit* that women are the 'irony [in the life] of the community' – necessary to sustain the realms of the public and human, but suppressed in these realms.[64] Antigone carries out the duties accorded to women – to bury and memorialize the dead – but it is precisely this enactment of her duties that leads to her being sentenced to a living burial. Her duties as a woman, while necessary for the community, become the very means by which she loses her membership in the community. While her loyalties are not recognized within the realm of the play, Irigaray also argues that Antigone is misread by the dominant philosophical tradition of Hegel and Lacan so that misrecognition of her actions continues long after Sophocles' play concludes. In opposition to Hegel and Lacan's readings, Irigaray argues for Antigone's position as presenting an alternative, but an alternative that is not recognized by dominant readings. Her defiance and standpoint are erased in the play as being without warrant – despite its essential place in preserving the community – and Irigaray argues, her standpoint continues to be erased long after by philosophers who describe Antigone as acting apolitically or anarchic.

Irigaray argues that in differing ways both Hegel and Lacan erase Antigone's agency.[65] She explains that Antigone is painted as 'a sort of young anarchist, on a first-name basis with the Lord', whose enthusiasm for divine laws removes her from 'her share of responsibility in the here and now, and thus also in the order of the polis'.[66] Indeed, Hegel argues that Antigone's unburial of her brother is a perversion of the public realm from her place in its opposite – the realm of the family.[67] Kimberly Hutchings explains that for Hegel, *Antigone* is the most perfect example of the tragedy that occurs when 'the two realms cease to be complementary and divine and human law come into conflict'.[68] Hegel argues that Antigone's act of burying her brother is the fulfilment of her familial ethical duty (the unique responsibility of women).[69] In the same way that Hegel positions Antigone's act as outside the political, Lacan too denies that Antigone's burial of her brother can be read as political.[70] For Lacan, Antigone represents an ethics of pure desire and her burial of Polyneices represents motivation without motive; this makes Antigone in Lacan's thinking, a 'terrible, self-willed victim' that disturbs and startles.[71] Lacan argues that Antigone explains her act without recourse to any laws; it is her brother and that it is her brother is enough.[72] As Miriam Leonard explains, Lacan does not read Antigone as being in a dialectical relationship with Creon, as Hegel does, but he too relegates her to a space beyond the political, 'disinherited from any *moral* logic'.[73] Lacan's depiction of Antigone's desire, described by Irigaray as 'a rather suicidal familial and religious pathos, which only her innocent, virginal youth can excuse, or perhaps even make attractive', bars her from being political.[74]

Irigaray argues against this erasure and instead insists on Antigone as a civic subject, as an actor in the political, public sphere (precisely the identity denied her by both Lacan and Hegel). As Leonard argues, Irigaray points to the phallogocentric bias of both Hegel and Lacan and instead suggests that 'Antigone's exclusion from the political is not self-willed exile, but is rather the result of the prejudice of her readers from Hegel to Lacan and beyond'.[75] Irigaray states that neither Hegel nor Lacan can recognize Antigone as a citizen precisely because she challenges the dominant male-defined model of citizenship. She draws on Antigone to rethink the politics of women's inclusion, as a 'way of articulating what it means to be/become woman in clear distinction to masculine accounts of what it means to be a subject'.[76] Irigaray calls for us to 'listen' to what Antigone has to say, insisting that despite Hegel and Lacan's readings, she is indeed saying something political.[77] Irigaray argues that Antigone expresses her own value system and 'will choose to die a virgin, unwedded to any man, rather than sacrifice the ties of blood'.[78] In language not unlike Woolf's, Irigaray suggests that Antigone represents a viable political alternative to the perverse laws of Creon as 'the voice, the accomplice of the people, the slaves, those who only whisper their revolt against their masters secretly'.[79] That Antigone cannot be understood as anything other than an anarchist or suicidal and that Hegel and Lacan cannot read the burial of her brother as the action of a citizen, is precisely because Antigone represents the unread potential of feminist citizenship – the "not-yet". Sitting outside the dominant model of citizenship, Antigone's actions are unintelligible as public and political, hence for Irigaray, they represent 'the need to redefine the objective content of civil rights as they apply to men and women – since the neutral individual is nothing but a cultural fiction'.[80]

Irigaray, in the same way as Woolf, draws on Antigone's position as "not-yet" and takes the failure of recognition in both Hegel and Lacan as a place to begin – starting with Antigone's failure to be seen as political is to insist that Antigone's plight continues to haunt the possibility of female political subjectivity. Indeed, it is precisely this outsider status, this "not-yet", and this uninhabitable space that Antigone speaks from that is a symptom of what Antigone represents, yet has also never been. It is because of this insistence that she has in some sense yet to be made present, despite how far in the past she is, that feminists must continue to reiterate her critique of the state. Similar to how Freeman argues *Shulie* becomes an instance for thinking about how our political present may not be so coherent as we sometimes characterize it as, these returns to Antigone indeed go so far as to intrude on our political present by insisting that Antigone, as a historical figure, is in some sense still "not-yet".

Butler's Antigone

The last place where I turn to consider feminist evocations of Antigone is in Judith Butler's *Antigone's Claim*. In many ways Butler's reading is a strong counter to the two that I have already considered, in that she argues against Antigone's representational status. She explains that although she initially turns to Antigone as 'a counterfigure to the trend championed by recent feminists to seek the backing and authority of the state to implement feminist policy aims', she finds that Antigone cannot do this work.[81] Unlike Woolf, and in direct dialogue with Irigaray, Butler describes Antigone as being incapable of representing this kind of opposition. While both Woolf and Irigaray use Antigone as a clear oppositional voice for feminism, Butler argues that there are no clear oppositions in the play. She argues instead that Antigone troubles the norms of kinship through the very fact of being Oedipus' daughter and troubles the norms of the state through her adoption of the language of sovereignty. Butler argues that she confounds the boundaries of kinship and the state, perverting both realms through her defiance of Creon's edict.

For Irigaray, Antigone sits on the side of blood, with her allegiance representing a stark alternative to Creon. Woolf too sees Antigone as a force that speaks against fascism and patriarchy – rebellious in her insistence on radically alternative values. However, for Butler, Antigone sits uncomfortably and uneasily on neither the side of kinship nor the state. Butler argues that while 'entangled in the terms of kinship, she is at the same time outside those norms'.[82] As a product of incest, being neither simply sister nor daughter to Oedipus, and insisting herself that it is only for her brother – and no one else – that she would be so defiant of Creon, Butler argues that Antigone's status as representative of kinship is called into question. While previous readings of Antigone have unquestionably placed her on the side of kinship, with Creon sitting firmly on the side of the state, Butler insists that this cannot be the starting point.[83] Antigone cannot properly represent a kinship that opposes the state because Antigone herself is a perversion of kinship. Indeed, focusing on the incest taboo, Moya Lloyd explains that for Butler, Antigone 'as the child of Oedipus is a very peculiar champion of the family against the state'.[84] Evidencing that Antigone symbolizes a catachresis of familial time, Butler points to her name's meaning: 'anti-generation'.[85]

Further, Butler argues that Antigone's political speech cannot be seen as any pure or simple opposition, entangled as it is in Creon's language. Butler contends that Antigone's act is never fully hers because 'what gives these verbal acts their power is the normative operation of power that they embody without quite becoming'.[86] In other words, Antigone:

asserts herself through appropriating the voice of the other, the one to whom she is opposed; thus her autonomy is gained through the appropriation of the authoritative voice of the one she resists, an appropriation that has within it traces of a simultaneous refusal and assimilation of that very authority.[87]

Butler argues that Antigone cannot stand for pure opposition to power, seeing as her opposition is perverted. Adopting and perverting the language of the sovereign in speaking back to Creon and the language of kinship in burying her brother, Antigone's value lies in 'the social deformation of both idealized kinship and political sovereignty that emerges as a consequence of her act'.[88] Antigone's use of the language of the state in her opposition to Creon thus means that she acts in some sense through and not wholly outside of state power.

This perversion of the language of the state and the language of kinship means that Butler does not read Antigone as being an oppositional "not-yet" in the same way as the previous theorists. While others comment that she reveals the limits of the state, for Butler, as Lloyd puts it, 'Antigone is a figure that puts *both* kinship (and its related notions of gender and heteronormativity) *and* the state into question'.[89] Rather than represent kinship, Antigone, in Butler's reading, constitutes an interrogation of the category of kinship, as she 'upsets the vocabulary of kinship that is a precondition of the human, implicitly raising the question for us of what those preconditions really must be'.[90] What Antigone speaks to is precisely what qualifies as a speaking subject. Or, in other words, as the product of kinship gone wrong, with her condemnation coming before her action, she becomes from the start a figure who troubles signification. Butler argues that she 'is not of the human but speaks in its language'.[91] She instead argues that what Antigone makes visible is the way normative kinship is assumed and idealized in readers of Antigone. Butler thus reads Antigone as offering insight into the 'operation of political power that forecloses what forms of kinship will be intelligible, what kinds of lives can be countenanced as living'.[92] Relying on an understanding of Antigone as exceeding or sitting outside the social and political categories that render the "human" intelligible, Butler focuses on the ways her actions confound the laws of kinship and the state.

While her positioning of Antigone is unquestionably in opposition to those who place her on the side of kinship, Butler still reads Antigone as being a means to consider a possible future in which her signification might be possible. Indeed, Butler seemingly remains invested in the "not-yet" potential of Antigone precisely because she seems to point ahead to a more optimistic future. Thus, despite her opposition to reading Antigone as outsider to the state in the same way as Irigaray or Woolf, Butler persists in asking what it would mean for Antigone to matter. Antigone, for Butler, points 'not to politics as a question of representation but to that political possibility that emerges when the limits of representation and representability are exposed'.[93]

While not quite representative, Antigone is a space for considering the limits of our categories, and as such she remains a threat to the status quo. In asking what it would take for her to matter, Butler indeed questions what the space of the "not-yet" might do to demolish our understandings of the preconditions of the human.

That Butler's reading of Antigone retains some vestiges of those that precede it is the critique that Lee Edelman makes. As Edelman points out, Butler, just as much as those before her, is intent on allegorizing 'the steady pressure of a catachresis that moves [Antigone] beyond intelligibility and so toward new forms of social relation'.[94] This future-oriented interpretation of Butler's is precisely what Edelman takes issue with in *No Future*. For Edelman, Butler's account of Antigone can only widen the realm of what can be intelligible but it maintains the same temporal privileging of the future that Edelman argues does not challenge the remit of the political. As Edelman sees it, Antigone emerges from her tomb only by becoming intelligible through the very institutions that she renounces, 'confirming, in the process, the legitimacy of the institutions of legitimation, however much what counts as legitimate must undergo change with time'.[95] In other words, Antigone in this view can only widen the realm of intelligibility without challenging the process of becoming intelligible. For Edelman, Butler's reading is not so dissimilar to either Woolf's or Irigaray's in that all of these appropriations of Antigone use her to argue for an expansion of what qualifies as a speaking, political subject. In this, they draw on the possibility that Antigone opens up a future in which what is unthinkable can become recognizable. In each case, Antigone represents the as-yet-unrealized and thus turns to Antigone place hope in the possibility of a future realization (for women, feminist political subjects, queers). Thus, for Edelman, Butler's reading, as much as any other, confirms the liberal politics that are structured by the future – 'as affirming the identity of the future with the *promise* of meaning itself'.[96] Edelman, on the other hand, suggests that a more radical – more queer – reading might resist this future-orientation. He desires that Antigone not signify a future in which she might be meaningful. Instead, his hope for her is that she remains outside of signification – that she is not a "not-yet" but perhaps a "never". This, for Edelman, is Antigone's most radical potential.

While Edelman's reading is compelling, what it leaves out is the collective practice that has built up around Antigone in feminism. Edelman's version of queer has been criticized for its refusal to consider the queer possibility of collectivity.[97] In his focus on Antigone as a text, rather than a collective practice, Edelman ignores how feminists' turn to Antigone as a figure of futurity is an ongoing practice of turning back. Ignoring the effects of this collective practice misses out on an opportunity to consider how, as a practice, dragging Antigone does not so simply point in the direction of futurity. In constantly returning to Antigone, a figure from the past, feminist iterations of Antigone's ability to disrupt the present do not read so simply as moves into the future. Taken as a collective archive, feminism's relationship with Antigone is far weightier than Edelman gives it credit. Focused as he is on Butler's individual reading, Edelman is blind to the collective feminist turns to Antigone – he is blind to the possibility that Antigone is not a text for feminism but a practice of unsettling the present not with the promise of the future but with the ever-unstable past. As a collective practice, feminist reiterations of Antigone, much like interpretations of Callé's break-up letter and Freeman's temporal drag, do not only point toward the future, but also are definitively oriented backwards – they are stuck, dragging, and resistant to moving on.

Un-remembering

Antigone's greatest defiance might not be her speaking out against Creon's edict, but her refusal to be singular in time. To turn back to Antigone and read her importance to feminists alongside Freeman's work, it becomes possible to read in feminist engagements with Antigone the persistent claim that there is something "not-yet" about her. These readings of Antigone insist that in some sense Antigone's unintelligibility, or her "not-yet" status, is precisely the challenge she brings to our categories of the state, citizenship, and kinship. These continual returns to Antigone, these praises of her defiance and performances of her critical speech, indeed seem to function not as a repetition of her original act but in much queerer ways. Far from merely citing Antigone as an original voice or placing her in a feminist genealogy of defiant women, Antigone's presence in contemporary feminism is, I would argue, much more complex. Holland argues that in feminist engagements with her, Antigone is situated as a sort of lost past, 'a past that feminist action in the present might to some degree reinstate'.[98] However, similar to Freeman's assertion that *Shulie* does not so much recreate the original as it unearths the surprising way that the past disrupts the present's presumed singularity, feminist reiterations of Antigone might be read not as confirming the past's ontological status. She appears in feminist theory as a figure who may be from the past, but who is not past. She is a figure that inspires feminist theory not only in her defiance against Creon or her speech acts, but precisely through her status as "not-yet". Moreover, the practice of dragging Antigone in feminism provides a model for a feminist temporality that refuses to use the past as ontological ground.

   In the introduction to this book, I explore how generational models of feminism's timing, in their insistence on coherence, fail to account for feminism's temporal complexities. As a final comment on this practice of refusing to "settle" the past, I want to consider a recent example of a call to resist presuming that the past is a known territory. A refusal to "properly mourn" might be conceptualized as a feminist tactic to question desires for coherent narratives. In 2007, the journal *GLQ: A Journal of Lesbian and Gay Studies* published a memorial issue dedicated to Monique Wittig.[99] In the issue, Wiegman's article 'Un-Remembering Monique Wittig' stands out because she troubles the issue's attempt at memorialization. Wiegman describes the memorial issue as unusual because she feels she is tracing what has already been lost, explaining that 'Monique Wittig has already been "positioned" by us, which makes this volume's task of memorialization a strange encounter with what we have already done to and with her'.[100] She points to the infrequency with which Wittig is cited in *GLQ* as well as her students' resistance to referencing Wittig in their work, suggesting that 'the kind of critical alterity her work projects seems, to them, to be a future we have already outgrown'.[101] Wiegman's call to "un-remember" gains its force not through an insistence that Wittig needs to be "properly" re-buried or remembered, but through disrupting what has already been "settled".

Moreover, through interrupting the text with institutional stories of racism, sexism, and discrimination, and through drawing attention to the paradox of memorializing a figure that has already perhaps been positioned in feminism and queer theory, Wiegman argues for the impossibility of conceptualizing feminist time as cohesive and linear. Wiegman's stance is not to insist on coherence, or narrating the story "correctly", but instead to argue for the necessity of grappling with these incongruences, poignantly asking: 'Might there be something instead important about refusing to ignore the losses that our investments in producing coherence entail?'[102] Echoing Freeman in this final question, Wiegman insists on the excess produced by models of temporality that presume certain things remain comfortably and unquestioningly in the past. In feminist returns to the myth of Antigone, a model of feminism's temporality is produced which refuses this coherency. Dragging Antigone, feminists draw on the incoherent temporality of Antigone to produce their own challenges to the present's coherence. Moreover, as a collective practice, these returns to Antigone evidence a queer feminist timing, in which the future becomes not about leaving the past behind, but instead insisting on its unsettling.

Notes

1 Sophie Callé, *Take Care of Yourself* (London: Whitechapel Gallery, 2009).
2 Ann Cvetkovich, *An Archive of Feelings: Trauma, Sexuality and Public Cultures* (Durham, NC and London: Duke University Press, 2003), p. 16.
3 Jacques Derrida, *Archive Fever: A Freudian Impression*, trans. Eric Prenowitz (Chicago and London: University of Chicago Press, 1996), p. 18.
4 Sophocles, *The Oedipus Cycle*, trans. Dudley Fitts and Robert Fitzgerald (Harcourt Brace & Company, 2002).
5 Judith Butler, *Antigone's Claim: Kinship Between Life and Death* (New York: Columbia University Press, 2000).
6 Jean Bethke Elshtain, 'Antigone's Daughters', in *Feminism and Politics*, ed. Anne Phillips (Oxford: Oxford University Press, 1998), pp. 363–77 (first published in *democracy*, 2 [1982], 46–59); Jean Bethke Elshtain, 'Antigone's Daughters Reconsidered: Continuing Reflections on Women, Politics, and Power', in *Life-World and Politics: Between Modernity and Postmodernity*, ed. Stephen K. White (Notre Dame, IN: University of Notre Dame Press, 1989), pp. 222–35.
7 Virginia Woolf, *The Years* (London: Vintage Books, 2004); Virginia Woolf, *A Room of One's Own and Three Guineas* (London: Vintage, 2001).

8 Cecilia Sjöholm, *The Antigone Complex: Ethics and the Invention of Feminine Desire* (Stanford, CA: Stanford University Press, 2004).

9 Catherine A. Holland, 'After Antigone: Women, the Past, and the Future of Feminist Political Thought', *American Journal of Political Science*, 42.4 (1998), 1108–32.

10 Rosiska Darcy De Oliveira, *In Praise of Difference: The Emergence of a Global Feminism* (New Brunswick, NJ: Rutgers University Press, 1991); Elshtain, 'Antigone's Daughters'; Luce Irigaray, *Speculum of the Other Woman*, trans. Gillian C. Gill (Ithaca, NY: Cornell University Press, 1985).

11 De Oliveira, p. 18.

12 Katie Fleming, 'Fascism on Stage: Jean Anouilh's *Antigone*', in *Laughing with Medusa: Classical Myth and Feminist Thought*, ed. Vanda Zajko and Miriam Leonard (Oxford: Oxford University Press, 2006), pp. 163–86 (p. 164).

13 Ibid., p. 184.

14 Fanny Söderbäck, 'Introduction: Why Antigone Today', in *Feminist Readings of Antigone*, ed. Fanny Söderbäck (Albany: SUNY Press, 2010), pp. 1–14 (p. 2).

15 Elizabeth Freeman, 'Packing History, Count(er)ing Generations', *New Literary History*, 31.4 (2000), 727–44. This article appears in an expanded form as Chapter 2 in *Time Binds: Queer Temporalities, Queer Histories* (Durham, NC and London: Duke University Press, 2010). I reference the earlier version throughout this chapter as it contains the narrative of the lesbian student, omitted from the chapter in *Time Binds*.

16 George Steiner, *Antigones* (Somerset: Messrs. Cox, Sons & Co. Ltd., 1979), p. 12.

17 George Steiner, *Antigones* (Oxford: Clarendon, 1984), p. xi.

18 Fleming, p. 165.

19 Bonnie Honig, *Antigone, Interrupted* (Cambridge: Cambridge University Press, 2013), p. 2.

20 Monique Wittig, *Les Guérillères*, trans. David Le Vay (London: Women's Press, 1979); Angela Carter, *The Passion of New Eve* (London: Virago, 1982); Angela Carter, *The Magic Toyshop* (London: Virago, 1981); *Fire*, dir. by Deepa Mehta (Zeitgeist Films, 1996).

21 Amber Jacobs, *On Matricide: Myth, Psychoanalysis, and the Law of the Mother* (New York: Columbia University Press, 2007), p. 16.

22 See Claude Lévi-Strauss, *Myth and Meaning* (London: Routledge, 2001).

23 Jacobs, p. 18 (emphasis in original).

24 Luce Irigaray, quoted in Elaine Hoffman Baruch and Lucienne J. Serrano, eds, *Women Analyze Women: In France, England and the United States* (New York: New York University Press, 1988), p. 159.

25 Vanda Zajko and Miriam Leonard, 'Introduction', in *Laughing with Medusa: Classical Myth and Feminist Thought*, ed. Vanda Zajko and Miriam Leonard (Oxford: Oxford University Press, 2006), pp. 1–20 (p. 2).

26 Zajko and Leonard, p. 2.

27 Holland, p. 1110.

28 Söderbäck, p. 2.

29 Judith Roof, 'Antagone: A Play in Three Acts', *CR: The New Centennial Review*, 2.1 (2002), 259–66 (p. 263)

30 Ibid., p. 265.

31 Holland, p. 1114.

32 Ibid.

33 Ibid., p. 1115.

34 Zajko and Leonard, p. 4.

35 Freeman, 'Packing History, Count(er)ing Generations', p. 728.

36 Judith Butler, *Gender Trouble* (New York and London: Routledge, 1990), p. 187.

37 Freeman, 'Packing History, Count(er)ing Generations', p. 728.

38 Ibid., p. 727.
39 Ibid., p. 728.
40 *Shulie*, dir. by Elisabeth Subrin (Video Data Bank, 1997).
41 Freeman, 'Packing History, Count(er)ing Generations', p. 742.
42 Ibid.
43 Ibid., p. 743.
44 Freeman, *Time Binds*, p. xvi.
45 Sophocles, p. 214.
46 Peggy Phelan, *Mourning Sex: Performing Public Memories* (New York and London: Routledge, 1997), p. 13.
47 Ibid.
48 David Hopkins and Tom Kurzanski, *Antigone* (Silent Devil, 2006), p. 6; *The Ring,* dir. by Gore Verbinski (DreamWorks, 2003).
49 Madelyn Detloff, ""Tis Not My Nature to Join in Hating, But in Loving": Toward Survivable Public Mourning', in *Modernism and Mourning*, ed. Patricia Rae (Lewisburg, PA: Bucknell University Press, 2007), pp. 50–68 (p. 57).
50 Sybil Oldfield, 'Virginia Woolf and Antigone: Thinking Against the Current', *South Carolina Review*, 29 (1996), 45–57.
51 Quoted in Oldfield, p. 50.
52 Diana L. Swanson, 'An Antigone Complex? Psychology and Politics in *The Years* and *Three Guineas*', in *Virginia Woolf Texts and Contexts,* ed. Beth Rigel Daugherty and Eileen Barrett (New York: Pace University Press), pp. 35–39 (p. 38).
53 Barbara Andrew, 'The Psychology of Tyranny: Wollstonecraft and Woolf on the Gendered Dimension of War', *Hypatia*, 9.2 (1994), 85–101 (p. 90).
54 Woolf, *Three Guineas*, p. 120.
55 Swanson, p. 38.
56 Woolf, *Three Guineas*, p. 180, n. 40.
57 Ibid., p. 273, n. 39.
58 Woolf, *The Years*, p. 43.
59 Woolf, *Three Guineas*, p. 133.
60 Woolf, *The Years*, p. 42.
61 Ibid., p. 117.
62 Ibid.
63 Patricia Cramer, '"Loving in the War Years": The War of Images in *The Years*', in *Virginia Woolf and War: Fiction, Reality and Myth*, ed. Mark Hussey (Syracuse, NY: Syracuse University Press, 1991) pp. 203–24 (p. 135).
64 G. W. F. Hegel, *The Phenomenology of Spirit*, trans. A. V. Miller (Oxford: Clarendon Press, 1977), p. 288.
65 For more detailed analyses of Irigaray in relation to Hegel and Lacan, see Butler, *Antigone's Claim*; Kimberly Hutchings, *Hegel and Feminist Philosophy* (Cambridge: Blackwell Publishing Ltd, 2003); Sjöholm.
66 Luce Irigaray, *Thinking the Difference: For a Peaceful Revolution*, trans. Karin Montin (London: The Athlone Press, 1994), pp. 67–68.
67 Hegel, p. 288.
68 Hutchings, p. 83.
69 Along with Irigaray's analysis, further feminist perspectives on Hegel's reading of Antigone can be found in Seyla Benhabib, 'On Hegel, Women, and Irony', in *Feminist Interpretations of G.W.F. Hegel*, ed. Patricial J. Mills (University Park: Pennsylvania State University Press, 1996), pp. 25–43; Butler, *Antigone's Claim*; Patricia J. Mills, 'Hegel's Antigone', in *Feminist Interpretations of G.W. F. Hegel*, ed. Patricia J. Mills (University Park: Pennsylvania State University Press, 1996), pp. 59–88.
70 Jacques Lacan, 'The Essence of Tragedy: A Commentary on Sophocles' *Antigone*', in *The Ethics of Psychoanalysis 1959–1960*, vol. VII, ed. Jacques-Alain Miller, trans. Dennis Porter (London: Tavistock/Routledge, 1992), pp. 243–90.

71 Ibid., p. 247.
72 Ibid., pp. 278–79.
73 Miriam Leonard, 'Lacan, Irigaray, and Beyond: Antigones and the Politics of Psychoanalysis', in *Laughing with Medusa: Classical Myth and Feminist Thought,* ed. Vanda Zajko and Miriam Leonard (Oxford: Oxford University Press, 2006), pp. 121–40 (p. 128, emphasis in original).
74 Irigaray, *Thinking the Difference*, p. 68.
75 Leonard, 'Lacan, Irigaray, and Beyond', p. 122.
76 Hutchings, p. 89.
77 Irigaray, *Thinking the Difference*, p. 70.
78 Irigaray, *Speculum of the Other Woman*, p. 218.
79 Ibid.
80 Irigaray, *Thinking the Difference*, p. 75.
81 Butler, *Antigone's Claim*, p. 1.
82 Ibid., p. 72.
83 Ibid., p. 2.
84 Moya Lloyd, 'Butler, Antigone and the State', *Contemporary Political Theory*, 4 (2005), 451–68 (p. 455).
85 Butler, *Antigone's Claim*, p. 22.
86 Ibid., p. 10.
87 Ibid., p. 11.
88 Ibid., p. 6.
89 Lloyd, p. 454 (emphasis in original).
90 Butler, *Antigone's Claim*, p. 82.
91 Ibid.
92 Ibid., p. 29.
93 Ibid., p. 2.
94 Lee Edelman, *No Future: Queer Theory and the Death Drive* (Durham, NC and London: Duke University Press, 2004), p. 102.
95 Ibid., p. 105.
96 Ibid. (emphasis in original).
97 See Judith Halberstam, *The Queer Art of Failure* (Durham, NC and London: Duke University Press, 2011); José Esteban Muñoz, *Cruising Utopia: The Then and There of Queer Futurity* (Durham, NC and London: Duke University Press, 2009).
98 Holland, p. 1114.
99 Brad Epps and Jonathan Katz, eds, Special Issue: Monique Wittig: At the Crossroads of Criticism, *GLQ: A Journal of Lesbian and Gay Studies*, 13.4 (2007).
100 Robyn Wiegman, 'Un-Remembering Monique Wittig', *GLQ: A Journal of Lesbian and Gay* Studies, 13.4 (2007), 505–18 (p. 507).
101 Ibid.
102 Ibid., p. 509.

2 Loss and futurity

Marge Piercy's *Woman on the Edge of Time*

Sarah Hall's 2007 novel *The Carhullan Army* opens in Rith, a fictional town in the British Lake District, home to the main character, known throughout as simply "Sister". In dystopian Rith, news is unreliable, resources are strictly rationed, communities are ruled by force, and women's reproductive capacities are tightly controlled – each woman is fitted with a coil as an extreme measure of population control. In the first pages of the book, Sister escapes her town to journey to the hills where she hopes to find Carhullan, an all-women separatist community. In Iain Robinson's reading, the novel's concerns are decidedly contemporary as the novel's society might be seen to extrapolate the present-day threat of climate change, oil dependency, and the 'perceived restrictions on civil liberties and the tightening of internal security that arrived in the wake of the British government's post-9/11 anti-terror legislation'.[1] He argues that the dystopian town of Rith is clearly related to contemporary Britain as 'a dystopian portrayal of what it might become' and that the novel is a 'proper attempt to imagine a possible and plausible future for the historical circumstances under which the author is writing'.[2] For Robinson, the 'critical sensibility of the novel is thus geared towards early twenty-first-century concerns'.[3] Yet, the novel's concerns are not only with the contemporary, but also with the recent past. That the novel invokes an all-women's separatist community as a possible alternative society puts the novel into dialogue with a very specific feminist literary and political history.

The separatist utopia has a history in feminist writing, and the novel seems to reference specifically Sally Miller Gearhart's 1979 work of fiction, *The Wanderground*.[4] The rural-urban divide that Hall demarcates in *The Carhullan Army* mirrors that of *The Wanderground*, in which the hill women live separate from the male-controlled cities. Yet, *The Carhullan Army* does not just attempt to rewrite the separatist utopian novel for the contemporary moment. The novel does more than just revisit the separatist utopian novel and instead locates itself in a time "after" the politics of separatism. In other words, the novel clearly recognizes that it comes at a time that is after lesbian separatist feminism. Sister locates her present as "post" 1970s feminism through describing Jackie and Veronique, the founders of Carhullan, as 'two retro-feminists'.[5] In the time of the novel then, 1970s feminism has seemingly occurred and Sister identifies the separatist politics of Jackie and Veronique as outdated, belonging to the past – a retro-politics. Despite having qualified Jackie and Veronique as outdated, it is precisely this so-called past version of feminist politics that allows Sister to imagine an alternative future. First hearing about Carhullan when she was seventeen, Sister holds on to news clippings about the community for years before she escapes. As Sister reflects, '[l]ike those who has brought pictures of better times to their workstations and tacked them up on the panels of machines, I had kept Carhullan in my mind'.[6] It is the imagined possibilities of this brand of retro-feminism that Sister accesses as a way to imagine a way out of her oppressive present. Thus, if the novel might be said to offer a reading of the possible dystopian near future of Britain, Carhullan, as another possible future, is decidedly retro.

This contemporary novel is not only concerned then with the twenty-first century, but also with the recent feminist past. Through Sister, it imagines another possible near future as a women's only separatist community. Yet, this alternative community is not necessarily a move forwards. As Sister explains: 'There was something better out there. I knew what it was and where to find it. Even if it meant looking behind me, to a venue that had long been forgotten in the aftermath of catastrophe, and the desperate rush to subsist.'[7] Here, the novel gestures to the politics of Carhullan as that which was lost, that which had been forgotten. Just as much as the novel is concerned with this historical present, it is also invested in exploring the lingering after-affect of lesbian utopian separatism as a possibility for the present. Importantly, this community is not idealized – it does not offer the perfect utopia to counter Rith. Sister does not find the sisterhood she imagines and Carhullan is no utopia. Yet precisely because the so-called retro-politics of the past are not idealized, they become interlocutors in a conversation about the present. This novel resists this nostalgic approach, an approach that would keep the past frozen as something lost to the present. The retro-feminism of separatist communities becomes not the idealized solution to the present, but, through Hall's novel, part of an ongoing conversation about what other kinds of futures we might imagine. Hall's novel asks us to consider whether and how histories of 1970s feminism might infuse twenty-first-century critical sensibilities.

Similar to how Hall's novel explores the links between an all-women's separatist community – a "retro-feminism" – and the contemporary moment, this chapter is concerned with bringing the feminist utopian novel into contemporary feminist and queer discourse about futurity. As I outlined in the introduction to this book, towards the end of the millennium, the question of feminism's futurity became the focus of much scholarship, with dominant discourses suggesting that feminism's present tense was one marred by failure and disease.[8] This conception of feminism's timing has been critiqued by Robyn Wiegman as an 'apocalyptic' register which demands that the feminist future be not only a forward move, but one that is produced out of the successful achievement of the political goals of the present – suggesting that we might already know in advance what feminism's future will look like.[9] It is a conception of futurity that demands a linear move forwards, building a future out of the successful attainment of the goals of the past. Yet, emerging out of the millennial fears about a failed future have been a number of attempts to rethink feminist futurity outside of linear models.[10] Resisting notions of futurity as arising out of a linear relationship of success to the desires of the past or present, there has been an increased interest in considering a less linear version of feminist futurity. In Sara Ahmed's words, a feminist futurity might best be realized not through moving on from the past but instead by 'attending to the multiplicity of the pasts that are never simply *behind* us, through the traces they leave in the encounters we have in the present'.[11] The future then becomes only realizable as a complicated interrelation with the past, meaning that in Rebecca Coleman's words, 'a tendency towards the future does not mean that feminist theory disregards the past and present but that it engages these temporalities in different, or "new", ways'.[12]

In light of these recent arguments about feminist futurity, I turn to reread the 1970s feminist utopian novel, and specifically Marge Piercy's *Woman on the Edge of Time*. Drawing on Elizabeth Freeman's insistence that the past might contain 'undetonated energy', I have chosen a text from the feminist 1970s to consider the question of the future, in a move to complicate the dominant narrative that would see the present as having moved on from this time and to insist instead on the genre's possible contribution to contemporary feminist theory.[13] Connie, the protagonist of the novel, sojourns into the future with the strange Luciente, resident of Mattapoisett from the year 2137, who has come to enlist Connie in a war for the future. Connie's special ability to "catch", described as a heightened emotional sensitivity, combined with Luciente's "sending" powers enable Connie to be brought into the utopian village of Mattapoisett, where she is confronted with the vast changes that the future has brought to all aspects of life, including education, work, kinship, gender, and sexuality. Through her travels to Mattapoisett, Connie glimpses the possibility of an alternative to her present and mobilizes a fight against the hegemonic and institutional oppression that she faces locked away in a mental institution.

This chapter explores the limitations of a dominant tendency to read the 1970s feminist utopian novel in relation to its contemporary feminist moment. I suggest instead that the genre might speak to contemporary feminist and queer theorizing on the relationship between futurity and the past. In my reading, *Woman on the Edge of Time* brings loss, mourning, and futurity into close contact with each other – so that Connie's past losses are formative and productive of the future. In other words, I argue that the novel is an example of precisely the kind of futurity that resists linearity and instead engages in a more complex relationship with the past. Far from speaking only to its contemporary feminist moment, the novel speaks to contemporary theoretical interests in a feminist futurity that engages in more manifold ways with the past. Just as Sister imagines that an alternative future might be found "behind" her, I consider how *Woman on the Edge of Time* offers an alternative model of feminist futurity that speaks to contemporary concerns. I first trace through the critical approaches which contain the feminist utopian genre in the 1970s before turning to consider a reading of Piercy's novel which draws out how it might further feminist thinking on models of non-linear futurity. Finally, through a reading of Connie and Luciente's time travel, I posit that the novel's version of feminist futurity might also be read as queer, bringing together a feminist version of futurity with queer thinking on the embodied erotics of time travel. This chapter argues that critiques of generational models of time in feminism and queer thinking on the body's relationship to time open up the genre to rereading. At the same time, I suggest that the genre might speak back to both these disciplines, furthering thinking on what it means to consider non-linear relationships between the past and the future.

The feminist utopian genre

Piercy's writing emerged in the 1970s alongside a peer group of feminist utopian writers including Joanna Russ, Ursula K. Le Guin, and Octavia Butler. These authors are commonly grouped together as belonging to, what was in 1970, an emergent community of feminist writing. Jean Pfaelzer, for instance, highlights the commonalities between authors of feminist utopias, arguing that they 'arose within the context of the contemporary struggles for equal pay, reproductive rights, wider access to both professional and non-traditional jobs, shared housework, childcare, and the removal of cultural stereotypes'.[14] The feminist utopia is, in this way, traditionally described as having a close relationship to feminism's criticisms of patriarchy. The genre is frequently narrated as emerging out of the necessity of women imagining alternative social arrangements from the point of view of their experiences. This emphasis can be found in two genre-defining examples: Carol Pearson's seminal piece on the genre of feminist utopias, 'Women's Fantasies and Feminist Utopias', and Joanna Russ's 'Recent Feminist Utopias'.[15]

Pearson emphasizes the community inherent in the feminist utopian writers, drawing out their related critiques of patriarchy and their attempts at creating alternatives to the dominant order. Grouping together diverse texts by James Tiptree Jr, Ursula K. Le Guin, Joanna Russ, Marge Piercy, and Mary Staton, among others, Pearson highlights their mutual concerns with "woman's work", sexual assault, the private/public split, kinship, and technology. She explains that the feminist utopian novel emerged from women's experiences and privileges reimagining areas of society in which women are most directly affected. In similar language, Russ argues that the feminist utopias and the women's movement arose contemporaneously, remarking that the feminist utopian authors 'form a remarkably coherent group in their presentation of feminist concerns and the feminist analyses which are central to these concerns'.[16] Russ describes how the modern feminist movement made feminist utopian fictions possible, arguing that both genres of writing ask the same questions and 'provide similar answers and remedies'.[17] In the same way as Pearson, Russ groups the feminist utopian writers as a distinct community and similarly connects this community to its contemporary feminist movement. In linking the genre with its contemporary feminist movement, the utopian genre is described as almost the fictional counterpoint to the politics of women's liberation. Feminist utopian novels, in this narrative, were made possible by the politics of the women's movement, and in a fictional realm, they were posing similar questions.

Thus, founding gestures in feminist utopian literary criticism emphasized the connection between the fictional utopias produced in the 1970s and their contemporary feminist context. Pfaelzer argues that utopias 'embody our relationship to the realities of the present' and as readers of utopian fictions, our task is to 'explore how authors of utopian narratives, at particular historical moments, interrogate and inscribe our fate'.[18] In this work, Pfaelzer argues for the importance of reading utopian fiction alongside its historical present. This strategy of reading 1970s feminist utopian fiction as responding to its historical present is not only a founding gesture but it continues to be an important means through which the genre is discussed.[19] Examples of this are widespread, and can be found, for instance, in Tatiana Teslenko's 2003 book, *Feminist Utopian Novels of the 1970s*, in which she argues that the feminist utopian novels provided the conceptual space to test out some of the feminist ideas that were being put forth in theoretical terms. Teslenko explains that the challenge that these novels pose to the patriarchal utopian novel is made possible precisely because of feminist theory's expressed desire for 'social dreaming'.[20] In this, she connects feminism's emphasis on the possibility of other social worlds to the utopian genre's fictional imaginings. Similarly, Susan Magarey argues in 2007 that feminist utopian fictions of the 1970s were where many feminists went to find answers to the questions that were circulating in feminist theory about what a society without sexual difference might look like. According to Magarey, feminist utopias rendered 'dreams of new modes of living imaginatively concrete and detailed'.[21] This historicizing within a particular feminist moment is evident as well in larger surveys which situate feminist science fiction within a developmental narrative of cyberfeminism. For instance, in *Reload: Rethinking Women + Cyberculture*, feminist science fiction is positioned as a precursor to more contemporary cyberfiction writing. Mary Flanagan and Austin Booth explain that '[s]cience fiction was a form in which women writers could tease out the implications of second-wave feminism' and thus expose the sexist assumptions 'of the world in which they lived'.[22] In these engagements with 1970s feminist utopias, the stories are conceptualized primarily in terms of being a fictional space for testing out the revolutionary politics of the feminist seventies. In this emphasis on the genre of feminist utopian fiction as intrinsically related to, evolved from, and further contributing to 1970s feminist critique, the genre is housed in a particular feminist historical moment and, notably, attached to a specific set of political questions and aims.

In relation to *Woman on the Edge of Time*, Piercy's novel is frequently read alongside Shulamith Firestone's *The Dialectic of Sex*. In these readings, the novel is seen as fictionalizing the radical elimination of biological essentialism – an elimination that is called for in Firestone's theoretical work. In the utopian society of the novel, technology has evolved so that biological bodies no longer determine who can mother or even who can breastfeed, and thus traditional gender roles around mothering in Mattapoisett have been entirely done away with. Joan Haran thus reads Piercy's novel as being in dialogue with Firestone's theories, particularly the politics of childrearing and birth, in which Firestone calls for a radical democratization.[23] Haran argues that the technology in Mattapoisett 'is clearly a response to the potential for entrapment within the mothering role, as well as to the concerns felt in the 1970s by some feminists that the virtual exclusive rearing of children by their mothers is a further source of problematic and unequal power relations'.[24] In Haran's reading, Mattapoisett is generated out of the demands of Piercy's contemporary feminism – it takes its shape from the politics in which Piercy was writing. Haran is not alone in postulating this as an important entry-point into *Woman on the Edge of Time* and Lucy Sargisson too suggests that Firestone's thinking on the need to end biology's cultural significance is mirrored in Mattapoisett, where culture is not biologically defined. Sargisson thus argues alongside Haran that Piercy's novel can be 'read as a fictional exploration and extension of Firestone's theory'.[25]

Moreover, Piercy's novel is criticized in the same terms as 1970s feminist theory which further links the novel to its contemporary moment. Not only are the novel's strengths indebted to contemporary feminist theorizing but so too are its weaknesses. Haran argues that some of the shortcomings of *Woman on the Edge of Time* are the product of Piercy's situation within a specific feminist theoretical time. Haran's critique is worth quoting at length:

> Piercy is struggling to articulate a theory that she hopes will enable feminist praxis, and she does so in dialogue with contemporary understandings of sexual inequality. It would be unfair to expect her to anticipate later debates, although her attempts to explore other indices than gender, including race and class, show that her vision of feminism, like that of the 1980s and 1990s aims to be genuinely anti-oppressive, not narrowly self-interested.[26]

In this passage, Piercy's novel is made meaningful through a well-told narrative of feminism – a move from the narrow 1970s into the much more inclusive 1980s and 1990s. As Clare Hemmings argues in *Why Stories Matter*, this narrative is a dominant feminist story that circulates about the feminist seventies, eighties, and nineties.[27] While Haran suggests that Piercy surpasses some of the essentialism of the feminist seventies through exploring race and class, thus situating her outside of the feminist seventies, she emphasizes that these critiques can only be "attempts" and "aims". These aims and attempts cannot be entirely successful because Piercy cannot be expected to transcend her time, the "narrowly self-interested" feminist seventies.

Perhaps this emphasis on the feminist utopian novel's connection to its contemporary moment is unsurprising, given that utopian fiction is often read as offering critical distance on the present's inevitability. As Fredric Jameson explains it, the utopian form is 'the answer to the universal ideological conviction that no alternative is possible, that there is no alternative to the system'.[28] It is through the enactment of a break with the present that the genre is able to argue that 'radical difference is possible and that a break is necessary'.[29] Moreover, feminist utopian novels in particular have been framed through an emphasis not on imagining perfect societies but as discursive practices of resisting the present. Gearhart argues that a feminist utopian fiction is one which 'contrasts the present with an envisioned idealized society' and 'offers a comprehensive critique of present values/conditions'.[30] Further, as Sargisson explains, feminist utopias do not aim for finality but instead engage with the contradictions and politics of their contemporary times.[31] For Tom Moylan, feminist utopian fiction belongs to a 'critical' utopian tradition that is 'rooted in the unfulfilled needs and wants of specific classes, groups, and individuals in their unique historical contexts'.[32] In opposition to over-arching theories of utopia as a "distant" or "perfect" world, these arguments emphasize utopia as a discursive practice of imagining historically specific and situated alternatives.

This emphasis on utopian concerns changing with feminist ones is evident in how *Woman on the Edge of Time* and Piercy's later novel *He, She, and It* are often respectively read as representative of decade-specific concerns – namely a move from radical feminist utopianism to a focus on cyborgs and a more postmodern dystopianism.[33] As Booth and Flanagan explain: 'If feminist utopias of the 1970s and 1980s emphasized women's freedom and autonomy, the dystopias of the 1980s and 1990s accentuated the social and political consequences of the denial of that autonomy.'[34] Having read *Woman on the Edge of Time* alongside Firestone's *The Dialectic of Sex*, Haran reads Piercy's following novel *He, She, and It* alongside Donna Haraway's 'A Cyborg Manifesto', emphasizing a link between feminism's movement through time and Piercy's writing. Such a narrative of Piercy's development not only contains *Woman on the Edge of Time* within the 1970s, it also contains the text's value as being very specific to that time period through showing how Piercy's work supposedly moves on with feminist critiques. M. Keith Booker makes a similar analogy, explaining:

> *Woman on the Edge of Time* was written in the mid-1970s and reflects some of the utopian optimism of the women's movement of that era [...] *He, She, and It*, meanwhile, was written at the end of the 1980s, for many a decidedly dark decade for women's causes.[35]

Reading *He, She, and It* as a darker text than *Woman on the Edge of Time*, Booker reflects that this change in emphasis from utopian to dystopian reflects a changing feminist political landscape. Booker, similar to Haran, describes Piercy through the framework of distinctly separate feminist decades. In analyses such as these, feminist science fiction and feminist critical theory run along a similar timeline – where feminist fiction mirrors the feminist theory of its time.

I am not suggesting that there is something incorrect about this narrative or this approach to feminist utopias. More specifically, there is nothing necessarily objectionable about readings of 1970s utopian fiction that describe it as belonging to a particular feminist community and having a particular relationship to the women's movement. However, what I do want to suggest is that the dominance of this critical approach affirms the fictional texts as "belonging" to 1970s feminism. This kind of theoretical entombment potentially produces novels such as *Woman on the Edge of Time* as valuable to and in feminism only as a historical case study. The feminist utopian novels of the 1970s are thus understood as being windows into a "past" time, as having something to tell us in the present about the feminist struggles in another time. As fictional explorations of 1970s feminist politics, the genre is, in this narrative, decidedly "past". This, I think, makes it exceedingly difficult for the genre to be seen as able to speak to or alongside contemporary concerns. Indeed, the overwhelming prominence of historically situating the 1970s feminist utopia within its particular moment is both an effect of the dominance of linear models of feminism's timing and also makes it difficult to see how the novel itself might offer up other kinds of timing. While I have no intention of arguing that the genre is not influenced by its contemporary feminist critiques or that there is something inherently incorrect in these readings, this entry-point into the genre has perhaps limited the kinds of future relationships that might be thought between feminist writing and feminist theory.[36]

The genre's entombment within the 1970s is particularly salient because of the way this decade has been and continues to be vilified as an essentialist and perhaps even shameful time in Western feminist history. In other words, the feminist decade which the genre is defined in relation to has, in recent decades, been one that has been frequently described as not worth returning to. Hemmings argues that the dominant characterization of the feminist seventies 'is of course essentialism, an accusation so frequently repeated, that it can actually stand as justification for not reading texts from the feminist seventies at all any more'.[37] Hemmings points out that 'Western feminist theory tells its own story as a developmental narrative, where we move from a preoccupation with unity and sameness, through identity and diversity, and on to difference and fragmentation', with these shifts grounded in the 1970s, 1980s, and 1990s respectively.[38] She goes on to argue that regardless of which narrative of feminism's present is being told – one of an improvement on the past's essentialism and racism or one of a lost radical critique – the past is frequently utilized instrumentally in feminism as a means to accomplish a certain contemporary framing, a framing that works to secure an argument about the present. In order to secure this dominant story in feminism, the seventies have to be over in order to describe the present as an improvement or as a loss.

Hemmings' argument reveals how a decade-specific approach to feminism consigns certain theorists and debates to the past. Yet, what has been under-explored is how this narrative has affected the way in which feminist cultural production from the recent past is or is not approached. In other words, not only is the 1970s feminist utopian novel incessantly historicized in its con-temporary moment, but this moment itself is frequently over-inscribed with a narrative of essentialism that buries it as a time that needs no revisiting, that is better left in the past. The persistent framing of the genre within the fem-inist seventies makes it difficult to think through how texts that are labelled "feminist utopias" might travel through feminist time and speak to different contexts and forge alternative relationships to feminist literary and critical theory. Indeed, it seems to prevent this very work. I want to attempt to shift some of the possibilities of reading 1970s feminist utopias in the present by focusing less on situating the genre within its specific contemporary feminist moment. Instead, I read *Woman on the Edge of Time* through contemporary feminist and queer challenges to linear models of time. In the genre's concern with the relationship between various temporal presents and the relationship across these times, the genre is more than a site for imagining possible futures, it also tells stories about relationships to and with time. It is precisely this focus on the novel's concern with relationships between and across temporal boundaries that has been underexplored in critical work. An interest in link-ing the novel's utopian imaginings to its contemporary feminist moment has meant that, crucially, the novel's exploration of time has been almost com-pletely ignored. Piercy's novel works out a relationship between past and future through the themes of loss, mourning, and contingent touching across time. These themes have been under-researched in Piercy's work and speak heavily to contemporary questions surrounding precisely how to conceive of queer and feminist futures that resist privileging progress and the new. *Woman on the Edge of Time* might thus be read not only as a situated critique of its historical present but might also speak to contemporary feminist and queer theorizing on futurity.

Living on

In the first instance, the novel's protagonist is an unlikely figure of futurity. Institutionalized in a mental hospital for the majority of the novel, Connie's life is in many ways already negated. In *Precarious Life*, Butler argues that precarious life is expendable because it is life that has stopped counting, or that never counted in the first place. Butler explains: 'If violence is done against those who are unreal, then, from the perspective of violence, it fails to injure or negate those lives since those lives are already negated.'[39] This 'derealization' produces subjects that are indeed 'neither alive nor dead'.[40] The novel emphasizes the vulnerability of Connie's life in the ward, with the doctors and her family deciding the very fate of her body – which medicines to put her on, how conscious she is allowed to be, or whether to enrol her in medical trials. Facing a medical trial where electrodes would be inserted into her brain to control her behaviour, and having watched her fellow inmates lose control over their emotions following this procedure – with one being driven to suicide – Connie is confronted with her ultimate vulnerability:

> She remembered something she had heard Dr. Redding say to Super-intendent Hodges: that they had used up five thousand monkeys before they began doing these operations on patients. Used up. [...] Thus, after the five thousand monkeys, they [the human patients] were being used up one at a time.[41]

In this conversation about her that she is not privy to, but overhears, Connie learns something of the value placed on her life. As an object waiting to be used up in the same manner as the five thousand monkeys before her, Connie is in a position where her life indeed does not seem to count. The precarity she experiences in the mental institution is connected to the precarity she experiences throughout her life. From the loss of her lover Claud while he is in prison, to the loss of her daughter Angie to foster care, to the loss of her niece Dolly to her pimp boyfriend Geraldo, Connie's life is one of continuous survival of loss. After the implantation of the dialytrode, Connie describes how she 'lives on' despite the fact that she 'was no more' (*WT* 302). Legible through Butler's concept of precarious life, the character of Connie lives a life that has already been negated even as she lives on.

The novel's insistence on Connie as a figure of unbearable loss and precarious life perhaps marks her as a strange figure of feminist futurity. Her losses drag her down and indeed she is pulled back into her present at times when she feels overwhelmed or overcome with negative affect. As Libby Falk Jones writes, '[t]o exist in this novel means to feel'.[42] However, it is Connie's ability to feel that enables her to journey with Luciente into the future in the first place. She is chosen by the future for her ability to "catch" Luciente from Mattapoisett – an ability that is unique and particularly strong in her. Luciente describes Connie as a 'top catcher' due to her open and receptive mind (*WT* 42). This openness and receptability is not clearly explicated in the novel, but, given Connie's characterization as a figure of precarity, her superior catching ability seems likely to be a result of her affinity to affects of loss and mourning. In other words, the affective structures of loss and failure do not leave her in the past, but instead attach her more than others to the future. It is precisely her proximity to loss that makes her particularly able to make contact with the future. While loss and mourning might traditionally be understood as holding us back from moving into the future, from moving on, the novel gestures toward loss and mourning as precisely the qualities that bring Connie in touch with the future.

Loss may thus be an enabling factor in Connie's ability to be brought into the future; perhaps it is the unbounded nature of loss that makes her particularly ripe for crossing temporal borders. Freud argues that the process of grieving is long and arduous, in part due to the libidinal opposition to letting go of the love object. Distinguishing between the two terms in 'Mourning and Melancholia', Freud argues that mourning differs from melancholia in that eventually the reality of the object's absence wins over the refusal to let go and the clinging to the lost object ceases. At the end of the process of mourning, he explains that the ego indeed becomes 'free and uninhibited again'.[43] In melancholia, Freud suggests that the loss is often of a different kind, 'a more ideal kind', where the loss takes forms that exceed the death of a loved one.[44] In this loss, he explains that 'one cannot see clearly what it is that has been lost'.[45] Melancholic loss is often characterized by the inability to fully come to terms with what has been lost, 'in the sense that he knows whom he has lost but not what he has lost in him'.[46] While in mourning the libido withdraws from the lost loved object and is displaced onto another object, in melancholia, 'the free libido was not displaced on to another object; it was withdrawn into the ego'.[47] Thus, the melancholic individual refuses to let go of the object in part through identification with the object. The distinction between mourning and melancholia rests then on mourning being a process through which the ego is able to be free. Melancholia, on the other hand, is akin to failed mourning as the ego does not become free but incorporates the lost object.

However, as Butler points out, Freud's initial distinction between the two terms is blurred in later writing. Freud's subsequent 'The Ego and the Id' contains a revised version of the process of resolving grief. In this work he argues that the incorporation of the lost object 'has a great share in determining the form taken by the ego', contributing 'towards building up what is called its "character"'.[48] Thus, incorporation becomes not a barrier to the resolution of grief, but indeed may be 'the sole condition' through which this process may occur.[49] In this later work, Butler explains that letting go of the lost object no longer requires a break in attachment. Instead, she argues that Freud 'makes room for the notion that melancholic identification may be a *prerequisite* for letting the object go'.[50] This identification with the lost object becomes a psychic means through which the object is preserved. In other words, letting go becomes about a movement of the object from external to internal, preserving the object in the ego and blurring Freud's earlier distinction between mourning and melancholia. The object, as Butler explains, can be given up 'only on condition of a melancholic internalization or [...] a melancholic *incorporation*'.[51] What Butler marks in Freud's shift in understanding of the grieving process is that grief might never end in the simple way of an attachment breaking and being replaced with a new object. Grief and loss become creative forces in the ego so that, Freud explains, the ego 'is a precipitate of abandoned object-cathexes' containing 'the history of those object-choices'.[52] This complicates the notion of mourning being a project that can be completed in a way that leaves the subject untouched, so to speak, by the loss. Instead, loss becomes a creative subject-forming force rather than a process that one needs to end in order to move on.

What both later Freud and Butler suggest and what I identify in *Woman on the Edge of Time*'s preoccupation with loss is that there is something productive about mourning. If Freud's initial understanding of mourning involved seeing it as a process with a beginning and an end – a process that can be resolved – the later work surely moves away from this linear understanding of moving on. Indeed, to suggest that grief is never over but that the lost object is incorporated into the subject is to deny an endpoint to the process of mourning. To deny mourning an endpoint and to emphasize its productivity is to insist that mourning is one process that guarantees the lost object future presence. If the process of mourning carries objects into the future, then mourning contributes to creating futurity. This work on the productivity of mourning at the individual level has been expanded on within feminist writing to suggest that mourning is also productive of collective formation. Freeman's work, which was integral to the previous chapter's reading of Antigone's movements through feminism, articulates how the "losses" of the past find surprising life in the present, so that they productively haunt contemporary feminist identities.[53] Moreover, Ann Cvetkovich's writing explores how the affects associated with trauma serve 'as the foundation for the formation of public cultures'.[54] For example, in one chapter of *An Archive of Feelings*, Cvetkovich considers how lesbian public cultures have accrued around explorations of the complex links between sexual abuse and lesbianism. Through reading cultural texts such as performances by the punk band Tribe 8 and memoirs by lesbian survivors of sexual abuse, Cvetkovich shows how lesbian and queer representations of incest do not so much reject the association between lesbianism and sexual abuse but create public cultures around the possibilities of exploring a more complicated relationship between sexuality and trauma. Such work blurs the distinction between individual psychic processes and collective feeling, emphasizing that loss is not only a process that the individual goes through but that it can be formative of political, affective, and public communities.

In Piercy's text, Connie's losses refuse to settle in the past and instead move (her) into the future. Connie's losses find their doubles in Mattapoisett, where loss extends into the future and is constitutive of her experiences there. For instance, in Mattapoisett she engages in a love affair with a man called Bee, whom she has difficulty separating from Claud: 'She felt swollen equally with old tears and present wanting, the memory of Claud and the presence of Bee. Who was not Claud. But who made her remember' (*WT* 186). Connie's passion for Bee swells with her past love so that this future relationship cannot be easily separated from her memories of loss. Claud, whom Connie describes as the 'sweetest man she had ever had', dies after participating in a medical experiment while in jail – the hepatitis they inject in him in exchange for a shorter sentence eventually takes his life (*WT* 26). Connie mourns Claud in 'a haggard frenzy of alcohol and downers, diving for oblivion and hoping for death' (*WT* 61). In Mattapoisett, walking with Bee and laughing, Connie startles herself 'to hear that old happy laugh from her chest, that sensual laugh Claud had loved to feel with his hands against her' (*WT* 187). After making love to Bee, Connie tells him that he was 'giving [her] back Claud for a night' (*WT* 189). Connie not so much moves forward in time, past her losses, but instead, she moves backward into the past, recovering Claud. Her memories of Claud disrupt Connie's sense of time, where her mourning for Claud not only impacts upon Connie's present but also her experience of the future. Through her time-travelling into the future, Connie's losses move into constructing the future – translating mourning as a process that "takes time" into a claim on the future. Exploring the continued presence of Claud in Connie's experience of the future, the novel describes Connie's inability to leave him behind completely. Instead, loss is a constitutive force of her experiences in the future and thus characterizes the future as a space of loss.

Through an emphasis on a relationship between loss and futurity, Connie contributes to considering how a feminist futurity might require examining how the "incomplete", "unfinished", or even "failures" of the past do not threaten the future but open up unforeseen possibilities. If Connie's ability to be brought into the future of Mattapoisett is connected to her affective life – one overburdened by loss, failure, and mourning – then the novel, similar to psychoanalytic models, suggests that there is something productively unbound about loss. It is precisely this the productive possibilities of failure that Wiegman considers in 'The Intimacy of Critique', where she hypothesizes that a 'pedagogy of failure' might generate feminism's futurity.[55] Unpacking the rhetoric of feminism's failures, Wiegman suggests that perhaps repetition of failure is not a block to feminist futurity but instead its generative force. In other words, perhaps it is through, and not despite, claims of feminism having failed that feminism reproduces itself through time as continuing to be necessary, making failure 'the constitutive condition of feminism's futurity'.[56] This is a feminist futurity in which it is 'the spectre of loss that generates the desire for attachment'.[57] Casting failure as a site not for giving up or letting go, but as a site of continual attachment, Connie's losses in the present might be what contributes to her ability to make contact with the future. This is a representation and version of feminist futurity that is intimately tied to and enabled by past loss and mourning. This is a future that not only functions to critique the present, but is fundamentally built on Connie's relationship to, and experience of, loss.

Whose future?

The novel might thus be read as exploring a feminist futurity that does not move on, but is instead enabled by a cleavage to that which is lost. Yet,

Connie's relationship to loss becomes more complex when she finds herself situated in Mattapoisett as a past that the people of Mattapoisett were more than happy to have left behind – Luciente and her community describe Connie's time as 'The Age of Greed and Waste' (*WT* 240). Luciente explains while visiting Connie's apartment that she is afraid to eat Connie's food because of the horror stories of food 'full of poisonous chemicals, nitrites, hormones residues, DDT, hydrocarbons, sodium benzoate' (*WT* 54). Luciente similarly expresses disdain toward Connie's sewage system, describing Connie as 'primitive' before correcting herself and choosing instead to describe Connie's world as 'rudimentary' (*WT* 55). This framing of Connie's time as a primitive and ungrievable past continues in Mattapoisett where Connie continually is met with surprise and confusion over the practices of "her" time, such as when Jackrabbit, one of Luciente's lovers, marvels at the idea that individuals paired off into couples, which to him, 'looks tragic and blind!' (*WT* 125). Luciente responds by explaining that they should not be surprised, after all, the people of Mattapoisett have 'a more evolved society' (*WT* 125). In this narrative, Connie's present becomes primarily Mattapoisett's past – a rudimentary and less evolved version of what will eventually come to be. In defining Connie as belonging to a "past" stage of development, Luciente and the community of Mattapoisett more widely confirm their own superior "evolved" status and subsume Connie's present into Mattapoisett's time.

In this, the novel echoes the transnational critiques of Western feminist models of development which posit "Other women" as belonging to a prior stage of development in Western feminism's own history. Models of generational inheritance, in their presumption that the future will develop out of the politics of the present, have a tendency to foreclose the possibility that the future might be "other". Generational models of time, according to Judith Roof, are written with the future in mind, so that they attempt to produce 'a future that will be sufficiently attentive to the past to go in the direction imagined by the past'.[58] On a more global scale, a narrative of linear, progressive development forecloses the possibility that feminisms around the world might have very different trajectories from those of the West. When the epitome of feminist development is located in the West, this becomes the marker of futurity that everyone else must achieve. As Aili Mari Tripp argues, Western feminist movements often define feminism's global movement through privileging its own narratives of first and second waves, 'as though these phases occurred universally and as though Western movements were the precursors to similar movements in other parts of the world'.[59] This narrative not only works to make transnational feminist linkages difficult because it denies feminism's multiple and not necessarily coeval global movements, but further, it produces a particular kind of othering of non-Western feminist subjects. As Shu-Mei Shih argues in relation to Chinese women and feminism, the non-Western, 'Other woman' is often then seen as being 'trapped in the earlier phase of development of feminism'.[60] In other words, models of feminism in time which centre around the development of feminism in Western countries situate Western feminism's "present" as the necessary "future" of non-Western feminist development.[61] The future, then, is already determined in advance for non-Western contexts, where it is presumed that feminism will develop along similar lines as it has in the West. Generational narratives thus make it difficult to imagine how non-Western feminisms might have different, competing, and conflicting trajectories to Western feminisms' movements. As Ahmed explains, the challenge for transnational feminism 'might then not only be who is allowed to "make" feminist agendas, but also how can we keep such agendas open, such that they may be disputed by those who are yet to come'.[62] For Ahmed then, the '"we" of such a collective politics is what must be worked for'; it is a labour of 'getting closer'.[63]

Similar to many transnational feminist critiques of Western models of feminist progress, Connie critiques the notion that Mattapoisett might be "her" future. She neither recognizes Mattapoisett as the future nor is particularly desirous of what it has to offer. Her first glimpse of Mattapoisett leaves her confused about exactly what time she is in – Mattapoisett is markedly different from the future she expects. Connie sees Mattapoisett's agricultural paradise as not that far removed from her and her family's past – the rural farming life that they worked so hard to escape. Connie exclaims with disbelief: 'You sure we went in the right direction? Into the future?' (*WT* 68). Thinking she'd see '[r]ocket ships, skyscrapers into the stratosphere, an underground mole world miles deep, glass domes over everything' (*WT* 68), Connie is utterly taken aback by the sound of a rooster, clothes drying on clotheslines, cows, and vegetable plots. She sums up her confusion with the simple utterance: 'It's not like I imagined' (*WT* 68). This resistance to seeing Mattapoiset as her future challenges the narrative that her time is definable primarily through Mattapoisett – to resist Mattapoisett as her future is to resist seeing her present as locatable principally as Mattapoisett's past. Similar to how Tripp argues that a transnational feminism can only be forged through concepts of parallel rather than progressive movement, which can more fully account for feminism as a global project contains 'quite independent trajectories and sources of movement' (*WT* 52), Connie's response to Mattapoisett as her future is to remain distanced from this narrative, challenging instead the so-called developments that she finds.

This is nowhere more apparent than in relation to the politics of mothering that Connie finds in Mattapoisett. When taken for the first time to the brooder, a type of factory that produces and incubates foetuses, Connie's body is physically affected by the sight of the future residents of Mattapoisett: 'Connie gaped, her stomach also turning slowly upside down. All in a sluggish row, babies bobbed. Mother the machine' (*WT* 102). Connie cannot stand the sight of them, hating these 'bland bottleborn monsters of the future' (*WT* 106). Alongside her disgust at the machination of gestation, she is similarly unimpressed with motherhood becoming a practice for men as well as women. Unsatisfied with Luciente's explanation that motherhood was a power that needed to be seceded, a burden but also a tool that could potentially yield power, Connie explains: 'These women thought they had won, but they had abandoned to men the last refuge of women' (*WT* 134). Connie reacts viscerally when she sees a man breastfeeding: 'He sat down with the baby on a soft padded bench by the windows and unbuttoned his shirt. Then she felt sick' (*WT* 134). Connie's disgust at the fate of mothering in Mattapoisett results from being unable to identify with Luciente's narrative of motherhood as a realm of power for women.

As I outlined earlier, the so-called democratization of mothering in Mattapoisett has been understood as a fictional exploration of the theories of Firestone. Yet, the dominance of this reading obscures Connie's persistent ambivalence to this development. Connie's resistance to the discourse of motherhood that she finds in Mattapoisett might be resuscitated not as a "primitive" stance that is best left in the past, but as a considered challenge to Mattapoisett's narrative of progress through her refusal to be a past stage of development. Connie does not experience control over her reproductive or mothering capacities and she thus sees control over mothering as a desirable future for women. Connie's first pregnancy occurs in the middle of her schooling and marks the end of this pursuit, 'her pride, her hope' (*WT* 242). While the baby's father is free to leave her and the baby, which he does, Connie describes the pregnancy as a burden that negatively affects her and her future. Connie's experiences with medical communities contribute to feelings of alienation from her reproductive body. Both Connie and her mother are described by Connie as being 'robbed' (*WT* 47) of their wombs. In Connie's case, her womb is removed unnecessarily, simply 'because the residents wanted practice' (*WT* 45). The state deals the final blow in Connie's narrative of motherhood, when her daughter Angie is taken away from Connie and placed in a foster home after it was decided by psychiatrists that Connie was not fit to keep her. While Luciente describes the "past" act of giving birth as a remit of control for women, Connie's experiences counter this claim. Indeed, the men in her life, the medical community, and finally the child welfare office, all prevent Connie from having the control she so desires over her body, her womb, and her child. Connie, in her journeys to Mattapoisett, thus might be read as a past that refuses to be subsumed into the narrative of Mattapoisett's present – her experiences of motherhood counter Mattapoisett's narrative of the "past", and as an interlocutor in Mattapoisett, she refuses to "settle" in the past that Mattapoisett constructs.

Some of what I see as being at stake in intervening into dominant reading strategies of Piercy's novel becomes particularly apparent at this point. Through a focus on not only its contemporary feminist moment but the theme of time and the question of progressive narratives of feminism, Connie's revolt becomes legible. While the novel has been read as a fictional space for exploring the politics of its contemporary moment – a space for imagining utopic feminist futures – Connie's resistance to these "developments" has remained largely unread. Crucially, this critical blindness to Connie's resistance is a doubling of Luciente's conclusion that Connie's point of view is out of place or "backward". To take Connie's protestations seriously and to account for her critique of Mattapoisett's future is thus to see how Connie does not settle into Mattapoisett's narrative of what progress looks like. Indeed, it is to recognize that Connie critiques a model of linear progress that would imagine her time as the precursor to the desired future. This is a reading of Connie that is overlooked when the novel is understood as a fictional exploration of its contemporary feminist politics. In arguing against the politics of motherhood she finds in Mattapoisett, Connie holds out for a model of time that would allow her a different trajectory. The novel, I continue to insist, offers a number of frames through which to theorize feminist futurity, none of which imagine it as separate from the past, singular, or linear in the least. Moreover, as I will show in this final section, the future is imagined as queerly in touch.

The future is in touch

The process of history is, for Jacques Derrida, one that always creates excess in that 'one must filter, sift, criticize, one must sort out several different possibilities that inhabit the same injunction'.[64] Derrida argues that attempts to secure history in its place are always processes that fail, producing excess spectres which challenge the coherence of the present. Jameson explains in 'Marx's Purloined Letter' that Derrida argues against 'a world of pure presence, of immediate density, of things without a past'.[65] Wendy Brown explains that this process, this sifting and selecting, necessarily produces ghosts, ghosts which 'figure the impossibility of mastering, through either knowledge or action, the past or the present'.[66] The ghost or spectre confounds the logic of progress and ontology and is thus a figure for considering how to activate politically the remnants of the past that continue to exist in the present. As Victoria Hesford explains, mourning in this regard becomes not 'simply an act of remembrance, but also a way of resisting the hegemony of the present: the past becomes resource for the possibility of a different future'.[67] In other words, it is through heeding the ghosts in the present that the present's ontological certainty is disrupted.

However, in *Woman on the Edge of Time*, while Connie might be said to interrupt the narratives of Mattapoisett's model of progress, it is Luciente that is described through the language of spectrality. Similar to how mourning is constitutive of the future for Connie, the future comes to Connie in the form of a ghost – refusing to "remain". The novel begins with Connie in despair over Luciente's presence (who, at this point in the novel, she reads as a man): 'Either I saw him or I didn't and I'm crazy for real this time' (*WT* 9). Connie doubts Luciente's visit as one might doubt the presence of a ghost. Luciente's early visits come in spurts and traces; she is an ephemeral presence that is marked just as much by absence. Luciente's haunting presence is also experienced by Connie's niece, Dolly, who visits Connie shortly after Luciente to find the chair upon which Luciente had sat to be still warm. Connie, for her part, cannot recall when Luciente's visits began or whether there was even a beginning: 'The first time. Was there a once? The dreams surely began with an original; yet she had the sense, the first morning she awakened remembering, that there were more she had not remembered, a sensation of return, blurred but convincing' (*WT* 33). Similar to Derrida's spectre which is always 'a *revenant*' that '*begins by coming back*', Connie cannot be sure about Luciente's visits and cannot recall when (or if) they began.[68] However, in presenting us with a ghost from the future, *Woman on the Edge of Time* pushes the concept of haunting into a quality of not only the past. This suggests that the past is not the only temporality that might "undo" the present's coherence.

The challenge to Connie's ontological present by the future is emphasized through the language of touch. The connection between Connie and Luciente is persistently described through the language of physical contact. Moreover, time travel in the novel occurs when Connie and Luciente make contact with each other, described persistently through the language of touch. The first time Luciente successfully appears in Connie's time, Connie is convinced she is seeing things, but Luciente assures her by explaining, 'I am in touch with you, really' (*WT* 65). In one of the first instances where Luciente tries to make contact with Connie in her dreams, Connie awakes with memories of the touch; upon awakening, Connie 'remembered then the touch of the warm, gentle calloused hand on her bare arm' (*WT* 36). In her first time travel into Mattapoisett, Connie describes their connection by emphasizing this physical pressure and demand:

> She could feel Luciente concentrating, she could feel that cone of energy bearing down on her. It reminded her of the old intensity of a man wanting ... something – her body, her time, her comfort – that bearing down that wanted to grab her and push her under. (*WT* 67–68)

Connie connects the demands of the future to a physical demand on her body, a desiring press on her present.

As a mode of making contact with the past, "touch" has featured centrally within queer historiography. For instance, Dinshaw argues historicism is queer when 'it grasps that temporality itself raises the question of embodiment and subjectivity'.[69] In particular, Dinshaw is interested in moments in which the past might touch the present, might contribute to an expansion of the now. These moments, for Dinshaw, have an 'affective or an erotic component'.[70] Thus, she argues that 'queerly historical' questioning might explore what it means when the 'past touches the present'.[71] Dana Luciano suggests that an example of this queer historiographic practice is the kisses left on Oscar Wilde's grave. These kisses, argues Luciano, might be read as a critical gesture which 'bend time', 'pressing up against a presence from the past, the present-ness of this being-otherwise'.[72] In other words, these kisses, as touches across time, queer historical method through exploring a relation to the past that challenges linearity and instead aims to explore the often startling destabilization of the present that might be found by making contact with the past. Similarly, Freeman describes as queer an approach to the past that 'uses the body as a tool to effect, figure, or perform'.[73] Again, a focus on touch is integral to Freeman's elaboration of 'erotohistoriography', 'a politics of unpredictable, deeply embodied pleasures that counters the logic of development'.[74] Freeman, with this concept, asks how we might see 'queer practices of pleasure, specifically, the bodily enjoyments that travel under the sign of queer sex', as 'portals to historical thinking'.[75] This historiography, in other words, encounters or even enacts history as a bodily relation.

Woman on the Ege of Time is insistent on the way in which the affective and bodily energies of the two women are necessary for time travel to occur. If queer historiography is imagined as a bodily encounter – an erotics – the novel makes the bodies of Connie and Luciente integral to their ability to make contact. Through their bodily encounters, their touches across time, Connie and Luciente's respective present tenses are opened up to a shared contemporaneity. Connie's first journey to Mattapoisett is also the scene in which Connie discovers that Luciente is not a man, but a woman – marking the scene as more than a bit queer. The two women are described as travelling through time with their bodies in an embrace: 'Luciente drew her against him and held her in his arms so their foreheads touched' (*WT* 66). Standing forehead to forehead, the two women face each other with their bodies aligned. It is precisely at this moment that Connie discovers the surprising facts of Luciente's body: 'Pressed reluctantly, nervously against Luciente, she felt the course fabric of his shirt and … breasts! She jumped back' (*WT* 66). Thus, Connie's first sojourn into the future is also a queer moment of recognition – it is precisely the moment at which Connie touches the future that she realizes she has been desiring a woman. Dinshaw explains that the queer touch works by 'knocking signifiers loose, ungrounding bodies, making them strange, working in this way to provoke perceptual shifts and subsequent corporeal responses in those touched'.[76] This queer touching is a moment of discontinuity and strangeness, where Connie's understandings of desire, gender, and sexuality are forced to shift. The press of the future queers Connie's experience of her body and her desire. Connie literally jumps back in response to this queer touch and is forced to rethink her own assumptions about Luciente's gender and sexuality: 'She stared at Luciente. Now she could begin to see him/her as a woman' (*WT* 67).

The queer touch does more than shake Connie's certainty about her sexuality and desires. The specificity of Luciente as a spectre from the future means that the queer touch comes to challenge Connie's ontologically certain present. While Dinshaw, Luciano and Freeman explore the way in which the past might destabilize a coherent present, and seek out approaches to the past that might make visible the ways in which history might produce a queer relationship, *Woman on the Edge of Time* elaborates on the destabilizing queerness of the future. The connection in the novel between time travel, erotic touching, and a queer instance of recognition suggests that the future presses on the present in intimate ways – Connie describes refusing Luciente's touch would be like 'refusing to answer the door to a friend who knew she was at home' (*WT* 97). However, this knock at the door is not easy to embrace. Indeed, the queer touch of the future might dislodge and disrupt the one being touched. It might indeed be a touch that one recoils away from, as Connie initially does, fearing the queerness of the future bearing down on the present. It might be a moment of disidentification that does not entirely resist the future, but does not embrace it either. The future, in other words, does not remain out of reach, but presses on and makes demands of the present, demands that are not always comfortable or utopian.

Conclusion

Reading Piercy's novel through the themes of mourning, loss, and spectrality, I argue that the novel is an instance to consider the multiple desires and attachments that populate the concept of the future. Mourning, as articulated by Freud and Butler, is a productive, subject-forming force. The creative dimension of loss becomes, in Connie's story, a means to consider the future's connection to the desires and figures of the past. Connie confuses easy distinctions between the past, present, and future – bringing her desires into the future, feeling the future as her world's past, and being made to feel as if her arrival in the future is unwelcome. In thinking about time in feminism, *Woman on the Edge of Time* is an example of the various ways desires, attachments, and political dreams cross temporal boundaries, blurring these boundaries as they travel. Our feminist present might be best imagined as persistently interrupted by the demands of the future – haunted by the promise of something different and something more. Connie's experiences and the language of mourning provide models for thinking about the inevitable ways we are always out of time, giving us language to experience the multiplicities of our present, the residues of our past, and the loss of a future we have yet to know.

Notes

1 Iain Robinson, '"You Just Know When the World Is About to Break Apart": Utopia, Dystopia and New Global Uncertainties in Sarah Hall's *The Carhullan Army*', in *Twenty-First Century Fiction: What Happens Now*, ed. Siân Adiseshiah and Rupert Hildyard (Basingstoke: Palgrave Macmillan, 2013), pp. 197–211 (p. 198).
2 Ibid., p. 197.
3 Ibid., p. 200.
4 Sally Miller Gearhart, *The Wanderground: Stories of the Hill Women* (Watertown, MA: Persephone Press, 1979).
5 Sarah Hall, *The Carhullan Army* (London: Faber and Faber, 2007), p. 50.
6 Ibid., p. 54.
7 Ibid.

8 See Cathryn Bailey, 'Making Waves and Drawing Lines: The Politics of Defining the Vicissitudes of Feminism', *Hypatia*, 12 (1997), 17–28; Susan Gubar, 'What Ails Feminist Criticism?', *Critical Inquiry*, 24.4 (1998), 878–902; Martha Nussbaum, 'The Professor of Parody: The Hip Defeatism of Judith Butler', *The New Republic*, 22 February 1999, pp. 37–45; Lynne Segal, 'Only Contradictions on Offer', *Women: A Cultural Review*, 11.1–2 (2000), 19–36.

9 Robyn Wiegman, 'Feminism's Apocalyptic Futures', *National Women's Studies Association Journal*, 14.2 (2000), 805–25 (p. 811).

10 See Sara Ahmed, 'Imaginary Prohibitions: Some Preliminary Remarks on the Founding Gestures of the "New Materialism"', *European Journal of Women's Studies*, 15.1 (2008), 23–39; Elizabeth Freeman, *Time Binds: Queer Temporalities, Queer Histories* (Durham, NC and London: Duke University Press, 2010), especially Chapter 2: 'Deep Lez'; Clare Hemmings, *Why Stories Matter: The Political Grammar of Feminist Theory* (Durham, NC and London: Duke University Press).

11 Sara Ahmed, 'This Other and Other Others', *Economy and Society*, 31.4 (2002), 558–72 (p. 559, emphasis in original).

12 Rebecca Coleman, '"Things That Stay": Feminist Theory, Duration and the Future', *Time & Society*, 17.1 (2008), 85–102.

13 Freeman, *Time Binds*, p. xvi.

14 Jean Pfaelzer, 'The Changing of the Avant Garde: The Feminist Utopia', *Science-Fiction Studies*, 15.3 (1988), 282–94 (pp. 282–83).

15 Carol Pearson, 'Women's Fantasies and Feminist Utopias', *Frontiers: A Journal of Women's Studies*, 2.3 (1977), 50–61; Joanna Russ, 'Recent Feminist Utopias', in *Future Females: A Critical Anthology*, ed. Marleen S. Barr (Bowling Green, OH: Bowling Green State University Popular Press, 1981), pp. 71–85.

16 Russ, 'Recent Feminist Utopias', p. 71.

17 Ibid., p. 73.

18 Jean Pfaelzer, 'Response: What Happened to History?', in *Feminism, Utopia, and Narrative*, ed. Libby Falk Jones and Sarah Webster Goodwin (Knoxville: University of Tennessee Press, 1990), pp. 191–200 (pp. 198–99).

19 Notable exceptions to this can be found in Jane Elliott, *Popular Feminist Fiction as American Allegory: Representing National Time* (New York and Basingstoke: Palgrave Macmillan, 2008); Kim Trainor, '"What Her Soul Could Imagine": Envisioning Human Flourishing in Marge Piercy's *Woman on the Edge of Time*', *Contemporary Justice Review*, 8.1 (2005), 25–38.

20 Tatiana Teslenko, *Feminist Utopian Novels of the 1970s: Joanna Russ and Dorothy Bryant* (New York and London: Routledge, 2003), p. 34.

21 Susan Magarey, 'Dreams and Desires: Four 1970s Feminist Visions of Utopia', *Australian Feminist Studies*, 22.53 (2007), 325–41 (p. 327).

22 Austin Booth and Mary Flanagan, 'Introduction', in *Reload: Rethinking Women + Cyberculture*, ed. Mary Flanagan and Austin Booth (Cambridge, MA and London: MIT Press, 2002), pp. 25–41 (p. 2).

23 Joan Haran, '(Re)Productive Fictions: Reproduction, Embodiment and Feminist Science in Marge Piercy's Science Fiction', in *Science Fiction, Critical Frontiers*, ed. Karen Sayer and John Moore (Basingstoke: Macmillan, 2000), pp. 154–68.

24 Haran, p. 159.

25 Lucy Sargisson, *Contemporary Feminist Utopianism* (London and New York: Routledge, 1996), p. 165.

26 Haran, p. 159.

27 Hemmings, p. 5.

28 Fredric Jameson, *Archaeologies of the Future* (London: Verso, 2005), p. 232.

29 Ibid., pp. 231–32.

30 Sally Miller Gearhart, 'Future Visions: Today's Politics: Feminist Utopias in Review', in *Women in Search of Utopia*, ed. Ruby Rohrlich and Elaine Hoffman Baruch (New York: Schocken, 1984), pp. 296–310 (p. 296).
31 Sargisson, p. 20.
32 Tom Moylan, *Demand the Impossible: Science Fiction and the Utopian Imagination* (New York and London: Methuen, 1986), p. 1.
33 See M. Keith Booker, 'Woman on the Edge of a Genre: The Feminist Dystopias of Marge Piercy', *Science-Fiction Studies*, 21.3 (1994), 337–50; Haran; Heather Hicks, 'Striking Cyborgs: Reworking the "Human" in Marge Piercy's *He, She and It*', in *Reload: Rethinking Women + Cyberculture*, ed. Mary Flanagan and Austin Booth (Cambridge, MA and London: MIT Press, 2002), pp. 85–106; Anna M. Martinson, 'Ecofeminist Perspectives on Technology in the Science Fiction of Marge Piercy', *Extrapolation*, 44.1 (2003), 50–68.
34 Booth and Flanagan, p. 2.
35 Booker, p. 337.
36 This is not to say that turning to the past as "case study" does not hold critical value. For an elaboration on an approach to the past that resists a model of either alterity or continuity, see Valerie Traub, 'The Present Future of Lesbian Historiography', in *A Companion to Lesbian, Gay, Bisexual, Transgender, and Queer Studies*, ed. George E. Haggerty and Molly McGarry (Oxford: Blackwell Publishing Ltd, 2007), pp. 124–45.
37 Hemmings, p. 120.
38 Ibid., pp. 115–16.
39 Judith Butler, *Precarious Life: The Powers of Mourning and Violence* (London and New York: Verso, 2004), p. 33.
40 Ibid.
41 Marge Piercy, *Woman on the Edge of Time* (London: The Women's Press, 1979), pp. 220–21. Hereafter referred to in the main text as *WT*.
42 Libby Falk Jones, 'Gilman, Bradley, Piercy, and the Evolving Rhetoric of Feminist Utopias', in *Feminism, Utopia, and Narrative*, ed. Libby Falk Jones and Sarah Webster Goodwin (Knoxville: University of Tennessee Press, 1990), pp. 116–29 (p. 124).
43 Sigmund Freud, 'Mourning and Melancholia', in *The Standard Edition of the Complete Psychological Works of Sigmund Freud*, vol. XIV (1914–16), trans. James Strachey (London: Hogarth Press, 1957), pp. 243–58 (p. 245).
44 Ibid.
45 Ibid.
46 Ibid.
47 Ibid., p. 249.
48 Sigmund Freud, 'The Ego and the Id', in *The Standard Edition of the Complete Psychological Works of Sigmund Freud*, vol. XIX (1923–25), trans. James Strachey (London: Hogarth Press, 1961), pp. 3–68 (p. 28).
49 Ibid., p. 29.
50 Judith Butler, *The Psychic Life of Power: Theories in Subjection* (Stanford, CA: Stanford University Press, 1997), p. 134 (emphasis in original).
51 Ibid. (emphasis in original).
52 Freud, 'The Ego and the Id', p. 29.
53 Elizabeth Freeman, 'Packing History, Count(er)ing Generations', *New Literary History*, 31.4 (2000), 727–44.
54 Ann Cvetkovich, *An Archive of Feelings: Trauma, Sexuality and Public Cultures* (Durham, NC and London: Duke University Press, 2003), p. 10.
55 Robyn Wiegman, 'The Intimacy of Critique: Ruminations on Feminism as a Living Thing', *Feminist Theory*, 11.1 (2010), 79–84 (p. 82).
56 Ibid.

57 Ibid., p. 81.
58 Judith Roof, 'Generational Difficulties; or, The Fear of a Barren History', in *Generations: Academic Feminists in Dialogue,* ed. Devoney Looser and E. Ann Kaplan (Minneapolis and London: University of Minnesota Press, 1997), pp. 69–87 (p. 83).
59 Aili Mari Tripp, 'The Evolution of Transnational Feminisms: Consensus, Conflict and New Dynamics', in *Global Feminism: Transnational Women's Activism, Organising and Human Rights*, ed. Myra Marx Ferree and Aili Mari Tripp (New York and London: New York University Press, 2006), pp. 51–75 (p. 54).
60 Shu-Mei Shih, 'Towards an Ethics of Transnational Encounter, or "When" Does a "Chinese" Woman Become a "Feminist"?', *differences: A Journal of Feminist Cultural Studies*, 13.2 (2002), 90–126 (p. 95).
61 It might also be integral here to consider that "progress" or "futurity" can only be defined with an idea of what is "past". In other words, it is not just that there are competing temporalities but that they are articulated in relation to each other. For an elaboration of this, see Judith Butler, 'Sexual Politics, Torture, and Secular Time', *The British Journal of Sociology*, 59.1 (2008), 1–23.
62 Ahmed, 'This Other and Other Others', p. 569.
63 Ibid., p. 570.
64 Jacques Derrida, *Spectres of Marx*, trans. Peggy Kamuf (London and New York: Routledge, 1994), p. 18.
65 Fredric Jameson, 'Marx's Purloined Letter', in *Ghostly Demarcations: A Symposium on Jacques Derrida's Spectres of Marx*, ed. Michael Sprinkler (London and New York: Verso, 1995), pp. 26–67 (p. 58).
66 Wendy Brown, *Politics Out of History* (Princeton: Princeton University Press, 2001), p. 146.
67 Victoria Hesford, 'Feminism and Its Ghosts: The Spectre of the Feminist-as-Lesbian', *Feminist Theory*, 6.3 (2005), 227–50 (p. 230).
68 Derrida, *Spectres of Marx*, p. 11 (emphasis in original).
69 Carolyn Dinshaw, 'Temporalities', in *Oxford Twenty-First-Century Approaches to Literature: Middle English*, ed. Paul Strohm (Oxford: Oxford University Press, 2007), pp. 107–23 (p. 109).
70 Carolyn Dinshaw, *Getting Medieval: Sexualities and Communities, Pre- and Postmodern* (Durham, NC and London: Duke University Press, 1999), p. 50.
71 Dinshaw, 'Temporalities', p. 112.
72 Dana Luciano, 'Nostalgia for an Age Yet to Come: *Velvet Goldmine*'s Queer Archive', in *Queer Times, Queer Becomings*, ed. E. L. McCallum and Mikko Tuhkanen (Albany, NY: SUNY Press, 2011), pp. 121–55 (p. 123).
73 Freeman, *Time Binds*, p. 95.
74 Elizabeth Freeman, 'Time Binds, or, Erotohistoriography', *Social Text*, 23.3–4 (2005), 57–68 (p. 59).
75 Ibid.
76 Dinshaw, *Getting Medieval*, p. 151.

3 'I'm a waste of time'

Riot grrrl and *Ladies and Gentlemen, the Fabulous Stains*

In broad and loosely defined terms, riot grrrl is frequently described as a feminist alternative subculture that emerged in the United States in the early 1990s around bands including Bikini Kill, Tribe 8, and L7. It was a DIY (do-it-yourself) movement characterized by its feminist politicization of female adolescence, its critique of the male-dominated music scene, and its emphasis on young women being in charge of cultural creation (through music and zines in particular). In the last decade or so, there has been the release of a spate of documentary films which explore the significance of this feminist subcultural movement. These include Kerri Koch's 2005 film *Don't Need You: The Herstory of Riot Grrrl*, Kerthy Fix's *Who Took the Bomp? Le Tigre on Tour* and Amy Olden's *Grrrl Love and Revolution: Riot Grrrl NYC, From the Back of the Room*, both from 2011, and most recently, Sini Anderson's 2013 *The Punk Singer*, a film focused on Bikini Kill singer, Kathleen Hanna. These documentary films are matched by a focus on riot grrrl in scholarly texts, at numerous conferences, in exhibitions, and more informally online (on blogs, Tumblr, etc.). This interest in revisiting riot grrrl in the present leads Mimi Thi Nguyen to argue that riot grrrl is 'now becoming the subject of so much retrospection'.[1] As Nguyen argues, this proliferation of histories, documentaries, and knowledge about riot grrrl 'renders especially pertinent questions of how we remember'.[2]

In Nguyen's brilliant consideration of riot grrrl, she is interested in particular in the dominant narrative that suggests that critiques by women of colour interrupted the trajectory of riot grrrl. She traces through a less often told story of how a focus on girl–girl intimacy in the movement affected the kinds of collectivity that the movement imagined. In particular, she argues that the demand for collective intimacy had difficulty accommodating racial difference. She argues that 'the difference of race both confounded (and was contained by) the prescription of intimacy' and 'it became apparent that girl love could easily, intensely, perform as a feminist mode of control and psychic violence'.[3] As well as reconfiguring how the "interruption" of race is imagined, Nguyen also argues that women of colour in the movement did not just "interrupt" or "get in the way" – they created a co-present scene that considered race as central to cotemporaneous ruminations on mixed-race identifications, queerness, and migration histories (to name but a few). As well as offering a different narrative of race in riot grrrl, Nguyen is also concerned with the ongoing erasure of these co-present riot grrrl histories and trajectories in contemporary remembrances. In other words, she argues that how we continue to remember and narrate riot grrrl history is a political act. She takes the riot grrrl movement as an opportunity to consider more broadly questions about feminism and time, about the relationship between pasts and futures, and 'about lessons we might have – or should have – learned and those we did not'.[4]

This chapter aims to consider questions of feminism's timing and it does this in dialogue with riot grrrl cultural production.[5] Nguyen's piece focuses on feminism's ongoing failure to account for its own complicities and co-present movements, particularly in regards to race. I want to start by considering briefly the temporalities of Nguyen's article. Her reliance on a "then" and "now" temporal structure is a dominant approach in contemporary remembrances of riot grrrl. Moreover, the dominance of this temporal structure works to erase other possible ways of imaging feminism's timing. The first half of Nguyen's piece explores the "then" of riot grrrl subculture – taking "us" back to the time in which the movement was being created – and the second half considers the "now" – the remembering of this "then". In part, this is an effect of Nguyen's having been part of riot grrrl then and her ability now to converse with contemporary feminist theorists and frameworks (including Sara Ahmed, Laurent Berlant, and Robyn Wiegman) that produce her ruminations on the history of riot grrrl. This dual access to the "then" and "now" is a feature of a number of other revisits. Gayle Wald, for example, acknowledges her positionality in relation to riot grrrl by explaining that the riot grrrl movement encouraged her to begin to write academically about music culture and thus she has 'political, professional, and personal' investments in the topic.[6] Moreover, the director of *From the Back*, Amy Oden, similarly locates herself as a teenager within the DIY subculture, and Abby Moser, the filmmaker of *Grrrl Love and Revolution*, also identifies as having been part of the movement in the early 1990s. Not unlike Nguyen's article, these recent documentaries often use archival footage (the story then) alongside contemporary interviews (the remembering now) to create a dual temporality – what actually happened and what we now remember.

I make this connection neither as a critique, nor to suggest that everyone working on histories of riot grrrl was necessarily involved in the movement in the 1990s. Rather I aim to draw attention to the structure of "now" and "then". This structure stabilizes the past as something that we can have access to now. Indeed, it clearly divides the past from the present. The then generates the now in a linear model of development, where the then is not the now (despite how many similarities might exist between the two times). This is further exacerbated when the structure of remembrance is linked to individual subjects. What I mean here is that the past as the cause of the present becomes difficult to escape when it is linked to particular feminists who are not only narrating riot grrrl but also their own involvement in the movement. Even as Nguyen aims to resist 'progressive teleologies', the insertion of her own development as a subject in the narrative works to align riot grrrl with her own life course and thus a narrative of linear progression.[7] The past becomes a stage of development that has produced the contemporary speaking subject – solidifying a cause and effect relationship between the past and the present. In opposition to this "then" and "now" narrative, it seems to me that the story is much more circular. What I would instead suggest is the inherent circularity in these turns back – the turns back are in part enabled by the "grrrl" that existed in the past yet that "grrrl" is not the grounds for the present but produced by present demands. Perhaps this "grrrl" both guarantees the move from "then" to "now" while also troubles this linearity.

This brings me to my interest in riot grrrl, which has to do with the queer temporalities that might be found in its "grrrl" figure. I am not so much referring here to desire or sexual relationships within the community.[8] Rather, I aim to consider the queerness of resistances to reproductive, heterosexual temporalities. This chapter's exploration of the queer temporalities of riot grrrl cultural production is not concerned with what happened "then" and how we remember "now", but instead with an interest in considering what did not happen. In other words, if the now and then structure of remembrances works to "straighten" riot grrrl temporalities, align them with contemporary subjects, and demarcate the past from the present, perhaps we might consider the subculture through less linear approaches. In this, my entry-point into considering the queer temporalities of riot grrrl is a fictional 1981 cult film, *Ladies and Gentlemen, the Fabulous Stains.*[9] *The Fabulous Stains* tells the story of the rise to fame of an all-girl punk band, The Stains. The Stains, comprised of Corinne (Diane Lane), her sister Tracy (Marin Kanter), and Jessica (Laura Dern), escape their suburban American town to go on tour with two all-male bands – the ageing glam rock band, The Metal Corpses, and a young British punk band, The Looters. Despite only having had one band practice before going on tour, The Stains quickly gain notoriety through Corinne's media-savvy personality, outlandish "skunk" hairstyle and feminist politics (Fig. 3.1). Throughout the film, The Stains resist the demands to grow up, where growing up means growing into a timeline that has already been laid out before them. Instead, Corinne sings about the value of wasting time, of being a waster of time.

As I will go on to explore, the film is frequently named as a precursor to the riot grrrl movement, yet this is a retrospective claim that can only be made once riot grrrl has happened. Through a consideration of this film, I hope to consider what might be learned about riot grrrl without a desire to depict what really happened or to intervene in processes of historical remembrance. Instead, I want to focus on how the film has become a canonical riot grrrl film, even though it does not fit into the genealogy of the subculture. This timing might, I hope, open up an entry-point into the subculture that moves away from its ties to specific subjects and might instead enable a focus

Figure 3.1 Corinne 'Third Degree' Burns, *Ladies and Gentlemen, the Fabulous Stains.*
© Copyright 1981 Paramount Pictures. Reprinted by permission. All rights
reserved.

on the temporality (rather than history) of female rebellion. A focus on
representations of and mobilizations of girlishness in riot grrrl culture highlights the movement's emphasis on politicizing female adolescence. As Mary
Celeste Kearney argues, one of the key aspects of riot grrrl is 'the way it has
reformulated adolescent girlhood as a powerful location of cultural and political identity'.[10] If "girl" had been depoliticized, the snarling "grrrl", in
Marion Leonard's words, 'signified a feisty, assertive girl or woman, who
relished a political engagement with feminist issues'.[11] This politicization of
the girl has received much scholarly attention, particularly in relation to DIY
movements, capitalism, and the market economy.[12]

However, I hope in this chapter to consider the queer potential of calls to resist
growing up into "women". I draw on queer theorists including Judith Halberstam
to consider how the riot grrrl enables the envisioning of alternative timelines
that work in opposition to dominant heterosexual life courses.[13] Refusing the
imperative to find happiness in narratives of heterosexuality, female adolescent
rebels might be thought of, in Ahmed's words, as 'affect aliens'.[14] Drawing on
Kathryn Bond Stockton and Valerie Rohy, I argue that female fandom might
be read not only as a negative refusal but also as an alternative form of
reproduction – a sideways spread, or a queer subcultural meme. This chapter
does not aim to uncover alternative or transgressive correctives to riot grrrl
history. Challenges, such as Nguyen's, to dominant narratives are absolutely
politically integral. Yet, as I considered in this book's introduction, what
might be equally important is to explore the temporal structures through which
we frame these histories. It is here that I consider how the "then" and "now" of
riot grrrl narratives miss out on the possibility to see the movement's own
refusal of this linearity. As in previous chapters, this chapter explores how
recent critiques of generational time might illuminate a feminist archive of
cultural output. At the same time, I explore how this reading is possible
because of the already-thereness of the queerness of feminism's timing.

Trouble in/troubling the riot grrrl canon

I want to start by exploring a few of the strange temporalities of *The Fabulous
Stains.* In the first instance, the temporality of the film's release transgresses

the traditional route of theatre release to DVD to television spot. Despite the big names involved in the film, including Diane Lane (who by 1979 had already appeared on the cover of *Time* magazine), writer Nancy Dowd (*Slapshot, Coming Home*), director Lou Adler (record producer, manager, and producer of *The Rocky Horror Picture Show*), and members of The Clash and The Sex Pistols playing The Looters, the resulting film was initially a failed Paramount project, receiving a limited release in the 1980s. Many of the individuals involved in the film claim to have never seen it in its entirety and this initial failure had the film's writer believing it 'had gone to die in the Paramount vaults'.[15] However, the film has, in recent years, developed an audience thanks in part to late-night screenings on American television. The film was finally released on video in 2008, almost two decades after it was completed, and has since been screened at various film festivals.

Along with its almost backwards trajectory (from late-night screenings to DVD to festival screenings), the film's strange timing is also produced through its relationship to feminism. With its focus on an all-girl band and their in-your-face feminist style, *The Fabulous Stains* seemingly inserts The Stains into a history of riot grrrl subculture. While, as far as I know, there has been no scholarly attention paid to the film yet, this connection is made across both more informal sites (for example on numerous blogs, Tumblrs, and YouTube channels), as well as in the more formal marketing strategies of the film's distributor. In a review by Gary Morris for *Bright Lights Film Journal*, the film is described as a riot grrrl movie, with Corinne named as being in the 'upper tier of the riot girl canon'.[16] Furthermore, on the website of the DVD distributor, Rhino Home Video, the film is described as having inspired Bikini Kill, L7, and Courtney Love, thus placing The Stains as precursor to the riot grrrl movement.[17] Bikini Kill member Tobi Vail is quoted as describing the film as 'the most realistic and profound film I have ever seen'.[18] In popular culture and even riot grrrl subculture then, the film, as David Laderman argues, is conceptualized today as 'a visionary precursor of the 1990s riot grrrl music movement'.[19]

Of course, the similarities between The Stains and the riot grrrl movement are indeed striking. As numerous Bikini Kill songs attest (including 'I Like Fucking' and 'Don't Need You'), the riot grrrl movement in part involved a reclamation of female sexuality from patriarchal control. This is a message mimicked in Corinne's valuation of the experiences and identities of young women, and in particular her slogan, 'we don't put out'. This slogan, rather than acting as a rallying cry to virginity, is used by Corinne to refuse everything about patriarchal culture that defines her body, her sexuality, and her identity in ways that she aims to resist. Similar to how Bikini Kill would write "SLUT" across their midriff and many riot grrrls challenged notions of acceptable female display, Corinne's performances in see-through blouses, combined with her insistence that she does not 'put out', challenge and critique norms around female sexuality.

Moreover, the film's emphasis on an all-female band that spreads underground and takes control of their media representation resonates with the riot grrrl movement. Famously producing a mainstream media black-out, one of the key tenets behind the riot grrrl movement was that young women must have the means to control their own representation.[20] Vail, of Bikini Kill, writes in the liner notes of the CD version of the band's first two records:

We have been written about a lot by big magazines who have never talked to us or seen our shows. They write about us authoritatively, as if they understand us better than we understand our own ideas, tactics, and significance.

Alongside this insistence on the right to author their own movement, riot grrrl, as a term, was left open to contestation and this explicitly made it more difficult for popular media to pin it down in sound-bite form. As Kristen Schilt explains, 'while many women and girls took on the label "Riot Grrrls," they shied away from defining exactly what that identity meant, in an attempt to avoid allowing the media to co-opt the scene and create a static "Riot Grrrl" identity'.[21] This concern with mainstream media is mirrored in *The Fabulous Stains*, which offers its own critique of mainstream news for its inability to comprehend The Stains' success. In particular the film mocks the male newscaster who reports on The Stains' story yet cannot understand the band's significance or its politics.

Finally, similar to Nguyen's arguments that the riot grrrl movement had difficulty accommodating racial difference, the film seems unable to develop its own racial politics. The film's representation of Corinne's first tour manager, the Rastafarian Lawnboy (Barry Ford) – whose name is a less than oblique reference to his smoking habits – is incredibly stereotypical in its one-dimensionality. It is this character that gives Corinne her first break by taking a chance on The Stains, but who ultimately must be left behind in her ascendancy to stardom. In other words, as the sole non-white character, his abandonment might easily be read as The Stains needing to abandon race on their way to stardom. Lawnboy provides a kind of moral compass in the narrative – it is the betrayal of him that eventually leads to The Stains' implosion at the hands of the slick new manager, and it is Corinne's later giving of the tour profits to Lawnboy that is meant to signal a kind of recovery from the poison of commercial success. Nguyen opens her article by considering the parallels between the origin story of riot grrrl and the race riots following the shooting of a Salvadorian man by a police officer (both occurring in Washington, DC in 1991), as a way to demonstrate what has been seen as "periphery" to riot grrrl or what cannot "fit" into the dominant narrative.[22] The relationship between Corinne and Lawnboy is incredibly central to the plot in some respects, yet is a difficult fit for those who might want to celebrate the film's riot grrrl politics. In Lawnboy, the film both fails in its racial politics while also remaining profoundly ambivalent – it gestures toward a central relationship between race and riot grrrl, yet cannot, I suggest, finally settle the discordances and can only allude to them.

Not forsaking these similarities, *The Fabulous Stains* does not easily fit into the narrative of the riot grrrl movement. Despite the film's distributor, Rhino Home Videos, selling the film and Corinne as the 'archetypal' riot grrrl, there is something incompatible about this.[23] One of the first defining moments of riot grrrl is frequently cited as the International Pop Underground Festival held in the summer of 1991 by K Records of Olympia, where the first night was Girls' Night.[24] The film, finished in 1981, thus predates the movement's arrival by at least a decade. Moreover, as a fictional band created by Paramount, The Stains are an unlikely voice for a movement that was built so emphatically on the experiences and cultural creativity of young women. Further, the film itself might even be read as narrating the fall of riot grrrl, depicting as it does the band's increasing commercialization and eventual abandonment by their fans. The Stains are destroyed by their fans who turn on them when they realize that the alternative community they desired to be a part of has become mass-marketed and sold to them as blouses and hair dye. This narration of The Stains' demise is an uncanny precursor to the fight that the riot grrrls eventually had with media attention. The Stains, in the film, become sellable through a focus on Corinne as a fashion icon and her skunk style. Many in the riot grrrl movement feared precisely this kind of marketing of the movement – as a fashion or style that was emptied of its radical politics. *The Fabulous Stains* seemingly predicts and tells the story of the fall of the riot grrrl movement at least a decade before the subculture became identifiable as such.

Interestingly then, Corinne can only be claimed as the origin of riot grrrl after the fact. Indeed, the production of the film as the precursor to riot grrrl could only happen once riot grrrl itself had already happened. Corinne could only become the archetypal riot grrrl once the movement had occurred and riot grrrl became a recognizable politics and aesthetics – this could not have happened in 1981. The film is thus retrospectively the precursor to a movement that had to exist in order for it to achieve this label. This retrospective labelling is, I think, a moment in which a potentially disruptive narrative is made to fit into the dominant one. To return to Nguyen's insistence on the need to reflect on practices of remembering and troubling the dominant narrative of riot grrrl, including questioning 'the progressive teleologies of origin, episode, and succession', it seems that this film clearly demonstrates the discordances in narratives of feminism's linearity.[25] Yet, rather than argue that the film be more properly historically situated as belonging elsewhere, this strange timing might be an invitation to investigate further what kinds of temporalities it might direct us toward. I do not aim to tell a better story about the film but to instead consider what the film might contribute to challenging dominant narratives of feminism's timing. The film's circulation, rather than forecloses its ability to tell us anything about feminism's history, points us to consider the discordances and unevenness of feminism's temporality. I want to consider then for the remainder of this chapter not what *The Fabulous Stains* necessarily tells us about riot grrrl history, but what it might tell us about feminist temporalities.

In *The Fabulous Stains* I see a model for feminist time that works outside linear generations and instead generates queer relationships. As a film that follows the first tour of an all-female DIY punk band, I argue that the film's protagonist, Corinne, contributes to this book's archive of queer feminist timing. Through her resistance to growing older, her emphasis on wasting time, and her horizontal growth through the creation of a teenage girl community of "skunks", this chapter argues that Corinne challenges models of linear progress through time. I begin my reading of the film then not through the dominant narratives that circulate about riot grrrl but instead by arguing that Corinne's rebellion and resistance is of a temporal nature. I then trace through a reading of the film that considers it alongside the figure of the queer child, arguing for how Corinne furthers thinking about how this figure troubles linear narratives. Through the language of wasting time and a refusal to follow the path laid out in front of her, Corinne can be read as a queer feminist figure, refusing the timeline given to her, insisting on holding out for a "not-yet". Similar to previous chapters' explorations of genres and figures that have proven to be "sticky" in feminism, I suggest in this chapter that the appeal of riot grrrl subculture, one of the qualities that inspires continual returns, revivals, and revisits, might be its temporalities.

Corinne "Third Degree" Burns' timing

I first viewed *The Fabulous Stains* when it was screened in London at the British Film Institute's Lesbian and Gay Film Festival in 2010. Despite the curator of the event admitting that the film was not "about" gays or lesbians, she argued that there was indeed "something queer" about it. I would agree that there is a queerness to the film and that this queer aesthetic comes through what I identify as Corinne's queer timing. Corinne's queer timing is locatable in her resistance to dominant heterosexual temporality imagined as a means of moving "through" life. As Judith Halberstam argues, it is possible to consider queer time as running alongside and usually against what we might call hetero-temporality so that '[q]ueer uses of time and space develop, at least in part, in opposition to the institutions of the family, heterosexuality, and reproduction'.[26] Through asserting that queer subcultures work by allowing their participants to imagine their life courses as running alternative to the logic of 'birth, marriage, reproduction, and death', Halberstam creates a space for considering how queer bodies move in accordance with a different clock.[27]

The Fabulous Stains opens with the sound of a ticking clock. Accompanied only by a blank screen, the ticking of the clock becomes central to the opening seconds of the film. This opening alerts viewers to the importance that time will play throughout the narrative. The blank screen eventually opens to an image of a newscaster, who explains that the feature on Charlestown, Pennsylvania, which the news channel aired two days ago, has received a response of over 7,000 letters from teenagers. In the segment, which is replayed for viewers, Charlestown is described sentimentally as 'the town that will not die'. In the midst of the profile of the small town, a young girl working as a fry cook steals the show by throwing a tantrum and angrily declaring: 'This town died years ago!' The young girl, we learn, is Corinne Burns. This introduction to Corinne emphasizes her slanted timing – she literally has bad timing. Her personal outburst disrupts the flow and style of the news story thereby ruining the carefully constructed timing of the feature. More importantly, her outburst is itself a proclamation about and against a certain model of time – a rejection of the segment's narrative of time. Rejecting the idea that Charlestown is somehow romantically timeless, Corinne instead insists that not only is this untrue, but that Charlestown died years ago.

The newscaster explains that due to the response the segment on Charlestown generated from teenagers across the country, he has gone back to interview Corinne. The follow-up interview depicts Corinne mocking the newscaster and the questions he asks, and generally being unresponsive – or responsive in the wrong way. She does not play the part of interviewee as she spends the entire time putting on make-up, barely facing the camera, turning her gaze on it only to pull a face. While the newscaster probes Corinne about her life, her family, and her ambitions, Corinne seems entirely uninterested. Corinne's lack of life direction worries the newscaster who describes her activity as 'just sitting around at home wasting time' – a judgement she dismisses: 'I wouldn't call it a waste of time.' When he asks Corinne if her views might change as she grows older, she leaves a pregnant pause and then looks up with a vacant stare asking, 'Grow older?', as though the concept carries no meaning for her and she had never considered the prospect. The newscaster is insistent that Corinne sort out her life, seeing her as an orphan with a younger sister, no job, and no place to live. He is frustrated with Corinne's apathy in the face of what he considers a potential, if not literal, death. Agitated, the newscaster almost screams, 'What are you going to do?!' Corinne, calm, collected, and applying bright, brash red eyeshadow, is undisturbed by all of the things he finds utterly terrifying about her current situation, and says that she already is doing something – she's in a band. She proceeds to introduce herself as Corinne 'Third Degree' Burns, lead singer and manager of The Stains. The camera then turns to reveal two other people in the interview room: 'Dee Pleated' and 'Dizzy Heights', her sister and cousin, the other members of The Stains.

The opening interview with Corinne shows her poignant refusal of the timeline that is being narrated at her. Similar to how she refuses to see Charlestown as immortal, she also refuses to see her life as a waste of time by refusing to accept the interviewer's judgement that she is not doing anything. In so doing, she refuses his characterization of her life and life chances while at the same time makes a claim to a different use of time and another kind of timeline. She does not tell him what she "will" do – a future iteration that implies plans, a life course, and forward motion – instead telling him what she "is" doing. She changes the temporal frame of his question and refuses to move into a future ideal in favour of the present tense. She denies that she is wasting time and instead gestures towards her alternative value system, where her band consists of a "doing" that he does not recognize. This shift is also evident in Corinne's response to the question of growing older, where she refuses to be put into a position of valuing futurity – responding instead by denying any understanding of the concept.

This opening scene sets up Corinne as existing in a time that resists the future tense. Lee Edelman argues in his polemic *No Future* that a resistance to futurity is a queer resistance to the normative social order. The normative social order, according to Edelman, can only envision the future through the figure of the Child. In these terms, the needs of the future Child frame the political possibilities of the present. Edelman argues that this concept of futurity frames political debate in terms that negate the possibility of refusing the Child, imposing:

> an ideological limit on political discourse as such, preserving in the process the absolute privilege of heteronormativity by rendering unthinkable, by casting outside the political domain, the possibility of a queer resistance to this organizing principle of communal relations.[28]

For Edelman, queer subjects are placed in opposition to this social order, whereby 'the queer comes to figure the bar to every realization of futurity, the resistance, internal to the social, to every social structure or form'.[29] Edelman thus argues that queer must not accede to this 'reproductive futurism' that casts the future as the privileged time of politics – the production of which guides and radically limits the political landscape of the present.[30]

I hold back from reading Corinne as resisting reproductive futurity and instead consider how she does not reject futurity, but rejects the future that is being offered to her. Edelman's linkage of queer to a rejection of reproductive futurity and the figure of the Child in whose work normative politics is so frequently framed needlessly places queers on the side of negativity and anti-sociality. Many criticisms of Edelman's argument have come from feminists and queers of colour who emphasize queer horizons and queer world-building that relies on and draws strength from queer forms of intimacy and community.[31] Resisting Edelman's queer negativity, I am more interested in the alternative forms of kinship and community that queer bonds produce and that Corinne's feminist message creates. I thus read Corinne's refusal of the future as containing an opening for alternative (and collective) possibilities to the future that is offered up to her. Her wide-eyed, aped ignorance at the term "older" highlights Corinne's refusal to perceive her life in the terms that the interviewer sets up for her. While he can only see her wasting time, Corinne is actually painting her face with make-up – make-up that will later become her signature look as the lead singer of The Stains. As Halberstam argues, queer subcultural activity can seem 'pointless to people stranded in hetero temporalities'.[32] To the interviewer Corinne appears unfocused and tragic – he is unable to see that Corinne is in a band, cultivating her style, and preparing for the stage. The camera's close-up of Corinne during the interview hides what becomes apparent when the camera pans out as Corinne introduces her band mates – they have been sitting in on the interview the entire time. Neither the interviewer nor the camera sees them, but they are there. Their presence and existence as a band is not visible to the interviewer the same way that he cannot see Corinne doing anything.

Corinne's timing runs counter to the presumed life course that the interviewer suggests she should be concerned with following. In opposition to this timing, Corinne reclaims wasting time. The song that The Stains are shown performing on multiple occasions – perhaps the only song they have – is called 'Waste of Time'. The song, sloppily put together and featuring Corinne's low and scratchy vocals, can be read as not only espousing a punk aesthetic that celebrates being a waste, but importantly is also about a relationship to time. Corinne sings over and over 'I'm a waste of time', reclaiming on her terms the identity that is already placed on her from the beginning by the interviewer. Wasting time is always a judgement about what time should be filled with – what is valuable to do versus what is a waste. However, "wasting time" is not only a phrase that is related to being lazy or associated with the lull of adolescence, but also has a particular relationship with queer. Freud suggests that perversions develop when some external or internal factor 'hinders or postpones the attainment of the normal sexual aim'.[33] Stockton argues that, for Freud, perverts are 'people who either extend themselves beyond the normal "path" of "copulation" or linger at midpoints along the way', thus diverting askew of copulation and wasting time through these diversions.[34] In diverting its attention away from reproductive sex, queer sexuality has been understood as stuck in a mode of delay – a waste of time.

Moreover, a resistance to growing up has historically been cited as a characteristic of homosexuals, where, Stockton explains, being gay is described as being in a state of 'arrested development'.[35] In this reading, Corinne's reclamation of wasting time and her rejection of productivity are more than just expressions of a teenage or punk aesthetic of laziness and instead might be imaginable as a queer claim on temporality. When she gets on stage and screams at the audience, 'What's so great about getting old?', and they scream back, 'Nothing!', both Corinne and her fans reject a particular movement and alignment in time. When she screams, 'What's so wonderful about getting married?', and again the audience of teenage girls screams back, 'Nothing!', they collectively reject a life course that sees marriage as a privileged aim for young women. More than a refusal of futurity and a valorization of youth for youth's sake, I argue that Corinne's refusal to be "productive" should be read as a refusal to move through life along the course already set out before her.

Wasting time is a means of holding out for the "not-yet" – through "wasting time" Corinne and her fans hold out for an alternative future than the one offered to them. Moreover, they create the possibility of an alternative future in the present through the community they build around wasting time. These kinds of refusals do not necessitate forms of negative antisociality – refusals of shared timing can create and express alternative forms of community.

Alternative forms of community-building or shared timing are emphasized in Corinne's cover of one of The Looters' songs. The Looters, the all-male British punk band that The Stains are on tour with, also sing a song about resisting a particular kind of temporal existence. Their song, 'Join the Professionals', is about resisting the army draft and the lyrics are a protest against a certain kind of national time. Screaming lines such as, 'Who knows when your turn will be?', The Looters sing about resistance to a national timing where young men experience the always impending possibility that they will be drafted into the war. When Corinne later performs their song as an angry response to The Looters' attempt at replacing The Stains on their tour, her appropriation of the song changes its meaning. Halberstam argues that traditionally cover songs have functioned as tributes, re-enactments, interpretations, or revisions of classics.[36] Yet, she suggests that covering a song might be a queer practice. While there is nothing essentially queer about a cover song, she points out that the practice can open up ways of thinking about memory and history outside of linear models of legacy and transmission.[37] Covers create queer genealogies, argues Halberstam, as a cover song 'is not the progressive unfolding of a narrative of assimilation, it is a jagged story of cathexis and repudiation'.[38] While The Stains' cover of The Looters does not create the kind of queer genealogy that Halberstam has in mind, it does touch upon Halberstam's insight that covers function 'like a drag act, a way of inhabiting another persona or body or voice', doing more than aping an original copy.[39]

In particular, Corinne's cover highlights the gendered specificity of The Looters' original version. The song cannot have the same meaning when Corinne, a young woman, sings it, as when The Looters perform it. If Halberstam is right in positing that covers produce new temporal experiences, then Corinne's cover of The Looters' song about being drafted into the war surely enacts a queer covering. With dozens of girls in pop socks, heels, see-through blouses, and skunk hair dancing on the tables of the venue screaming 'Not me!' in response to Corinne's call-outs of 'Who knows when your turn will be?', The Looters' rejection of war and nationalism is re-visioned by Corinne's snarl as a new kind of fight – a war in which the young women are at the front lines. Moreover, while The Looters' lyrics focus on a singular response, 'Not me!', the audience participation that Corinne's version inspires creates a collective around this negativity – a collective that is missing from the male, punk version. The Stains' performance of 'Join the Professionals' is one of the most powerful scenes in the film. With hundreds of skunks chanting along with Corinne, the sheer scale of the community of skunks is felt for the first time. The phrases 'Who knows what you're gonna see? Who knows when your turn will be?' become the battle call for a girl revolution. As the girls chant their 'Not me!' responses, the song takes on a meaning of waiting in time, being stuck, not knowing when their turn will be. It becomes an anthem about how young women are placed in a position of delay – they are subjects-in-the-making who will be actualized upon marriage.

However, this temporality is reconceptualized by the skunks as a space of possibility. Their resistance to joining the professionals is more than a shared refusal and instead an anthem for a shared potentiality. Not knowing when their turn will be, the young women create a community that does not rely on their turn coming in a future tense, but can build in the present. Corinne's appropriation of the song turns it into an anthem that embraces and strives for an unknowable futurity. The "who knows" aspect of the song seemingly holds open a door for possible futures that cannot yet be imagined – the "not-yet". As Alicia, the newscaster, comments:

> These young women, who call themselves skunks, are not content to let old age bring them the specious wisdom of despair and in their rebellion, they have clearly decided that female existence should not be a rush to the grave – or worse, to the supermarket!

Corinne's performance accompanied by the participation of her skunk audience holds out for alternative possibilities for the future and for the present. Corinne rejects the narrative of growth that seems to be her only possible future and pushes for delay or, as Alicia says, she decides not to rush into this future. Instead, she and all of the skunks hold on to the future as a question – as a radical embrace of the possibility of something else.

Corinne rejects the promise of growing up – the promise of "what is to come" – through a feminist critique of the possible life courses available to young women. By rejecting growing up and asking what is indeed "so great" about it, Corinne's negativity can be read as a critique of the particular future that she is expected to grow into. Ahmed, in *Queer Phenomenology*, emphasizes that lives are oriented in particular directions, towards particular objects and away from others, so that certain lives are temporally directed towards certain things – a "valid" future becomes conceptualized through a correct orientation. Ahmed argues that 'life gets directed in some ways rather than others, through the very requirement that we follow what is already given to us'.[40] In terms of sexual orientation, she argues that 'orientations toward sexual objects affect other things that we do, such that different orientations, different ways of directing one's desires, means inhabiting different worlds'.[41] Ahmed uses terms such as 'off line', 'points of digression', and 'slantwise' to convey how queer desire is out of line with straightness and points in different directions.[42]

Ahmed argues in her later book, *The Promise of Happiness*, that negativity or unhappiness might be reclaimed not as a rejection of politics but as its very starting point. She challenges the notion that certain things or people cause happiness and instead argues that a discourse of "happiness" is attached to pre-conceived social goods. In this way, happiness is not the effect of certain orientations, objects, or places, but is rather its cause. These 'happiness-causes are attributed as the cause of happiness, which means they already circulate as social goods before we "happen" upon them, which is why we may happen upon them in the first place'.[43] Ahmed thus argues that the promise of happiness directs our orientations where being unhappy is seen as an effect of being improperly oriented. Corinne champions "wasting time", resisting the adoption of the life course that is offered to her. In this, she refuses and critiques the presumed orientation of happiness. The "promise" of happiness marks happiness as a future state that one attains if the correct path is followed – to waste time, to delay, and to refuse this movement forward is a refusal to be impelled by the pre-conceived path. Corinne's insistence on wasting time is a political stance for those whose identities, desires, and histories do not "line up".

At The Stains' first gig, Corinne confronts a woman in the audience, pointing at her and telling her that she is not fooled by her. Corinne says to her:

'You came here tonight thinking you'd see some cute and wonderful rock star and you hoped maybe he'd take one look at you from up on that stage and he'd fall in love with you, just like that. Then your saviour could take you out of this dump of a town you live in, you could be different from all the other girls.'

She then broadens her attack and screams out to the audience more generally: 'Suckers!' Corinne pierces the romantic narrative that she imagines the woman in the audience is hoping for with her own observation: 'These guys laugh at you. They've got such big plans for the world, but they don't include us! So what does that make you? Just another girl lining up to die.' Corinne does more in this scene than confront the other woman; she confronts a world where such a heterosexual imperative, such a path, is the only acceptable orientation for women. In *Bodies That Matter*, Butler theorizes that the normative subject is constituted by a heterosexual matrix that unifies gender, desire, and sex; subjectivity that falls outside of this matrix is unintelligible. This heterosexual imperative 'enables certain sexed identifications and forecloses and/or disavows other identifications'.[44] In screaming at the woman in the audience and at girls more generally, Corinne expresses her anger at the limitations of this imperative, where the kind of lining up of gender/sex/desire in this heterosexual matrix looks to her like "lining up to die". This refusal is repeated in her resistance to the narrative conclusion offered to her by Billy, the lead singer from The Looters, with whom she has a brief sexual relationship. By the end of the film, when The Stains have lost their fans and tour manager, Billy asks her to come with him on The Looters' tour as his girl, telling her that she's 'finished' and there's 'nothing left'. Crying, Corinne responds, 'Is that what I'm supposed to do now? Go be your groupie? Tune your guitar for you, be your old lady?' Just as she resists the newscaster's insistence that she stop wasting time, here too, Corinne resists the future that Billy offers her as his girlfriend. She rejects this life course as her only possible future.

Ahmed describes those figures that do not find "happiness" in its presumed sites as 'affect aliens'.[45] Her list of affect aliens (the "feminist killjoy", "unhappy queer", and "melancholic migrant") does not include a figure of adolescent angst, but I argue that while Corinne might fit into the category of feminist killjoy, Ahmed's framework sets up the possibility for Corinne to be an affect alien of a different kind. Ahmed's re-working of negativity and negative affect enables a reading of adolescent rebellion as a resistance to a temporal becoming that imagines maturation as the attainment of marriage, children, and a mortgage. In *The Promise of Happiness*, Ahmed considers a narrative of teenage girls, through her reading of the film *Lost and Delirious* as a narrative of unhappy queers.[46] The film is set in a boarding school and traces the relationship of roommates Tori (Jessica Paré) and Paulie (Piper Perabo) as they fall in love and then stop their affair due to Tori's felt pressure to "straighten up". The film ends with the suicide of Paulie and Ahmed reads these unhappy queers as critically important because their story functions to critique the world that describes being queer as an unhappy ending. Paulie and Tori are happy together before they are caught in bed together by Tori's sister, who threatens to tell her parents – a revelation that would cause immense unhappiness for her mother and thus for Tori. For Ahmed, this film highlights the continued importance of considering how unhappy queers are a product of the 'costs of happy heterosexuality'.[47] It is important then not to turn from these unhappy queers because they make it possible to critique the world that reads queer subjectivity as unhappy.

I would add to Ahmed's reading that Tori's logic in breaking up with Paulie – her intent on "becoming straight" – is inextricable from her argument to "grow up". The girls are young, at boarding school, and not only in love with each other, but as Tori describes it, they are also in a state of transition. This transitional state is highlighted by Tori as her reason for having to break up with Paulie, telling her that they need to be done with this now. Tori tells Paulie that they must grow out of their love for each other, explaining, 'It's just not right anymore.' In this, Tori emphasizes that their relationship is one that has particular temporal boundaries – it cannot be "anymore". For Tori, their love can only be a phase, something that she needs to move past in order to grow up, where growing up means entering into the heterosexual partnership that her family and society condone. Tori tells Paulie that although she will go to her grave knowing that she will never love anyone else as she loves her, 'this can never, it just can never, ever, forever be … It just can, never, ever, forever be.' Tori does not dismiss their love in the present, but instead she explains that it cannot move past this particular moment and into the future.

She does not claim that their love cannot be, but that their love cannot ever be forever – their love cannot endure, it has no future. Tori argues that they need to mature on to the kinds of relationships that are socially acceptable which in turn will make their lives bearable.

Paulie, similar to Corinne, not only refuses to let go of Tori but this refusal is intimately tied to a refusal to grow up. Paulie's rebellion is about her queerness as much as it is about age and refusing to see her sexuality and her love for Tori as a phase. Tori's unhappiness comes from the pressure that she feels to grow up and it is precisely this imperative to grow up that is also a pressure to align herself with more socially acceptable forms of happiness – namely a heterosexual relationship. In this way, aligning oneself with the accepted orientation – the heterosexual relationship – is not only about narrative end-ings, but is intimately connected with growing up. Particularly when queerness is imagined as a form of delay, to "stay" queer is to resist a linear trajectory that imagines queerness as a phase. Thus, to resist growing up in Paulie's case, to resist Tori's insistence that they can never be forever and that their time together is over, is also to resist the straight line of heterosexuality. It is at moments such as these that a refusal to move forward in time, when moving forward means aligning oneself along a specific (hetero) life course, is a queer refusal to grow into the life course that one is supposed to fit into as an adult.

It is precisely Corinne's sentiment of wasting time that can be recon-ceptualized as a queer refusal to grow up into the future that pre-exists her arrival – a future in which her destination has been pre-decided. Corinne makes evident what Ahmed's argument about unhappy queers gestures towards: that one means of resisting narrative conclusion and the unhappy ending is through a politics of wasting time and delay. Halberstam argues that through resisting the heteronormative imperative, queers spend more of their time devoted to subcultures, which challenges the idea that a subculture is a 'youth formation' and instead might 'expand the definition of subculture beyond its most banal significations of youth in crisis and, on the other hand, challenge our notion of adulthood as reproductive maturity'.[48] She thus argues for a reading of subcultural production as something other than a phase, but as 'preidentities to carry forward, inhabit, and sustain'.[49] I would be careful here to insist that my reading of Corinne does not rely on an idealization of adolescence as inherently or exceptionally a space of unbounded queer possibilities.[50] Instead, I am highlighting not Corinne's age as an essentially queer time, but her politics of delay and wasting time that might be mobilized as queer feminist critiques of hetero-temporalities.

Corinne's lateral community

To turn to the figure of the child is seemingly necessarily to be confronted with questions about models of linear growth, maturation, generation, history, and futurity. Erica Burman and Jackie Stacey point out that since individual teleology is often figured as a 'condensation of historical development', the figure of the child comes to bear a particular weight as 'the microcosm that condenses the yet-to-be'.[51] For Claudia Castañeda, the critical potential of the figure of the child comes from it being 'a potentiality rather than an actuality'.[52] She argues that the figure of the child appears across a range of cultural sites as 'an entity in the making', always working in service of the adult it will become.[53] Similarly, as Catherine Driscoll argues in relation to girls, '[f]eminine adolescence is always retrospectively defined, always definitively prior to the Woman it is used to explain'.[54] The staging of children as transformative discounts the possibility of the child existing outside of the privileged space of adulthood. When children are only conceptualized through adulthood – never distinct from the adult they will become – they are not permitted to be entities in their own right.

It is precisely this presumption that Corinne will become an adult woman that enables the newscaster to privilege the future tense. "Wasting time" becomes possible only because of the presumption that there is a teleology that she should be following. At the beginning of this chapter I argued for the possibility that *The Fabulous Stains* might tell us something about feminism's temporalities. Thus far, I have suggested that Corinne's feminist rebellion be read as a queer resistance to normative timelines. I want to now further expand on how the film might be read alongside queer theory on the child. Through this reading, I hope to continue to unpack how *The Fabulous Stains* might be read not as simply a riot grrrl film, but as a troubling of the very linearity that establishes it as "first" – thus producing queerer relationships in time. If Corinne resists the normative timeline that is laid out before her, she also might be read through queer theory on the child to make visible the alternative model of generation that she offers. In other words, while she resists the imperative to grow up, she manages to develop in alternative ways.

As I have already suggested in relation to Freud, the "narrative middle" has a history of being defined as opening up queer potentialities.[55] For Steven Bruhm and Natasha Hurley, teleological development which privileges adulthood opens up the possibility for 'childhood queerness': 'space for the figure of the child to be queer as long as the queerness can be rationalized as a series of mistakes or misplaced desires'.[56] Indeed, the centrality of the figure of the child in queer theory is a perspective famously argued for by Eve Sedgwick. She posits that there is childhood stigmatization inherent in "queer" which no amount of reclamation can cleanse it of, arguing that the word always carries with it the shame of a 'gender-dissonant or otherwise stigmatized childhood'.[57] In this, childhood is an intensely queer time, where "queer" can be most usefully understood as marked by childhood shame. Moreover, Sedgwick also suggests that the adolescent haunts the field of queer theory when, in the introduction to *Tendencies*, she argues that adults are always working to 'keep faith with vividly remembered promises made to ourselves in childhood'[58] and provocatively explains: 'I think everyone who does gay and lesbian studies is haunted by the suicide of adolescents.'[59] The primacy of the figure of the adolescent is such that for Sedgwick, the figure haunts not only contemporary queer identity but also the theoretical field of queer studies.

If Sedgwick brings queerness and the child into proximity, Stockton suggests that further resonances might be made. Similar to Castañeda's exploration of the child as 'a potentiality rather than an actuality',[60] Stockton argues that the child lacks a present tense: 'It is the act of adults looking back.'[61] It is here that Stockton suggests queer theory is a useful entry-point into this figure because of the figure of the "gay child":

> The phrase 'gay child' is a gravestone marker for where or when one's straight life died. Straight person dead, gay child now born, albeit retro-spectively (even, for example, at or after the age of twenty-five). This kind of backward birthing mechanism makes the hunt for the roots of queerness a retrospective search for amalgamated forms of feelings, desires, and physical needs that led to this death of one's straight life. And yet, by the time the tombstone is raised ('I was a gay child'), the 'child' by linguistic definition has expired.[62]

Stockton links the "problem" of children with gayness, drawing on how the "gay child" does not exist until the future "outing" of the gay adult, revealing the temporal problematic of all children: the child can only appear through a kind of "backward birth".[63] Her readings of the gay child open up new methodologies for thinking about the figure of the child that push beyond seeing this figure as knowable only through the act of adults looking back. She focuses on movement that is non-vertical, anti-linear, and de-privileges growing up – the taken for granted primary direction of childhood movement. If the child is traditionally seen as moving up towards adulthood and making this move only when adults say it's time, Stockton reads the child for the way growth happens in spite of this delay. She argues that focusing on these other kinds of movements (sideways growth, horizontal spread) enables readings of the child's motives and desires and thus gives shape to this figure outside of adult projections.

Stockton's theorizations of non-linear growth or growth that might exist in spite of delay open up the possibility of finding in Corinne's refusal to grow up other kinds of movements. If adolescence depends on adulthood for its meaning, only knowable retrospectively or understood as a stage on the way to adulthood, *The Fabulous Stains* asks what it might mean for adolescence to create itself and what this documentation might look like. Corinne's con-flict with the male newscaster's depiction of The Stains plays out the proble-matic of not-yet-adults being able to represent their motives and desires outside of the (literal) lens of adulthood. This form of documentation is insufficient for representing Corinne and The Stains at the same time as it opens up the possibility of manipulating this documentary technology to satirize this very point. The film's critique of the news media resonates then with the question of how to see the figure of the child outside of adult projections. This critique of and manipulation of news media also poses questions about the links between modes of representation and feminist ideology.

As I outlined in the beginning of the chapter, there have been a number of academic considerations of the DIY cultural output of riot grrrl subculture and the movement's aesthetic production of new representational strategies for the figure of the girl. Yet, the visual language of female fandom and participatory subcultural community might be another way in which the movement might threaten dominant representation strategies. In *The Fabulous Stains*, the visual language of female fandom becomes an alternative language to that of the mainstream news media. Moreover, this also represents an alternative language of growth, which resists the linear. For Stockton, a focus on the child on its own terms challenges linear narratives of maturation that posit the move towards adulthood as the only movement. The queer child, in Stockton, reconceptualizes the concepts of delay and growth so that delay and growth 'call us into notions of the horizontal – what spreads sideways – or sideways and backwards – more than a simple thrust toward height and forward time'.[64] Stockton thus challenges notions of linear progression and upwards growth using the horizontal. She argues that 'growth is a matter of extension, vigor, and volume as well as verticality'.[65] In this case, Corinne's sideways growth can be read alongside her refusal to grow up – extending herself through her fans, she forms a lateral community. The network of subcultural participation becomes a site for the skunks to grow and expand, to take up space, to build community, in a way that is not necessarily vertical growth upwards.

This emphasis on fattening can be connected to the community of skunks that form around Corinne. In the realm of "appropriate" reproduction, The Stains "reproduce" in a perhaps perverse way. While Corinne resists growing up and growing older as it requires an alignment in a heterosexual partnership and thus a particular understanding of progress in time, she does not resist growing altogether. Instead, as she gains notoriety, she grows sideways. Over the course of their tour, The Stains' audience grows so that at each performance more and more girls show up to their gigs mimicking Corinne's skunk hairdo, red see-through blouse, and black underwear. Eventually, the audience is literally a sea of Corinne look-a-likes (Fig. 3.2). This spread of Corinne's is attributed to her ability to give voice to particular desires. As one fan writes to the news channel, 'I think that girl is great. She said what I think all day long.' In one of the newscaster Alicia's interviews with a fan, the fan explains that Corinne 'said things that I've always wanted to say, and I haven't been able to ... she gave her honest opinion of how she felt about people. That's why I'm like her now.' Corinne reproduces herself through a kind of fattening, drawing attention to Stockton's emphasis on the movement available to children who cannot yet "grow up" – the horizontal. Corinne spreads herself, as an aesthetic and a politics, through her fans as they become "like her". If adolescence is unavailable in the present tense, if its documentability is questionable as

Figure 3.2 Skunks, *Ladies and Gentlemen, the Fabulous Stains*

always an act of retrospective creation, *The Fabulous Stains* uses the visual excess of female fandom as evidence of other kinds of development.

Finally, the sideways growth through subcultural spread in *The Fabulous Stains* highlights a further connection between the child or pre-pubescent subjects and queers – they do not reproduce sexually. Rohy argues that conservative fears about the spread of homosexuality are frequently underpinned by the assumption that homosexuality's non-reproductive sexuality will lead to the death of the human species.[66] However, she argues that claims that homosexuality's anti-reproductive nature threatens to render humanity extinct actually contain the opposite horror: '*they* [homosexuals] *are too fertile*'.[67] Fears that homosexuality will destroy the species contain the paradoxical fear that homosexuality is spreading and will spread to the point of wiping out heterosexual reproduction. Rohy argues that this creates the 'familiar rhetoric that – positing homosexuality as acquired, not innate – sees the queer population as capable of infinite growth, naturally inclined to expand its unnatural ranks through seduction, indoctrination, contagion, or recruitment'.[68] This fear of the reproducibility, the spread of homosexuality, makes homosexuality a threat to heterosexual reproduction – gays are turning people gay faster than heterosexuals can birth straight babies. Rohy's contribution to thinking through this rhetoric is to draw on Richard Dawkins' concept in *The Selfish Gene* of the meme as cultural spread.[69] Rohy explains that '[w]hile genes pass vertically from parent to child, memes can move horizontally through culture; homosexual generation could therefore proceed metonymically, spreading rapidly *across* a population'.[70] This terminology enables queer reproduction to be conceptualized not as a heterosexual reproductive inheritance but as a horizontal web of contagion and transmission.[71]

Rohy's concept of the queer meme brings a queer possibility to the notion of female fandom as it is frequently represented as a mad kind of disease. Stu, the male newscaster in *The Fabulous Stains*, can only read The Stains' idolization of Corinne as perverse, explaining that the story of The Stains makes him wonder about his profession:

> I mean you give a little air time to some nut on the big news and 24 hours later you've got a bunch of other nuts who are just making her into a hero. They see something on the media and they've got to do the same thing.

Denigrating Corinne's spread, he reads the fans as copying a nut and participating in some big fad. This response reveals Stu's anxiety over Corinne's reproduction. Indeed, he denies that she is responsible for the community of skunks, blaming instead the evils of mass media coverage: 'I mean they see something on the media and they've got to do the same thing [...] The power television has to create.' Stu's worry over the spread of The Stains is a fear of television's ability to contribute to their spread.

Making a return to the question of documentation, the female newscaster Alicia responds: 'Those girls created themselves.' In recuperating The Stains as creating themselves, Alicia does not deny the spread that has occurred through television coverage – she in fact encourages it by continuing to cover the story. However, she argues that the community of skunks is a production of The Stains – The Stains reproduce themselves. The sideways and meme-like growth of The Stains may be a form of reproduction that moves alongside or contra to linearity – where their message spreads like contagion, reproducing skunks through a queer kind of non-sexual and lateral spread. Fandom and the visual spectacle of the mass of skunks becomes a threat to heterosexual reproduction, building a community of resistant young women who threaten the status quo. This offers a potentially queer reading of what is traditionally read as a form of commodification or mass culture. Rather than read the copying, the mimicking, or the reproducibility of The Stains as a selling out, a gendered mass culture, perhaps through a queer lens, the threatening, all-consuming aspect of this mass of girls becomes legible for what it offers – an alternative form of reproduction.

Conclusion

In this chapter, I have been suggesting, through a reading of *The Fabulous Stains*, that we might read as queer the temporalities of female adolescent rebellion. *The Fabulous Stains* as a retrospectively produced origin point for riot grrrl subculture provides a generative opening point for taking this moment to consider what it means to remember in the present. Perhaps we might escape linear teleology, or the cause and effect inherent in the "now" and "then" narrative, by refusing the search for origins. Instead, we might start with what is less stable, what does not fit into linear narratives, or even what never happened. Through this, perhaps some of feminism's untimeliness can be explored. I want to conclude by reflecting briefly on the film's ending as a way to consider how the film, in the end, does not so successfully resist the refusal of linear teleology, or the "now" and "then" that predominantly structures how riot grrrl is currently being remembered.

The ending of *The Fabulous Stains* adds significant confusion to the final reading of the film. Originally, the film was meant to end after Corinne refuses to follow Billy and the rest of The Looters on tour. In this final scene a dejected Corinne watches The Looters' tour bus drive off while she stands in the parking lot. In the dust of The Looters' bus appears a motorcycle carrying energetic skunks. The appearance of these skunks suggests that though The Stains fail as a band they do not fail to reproduce – the skunks will carry on. However, an alternate ending was shot after the film was finished and this is the ending that the 2008 DVD contains. In this revised ending, the "last" scene is followed by credits and The Stains in an MTV music video for the song 'Join the Professionals'. Having left behind their skunk attire, Corinne and the band have adopted a more polished look that suggests a closer affinity to new-wave bands than to any riot grrrl group. This implies that the video has been made after time has passed – the band has moved on, and even "grown up".

I was tempted to disregard this ending because it does not seem to fit with the concluding scenes of the film. In the original ending Corinne realizes that the commercial fame that she gains in the end was a means through which her message was diluted and sold to young women – an ending that she did not intend or want for herself and The Stains. In contrast to this, the MTV music video shows The Stains as having learned how to become "professionals" – a polished and consumable all-girl band. The community of skunks disappears, Corinne's anger is translated into glamour, and as an MTV music video, the riot grrrl politics are seemingly erased. Thus this final archival document of The Stains seemingly erases over and provides a neat conclusion to the film's otherwise resistant temporalities. In this last instance the film contrasts not only a DIY culture with a polished MTV video, but a more complicated narrative about The Stains with a more positive conclusion. This is a disappointing ending not because The Stains become successful or sell-out, but because it gives the film the kind of narrative conclusion that Corinne resists throughout.

While disrupting the queerer temporalities of the film, this striking narrative conclusion also draws them even more to the fore. It also disappointingly returns the film to the "now" and "then" structure that I have suggested it might help us escape. The MTV music video becomes the "now" through which the entirety of the film's narrative becomes the "then". Through the inclusion of the MTV video, the film's narrative is placed as a then that we can look back at, now positioned years later. The ending is striking not only because it contradicts the riot grrrl aesthetic of the film but because it secures a narrative conclusion for a band that went to great lengths to resist the narratives of success and growth that were offered to them. In the end, the film's conclusion might serve as a reminder of desires for such narrative conclusions, upwards growth, success, linear development and maturation even in the face of perhaps our most radical option – resisting life as we know it.

Notes

1 Mimi Thi Nguyen, 'Riot Grrrl, Race, and Revival', *Women & Performance: a journal of feminist theory*, 22.2–3 (2012), 173–96 (p. 175).
2 Ibid., p. 188.
3 Ibid., p. 183.
4 Ibid., p. 188.
5 For further academic work on riot grrrl, see Anna Feigenbaum, 'Remapping the Resonances of Riot Grrrl: Feminisms, Postfeminisms, and the "Processes" of Punk', in *Interrogating Postfeminism: Gender and the Politics of Popular Culture*, ed. Yvonne Tasker and Diane Negra (Durham, NC and London: Duke University Press, 2007), pp. 132–52; Joanne Gottlieb and Gayle Wald, 'Smells Like Teen Spirit: Riot Grrrls, Revolution and Women in Independent Rock', in *Microphone Fiends: Youth Music and Youth Culture*, ed. Andrew Ross and Tricia Rose (London: Routledge, 1994), pp. 250–74; Mary Celeste Kearney, 'The Missing Links: Riot Grrrl – Feminism – Lesbian Culture', in *Sexing the Groove: Popular Music and Gender*, ed. Sheila Whiteley (London and New York: Routledge, 1997), pp. 207–29; Marion Leonard, '"Rebel Girl, You Are the Queen of My World": Feminism, "Subculture", and Grrrl Power', in *Sexing the Groove: Popular Music and Gender*, ed. Sheila Whiteley (New York and London: Routledge, 1997), pp. 230–55; Jessica Rosenberg and Gitana Garofalo, 'Riot Grrrl: Revolutions from Within', *Signs: Journal of Women in Culture and Society*, 23.3 (1998), 809–41; Kristen Schilt, '"Riot Grrrl Is ... ": The Contestation over Meaning', in *Music Scenes: Local, Translocal, and Virtual*, ed. Andy Bennett and Richard A. Peterson (Nashville, TN: Vanderbilt University Press, 2004), pp. 115–30.
6 Gayle Wald, 'Just a Girl? Rock Music, Feminism and the Cultural Constructions of Female Youth', *Signs*, 23.3 (1998), 585–610 (p. 593).
7 Nguyen, p. 175.
8 For an exploration of the "queerness" of the riot grrrl notion of "girl love", see Kearney, 'The Missing Links'.
9 *Ladies and Gentlemen, the Fabulous Stains*, dir. by Lou Adler (Paramount Pictures, 1981).
10 Kearney, p. 210.
11 Marion Leonard, *Gender in the Music Industry: Rock, Discourse, and Girl Power* (Aldershot: Ashgate, 2007), p. 117.
12 See, for example, Ellen Riordan, 'Commodified Agents and Empowered Girls: Consuming and Producing Feminism', *Journal of Communication Inquiry*, 25.3 (2001), 279–97; or Wald, 'Just a Girl?'
13 Judith Halberstam, *In a Queer Time and Place: Transgender Bodies, Subcultural Lives* (New York and London: New York University Press, 2005), p. 2.
14 Sara Ahmed, *The Promise of Happiness* (Durham, NC and London: Duke University Press, 2010), p. 42.
15 *Making of Ladies and Gentlemen, the Fabulous Stains*, dir. by Sarah Jacobson. <www.youtube.com/watch?v=lNYR_XlwEx0> (accessed 20 October 2014).
16 Gary Morris, 'Punk Girls on Film: Ladies and Gentlemen, the Fabulous Stains', *Bright Lights Film Journal*, 28 (2000). <www.brightlightsfilm.com/28/fabulous-stains.php> (accessed 20 October 2014).

17 Rhino Media. <http://rhinomedia.com/store/ProductDetail.lasso?Number=511847> (accessed 7 June 2012).

18 Rhino Media (online).

19 David Laderman, *Punk Slash! Musicals: Tracking Slip-Sync on Film* (Austin: University of Texas Press, 2010), p. 123.

20 For a tracing of these contestations between 1992 and 1995, see Schilt, '"Riot Grrrl Is … "'.

21 Schilt, p. 120.

22 Nguyen, p. 173.

23 Rhino Media (online).

24 Rosenberg and Garofalo, p. 809.

25 Nguyen, p. 175.

26 Halberstam, *In a Queer Time and Place*, p. 1.

27 Ibid., p. 2.

28 Lee Edelman, *No Future: Queer Theory and the Death Drive* (Durham, NC and London: Duke University Press, 2004), p. 2.

29 Ibid., p. 4.

30 Ibid., p. 2.

31 See José Esteban Muñoz, *Cruising Utopia: The Then and There of Queer Futurity* (New York and London: New York University Press, 2009); Judith Halberstam, *The Queer Art of Failure* (Durham, NC and London: Duke University Press, 2011).

32 Carolyn Dinshaw and others, 'Theorizing Queer Temporalities: A Roundtable Discussion', *GLQ: A Journal of Lesbian and Gay Studies*, 13.2–3 (2007), 177–95 (pp. 181–82).

33 Sigmund Freud, *On Sexuality: Three Essays on the Theory of Sexuality and Other Works*, ed. Angela Richards, trans. James Strachey (London: Penguin Books, 1977), p. 68.

34 Kathryn Bond Stockton, *The Queer Child, or Growing Sideways in the Twentieth Century* (Durham, NC and London: Duke University Press, 2009), p. 25.

35 Stockton, p. 22.

36 Judith Halberstam, 'Keeping Time with Lesbians on Ecstasy', *Women and Music: A Journal of Gender and Culture*, 11 (2007), 51–58 (p. 51).

37 Ibid., p. 52.

38 Ibid., p. 58.

39 Ibid., p. 52.

40 Sara Ahmed, *Queer Phenomenology: Orientations, Objects, Others* (Durham, NC and London: Duke University Press, 2006), p. 21.

41 Ibid., p. 68.

42 Ibid., p. 71; p. 72; p. 79.

43 Ahmed, *The Promise of Happiness*, p. 28.

44 Judith Butler, *Bodies That Matter: On the Discursive Limits of "Sex"* (New York and London: Routledge, 1993), p. 3.

45 Ahmed, *The Promise of Happiness*, pp. 41–43.

46 Ahmed, *The Promise of Happiness*, pp. 103–6; *Lost and Delirious*, dir. by Léa Pool (Greg Dummett Films, 2001).

47 Ahmed, *The Promise of Happiness*, p. 105.

48 Halberstam, *In a Queer Time and Place*, p. 162.

49 Ibid., p. 179.

50 For an exploration of the dangers of this perspective, see Angus Gordon, 'Turning Back: Adolescence, Narrative, and Queer Theory', *GLQ: A Journal of Lesbian and Gay Studies*, 5.1 (1999), 1–24 (p. 6).

51 Erica Burman and Jackie Stacey, 'Introduction: The Child and Childhood in Feminist Theory', *Feminist Theory*, 11.3 (2010), 227–40, p. 231.

52 Claudia Castañeda, *Figurations: Child, Bodies, Worlds* (Durham, NC and London: Duke University Press, 2002), p. 1.
53 Ibid.
54 Catherine Driscoll, *Girls: Feminine Adolescences in Popular Culture and Cultural Theory* (New York: Columbia University Press, 2002), p. 6.
55 For an exploration of this in relation to narrative more specifically, see Judith Roof, *Come as You Are: Sexuality and Narrative* (New York and Chichester: Columbia University Press, 1996).
56 Steven Bruhm and Natasha Hurley, 'Introduction', in *Curiouser: On the Queerness of Children*, ed. Steven Bruhm and Natasha Hurley (Minneapolis and London: University of Minnesota Press, 2004), p. xiv.
57 Eve Sedgwick, 'Queer Performativity: Henry James's *The Art of the Novel*', *GLQ: A Journal of Lesbian and Gay Studies*, 1.1 (1993), 1–16 (p. 4).
58 Eve Sedgwick, *Tendencies* (Durham, NC and London: Duke University Press, 1993), p. 3.
59 Sedgwick, *Tendencies*, p. 1.
60 Castañeda, p. 1.
61 Stockton, p. 5.
62 Ibid., p. 7.
63 Ibid., p. 6.
64 Ibid., p. 4.
65 Ibid., p. 11.
66 Valerie Rohy, 'On Homosexual Reproduction', *differences: A Journal of Feminist Cultural Studies*, 25.1 (2012), 102–30.
67 Ibid., p. 107 (emphasis in original).
68 Ibid.
69 Richard Dawkins, *The Selfish Gene* (Oxford: Oxford University Press, 2006).
70 Rohy, 'On Homosexual Reproduction', p. 109 (emphasis in original).
71 Ibid., p. 110.

4 The feminist manifesto

Valerie Solanas and *SCUM*

In 2007, feminist film scholar Mandy Merck published an article on Laura Mulvey's iconic piece from 1975, 'Visual Pleasure and Narrative Cinema'.[1] Mulvey's article, which first appeared in the film journal *Screen*, is widely recognized as a watershed text in film criticism and feminist film criticism more specifically. In it, she offers a psychoanalytic reading of classic Hollywood cinema, arguing that film is structured by the 'unconscious of patriarchal society'.[2] Concerned with the relationship between sexual difference and modes of looking, Mulvey explores how in 'a world ordered by sexual imbalance, pleasure in looking has been split between active/male and passive/female'.[3] As such, she argues that classic Hollywood cinema is structurally organized around the active male gaze and the image of women as '*to-be-looked-at-ness*'.[4] This argument, that viewing pleasures are highly gendered, almost single-handedly announced the beginnings of feminist film theory. Mulvey's piece has been anthologized, reworked, and critiqued numerous times and it is not my intention here to present either Mulvey's arguments in full nor the complex ways in which this text has travelled through film theory and feminist theory. My interest instead is in how Merck, returning to the piece over thirty years after its publication, focuses on revisiting not primarily the arguments Mulvey makes, but the generic form in which these arguments are made.

In order to understand the significance of Mulvey's article and its continued reverberations in the present, Merck argues for a return to the language of the piece – its rhetoric. As Merck notes in her essay titled 'Mulvey's Manifesto', there are many qualities of the article that give it a 'classic manifesto style' including the use of everyday language in the introduction, its call for change, and the use of the first person plural in reference to feminism, 'declaring her political solidarity with the collectivity on whose behalf this statement is written'.[5] While Merck acknowledges that she is not the first to suggest that the article be seen as 'polemical, programmatic, and unequivocal', she argues that the implications of it as a manifesto have rarely been considered.[6] Primarily, Merck argues that the piece's ongoing critical salience is due in part not only to the arguments that Mulvey puts forward, but to the pleasures of the manifesto. She describes the 'sensory pleasures' of reading

Mulvey's manifesto and suggests that the pleasures of reading the text are just as important to its endurance as the arguments that Mulvey makes.[7] For Merck, the manifesto contains its own 'enabling eloquence'; '[i]t is this provocative style, and not just the essay's paradigm-shattering influence, that incites both imitation and denigration'.[8] In other words, Merck suggests that any attempts to consider the ongoing endurance of Mulvey's text must consider not only its arguments but also its generic form. For Merck, the rhetorical strategies of the manifesto are central to the reading pleasure of 'Visual Pleasure and Narrative Cinema' and thus central to the piece's ongoing critical life.

This chapter, like Merck's article, is concerned with the feminist manifesto. I begin with Merck's revisit of Mulvey's manifesto in part because she explores how an attention to the form of the piece is integral to explaining the way it continues to circulate in contemporary theory. Merck's consideration of the critical salience of Mulvey's essay demands that the pleasures of the more popular manifesto be taken seriously. Indeed, it is in the sensory appeal of the manifesto's language that Merck locates the essay's staying power. Moreover, in drawing attention to 'Visual Pleasure and Narrative Cinema' as a manifesto, Merck reorients Mulvey's genealogical trajectory, putting her work in conversation with not only contemporaneous film theory but also a history of manifesto writing. As Merck points out, feminism's history 'rings with such calls to arms, from Mary Wollstonecraft's *Vindication of the Rights of Women* to Emma Goldman's "The Tragedy of Women's Emancipation" to Shulamith Firestone's *The Dialectic of Sex* to Mary Daly's *Gyn/Ecology*'.[9] This chapter is similarly interested in questions of feminist genealogy, staying power, and the manifesto. Merck attempts to explore the continued attraction to Mulvey's piece through a focus on the manifesto and this chapter aims to rethink Valerie Solanas' *SCUM Manifesto* along similar lines. If Merck aims to understand Mulvey's manifesto through a focus on the genre's seductive language, I focus in this chapter on the manifesto's timing. Solanas has become an iconic figure in recent feminist history yet I contend that she has been positioned within feminism in limited and limiting ways. Solanas tends to be either dismissed or embraced, where she is disregarded as a loner or claimed as absolutely central to second wave feminism. There is a tendency in these readings to focus on Solanas' timing as one of either historical belonging or unbelonging. In contrast to this, I argue that Solanas offers a far more complex model of feminist timing, and that this can be elucidated in part through a focus on the manifesto genre. Similar to how Merck argues that the endurance of Mulvey's manifesto requires a reading of its form, I suggest that Solanas' timing might be productively considered in relation to the formal qualities of *SCUM*.

SCUM Manifesto was self-distributed in the Village streets by Solanas in 1967 and first published by Olympia Press in 1968 and since then has been reprinted numerous times, most recently in 2004 by Verso with an introduction by Avital Ronell. While "SCUM" circulates as an acronym for "Society for Cutting Up Men" and the manifesto is now published with this subtitle, there is no evidence to suggest that this was Solanas' intended meaning of "SCUM". In an unpublished interview from 1975, Solanas supposedly claims that the acronym was created by her publisher Maurice Girodais.[10] The manifesto itself is a powerful, angry, witty, and filthy critique of patriarchy – a call to arms to destroy the system and eliminate the male. Solanas explains: 'The first part of the Manifesto is an analysis of male psychology, and the second part is like, you know, what to do about it.'[11] Solanas' popularity can be traced within feminist theory, popular culture, and across a number of forms. She has been labelled the archetypal radical feminist, a raving lunatic, the ultimate avant-garde artist, the 'bag lady of feminism',[12] or by her mom, as simply someone with a 'great sense of humour'.[13] There is a film focused on her (*I Shot Andy Warhol*), a 2006 play (*Valerie Jean Solanas for President of America*), various websites dedicated to her cause, a rumoured DC Comics adaptation of *SCUM Manifesto*, and ongoing mentions in various feminist and queer blogs and zines. Her shooting of Warhol on 3 June 1968 – supposedly due to his refusal to produce her play *Up Your Ass* and his loss of one of her only two copies of the play – is usually credited as the event which rocketed her into the public eye and secured her name in both feminist and avant-garde history. Indeed, her manifesto was only published after this act of violence. While she may have accrued some notoriety in Greenwich Village, New York before this – she appears in Warhol's films *I, A Man* and *Bikeboy* and was interviewed by the *Village Voice* – it was the shooting that secured her name in history. Before this act, there is considerable debate over how influential Solanas may have been in radical feminist circles, with Alice Echols arguing that feminists in New York Radical Women knew 'next to nothing' about Solanas.[14] The shooting imprinted her into pop culture history (her impact gaining iconic cultural status with Richard Avedon's portraits of Warhol's post-surgery body) and her *SCUM Manifesto* has similarly left lasting effects on popular culture and feminist history.

Precisely what these lasting effects are, however, remains open for contestation and it is my intention in this chapter to consider what Solanas might offer to contemporary theorizing of feminism's timing. While writing this chapter I came across an image on the photo-sharing website, Flickr, of a piece of graffiti placed on the outside wall of a sex shop in Sweden. The work is a simple stencil, reading: 'Valerie was right'. I have no other information about this work and no proof that it is about Solanas, but I cannot help reading this as an invocation of her. Perhaps it is my attraction to the simplicity of its claim – even the most generous readings of Solanas will very rarely and so succinctly say that she was "right". There is something both jarring and undeniably tempting about reading this graffiti as a claiming of Solanas. However, upon closer inspection, there is nothing simple about the proclamation that 'Valerie was right'. What was she right about, for instance? Was she right to shoot Warhol? Was she right in her analysis of patriarchy in her *SCUM Manifesto*? Or might we read this as a declaration of her sanity – was she right in the head? Moreover, it is the temporal register of the claim that strikes me most. Solanas "was" right. In which time was Solanas right? Was she right in the past? Can she continue to be right? Is she wrong now? Perhaps the text mourns for Solanas and for the time in which she was right. Or perhaps its past tense emphasizes that Solanas can never be right in the present. It might arguably lay her to rest at the same moment in which it evokes her, functioning as an epitaph or the last word on Solanas. The pale colour of the wall it is painted on combined with the simplicity of its message mimics a gravestone marker. One could almost envision the dates 1936–88 (her birth and death dates, respectively) scrawled underneath. This work casts Solanas as not only a controversial figure, but as a figure that has a complicated relationship to time, refusing to settle in the past but not quite being right in the present either.[15] In potentially mourning the loss of Solanas, this graffiti might mark the present as a time in which Solanas' project has some unfinished business. While it at once hints at her being in the past – she "was right" – its evocation in the present suggests a more complicated temporality.

It is this focus on Solanas' temporalities that this chapter takes. My starting point in this chapter is not to argue that we unbury Solanas and her *SCUM Manifesto* from the corners of history or from any sort of incorrect placing in history, feminist or otherwise. Too frequently this is the frame through which Solanas is approached. As I will show in the following section, Solanas is almost always discussed as either central to feminism's history or as absolutely marginal. This focus on her inclusion in or exclusion from feminist history – with correctly placing her in or out of feminist time – radically limits other possible readings of Solanas' timing. I move away from considering whether she is or is not part of feminist history and instead focus on what other temporalities Solanas might contain, particularly through a focus on the manifesto genre. Similar to the way the graffiti's polemic and assertive claiming of Solanas unravels at the same time it is spoken, I aim to explore the uncertainties of the manifesto genre – its performative failures – its inability to enact the future tense that it reaches for. This chapter first traces through dominant approaches to Solanas, approaches which debate whether or not Solanas should be understood as part of feminist history. I then pivot to thinking about what Solanas might reveal about feminism's timing, suggesting that she represents an anxiousness around feminism's ability to reproduce itself through time. In this, I consider her resonances with the temporality of the lesbian and this figure's potential difficult relationship to queer futurity. I draw out, through a focus on genre, the complex narrative of futurity that Solanas offers – one that "fails" to enact a leap forward but through this very failure suggests the difficulty of leaving the past "behind".

Valerie Solanas and feminism

It is difficult to tease out how and if Solanas was somehow "part" of radical feminism in the 1960s and 1970s – presuming of course we agree on what it means to "take part" in feminist politics. Yet, it is precisely this framework of "belonging" or "not belonging" that dominates approaches to Solanas. Catherine Lord argues that were it not for Solanas, the 'feminist movement would not have happened'.[16] Despite Lord's aim to resuscitate Solanas' importance in her publication of 2010, it is clear that there is a history of citational practice which places Solanas firmly in a history of radical feminism. These citations, ranging from the 1970s into the 2000s, work to solidify Solanas within narratives of feminism. Citation, Clare Hemmings argues, is the 'primary technique through which people and approaches are assigned an era, positioned as pivotal to key shifts in theoretical direction, or written out of the past or present'.[17] In terms of tracing Solanas' citational history, she frequently appears cited next to or with radical feminists, particularly in more recent anthologies. Ginette Castro in *American Feminism: A Contemporary History* quotes Solanas alongside radical feminists Ti-Grace Atkinson and Dana Densmore; Jacqueline Rhodes in *Radical Feminism, Writing, and Critical Agency* laments the publishing history of *SCUM Manifesto* alongside that of Shulamith Firestone's *The Dialectic of Sex*, a canonical example of second wave feminist theory; and *SCUM Manifesto* is reprinted in *Radical Feminism: A Documentary Reader* as well as in *Public Women, Public Words: A Documentary History of American Feminism*.[18] Solanas is also frequently discussed in feminist texts of the 1970s, excerpted in Robin Morgan's *Sisterhood Is Powerful* and championed by Joanna Russ in 'The New Misandry'.[19] Russ's article argues for and defends the inevitable misandry that she describes as being a part of the 'battle of the sexes' and suggests that in her anger towards the male, Solanas is an 'Everywoman'.[20] In *Lesbian Nation*, Jill Johnston describes Solanas as one of the 'only radical feminists around here worthy of the name', encircling her into radical feminist time through the 'pathological purity' of her rage.[21] National Organization for Women members claimed her as 'one of the most important spokeswomen of the feminist movement'[22] and the Boston radical feminist group, Cell 16, is particularly noted for bringing Solanas into second wave feminist circles and critique, reportedly reading *SCUM Manifesto* at their meetings 'as their first order of business'.[23] Echols recounts how Roxanne Dunbar of Cell 16 proclaimed the manifesto 'the essence of feminism' and visited Solanas in jail.[24] She also describes how Ros Baxandall in an interview referred to Solanas as 'our movement's Victoria Woodhull'.[25]

However, despite these citations and points of contact between Solanas and radical feminist history, Solanas' position in this history continues to be debated. While many argue for her centrality to feminist history, there are just as many who insist she does not belong. Distancing Solanas from feminism and feminism from Solanas, Jennifer Baumgardner dismisses the possibility of Solanas' *SCUM Manifesto* as a feminist classic, calling it instead a 'cult classic [...] an artefact, a relic from the heyday of Warhol and the revolutionary sixties'.[26] Rhodes argues that despite Solanas' text being read by second wave feminist groups Cell 16 and The Feminists, it was not 'overwhelmingly accepted into radical circles' and Solanas herself had no ties to women's liberation groups in New York.[27] For Rhodes, Solanas' manifesto 'was not produced as part of the women's movement'.[28] Contrasting Solanas with perhaps the most iconic second wave feminist, Shulamith Firestone, she uses Firestone's dismissal of Solanas to gesture towards a broader lack of acceptance of Solanas by second wave feminism, explaining that 'Firestone, for example, recalls that she did not particularly value Solanas' book because "it had a dangerous leaning towards what would become matriarchalist theory in the women's movement, a glorification of women as they are in their oppressed state"'.[29] Rhodes further argues that it was less the content of Solanas' feminist critique and more the politics of her trial that earned her attention from second wave feminism, explaining that after her arrest and trial, 'radical feminists saw her confinement in a mental hospital as indicative of the larger crime of male oppression'.[30] This description of feminists' interest in Solanas removes her as a subject of feminism and instead creates her as an object of feminist concern – someone who briefly caught the attention of the movement because of her oppression by state institutions.

Baumgardner and Rhodes argue that Solanas was marginal to feminism, as her perspective seemingly threatens the aims of the wider feminist movement. Yet, there are also those analyses which celebrate Solanas precisely because of this outsider status. For instance, Melissa D. Deem situates Solanas as an outsider figure to her contemporary feminist movement, describing *SCUM Manifesto* as 'an anomalous text, fitting neither into any organized component of the women's movement nor into any of its orthodoxies'.[31] Describing Solanas as living in 'displacement', '[o]utside of the fragile community of early Second Wave feminism', Deem paints Solanas as a true loner.[32] The anomaly of *SCUM Manifesto* makes Solanas' critique difficult to fit into narratives of feminist history for Deem who argues that her manifesto has 'never been adequately captured by the political narratives of Second Wave feminism'.[33] Breanne Fahs similarly articulates a certain difficulty in Solanas "fitting" into narratives of feminist history. In Fahs' use of Solanas' work in the name of an anarchistic asexuality, she argues that the master narrative of sexual revolution, where more sex = more freedom, leaves out 'other interpretations activists espoused for integrating sexuality and political freedom, particularly as radical feminists referenced the political goals of anarchism'.[34] Fahs argues that this situation continued into the 1980s where the sex wars divided feminists into two camps ("pro-" and "anti-sex") and 'these missing discourses of radical feminist mobilizations toward asexuality became even further silenced'.[35] In this view, Solanas' thinking does not fit easily within dominant narratives of feminist sexual politics and thus her contribution to theorizing female sexuality is obscured.

Emphasis is frequently placed on Solanas as a maverick figure in feminist history, lacking community and writing from the margins. In *Manifestos*, Janet Lyon argues that of all existing feminist manifestos, *SCUM Manifesto* is one of the 'most outrageously militant'.[36] She points out that despite the fact that the manifesto is addressed to 'People Like Her', Solanas is the sole signatory.[37] The manifesto, according to Lyon, essentially alienates any audience through pitting women against each other, reviling all men, espousing an intense homophobic description of gay men, and demeaning sexuality almost entirely. She explains that 'it seeks to polarize rather than negotiate its audiences; it fractures and diminishes its audience beyond coherence'.[38] For Lyon, the manifesto does the opposite of building community, distancing itself from communal politics so that the "we" in *SCUM Manifesto* can only be "Valerie Solanas".[39] In her introduction to the 2004 edition of *SCUM Manifesto*, Ronell similarly situates Solanas as an outsider, arguing that she is '[b]arely representable or representative, she was a speck and spectre on the margins of extremist writing'.[40] Ronell explains that 'Valerie Solanas was a loner', pushing her to the outer limits of representability as 'a psycho', '[b]utch-dykey angry, poor, and fucked up'.[41]

As a figure, Solanas continues to thus be both claimed for feminism and distanced from feminism in arguably equal measure. What remains constant is that this "belonging" or "not belonging" remains a primary frame through which Solanas is made meaningful in feminism. This focus on her place in feminist history imagines Solanas as either central to or outside "her time". In Chapter 2 I argued that the tendency to read Marge Piercy's *Woman on the Edge of Time* as having something to tell us, in the present, about a past moment in feminist history, makes it difficult to imagine how the novel might speak to contemporary concerns. Similarly, this tendency to consider Solanas' timing as bound to her contemporary moment makes it difficult to imagine how she might travel through feminism as anything other than a historic case study. I move away from focusing on whether or not Solanas should be seen as part of, or outside of, her contemporary feminist moment, to instead explore how Solanas might disrupt models of linear time. An emphasis on securing her status as either outside or inside of a particular feminist history misses an opportunity to consider the much less settled, less linear temporality that she might offer to contemporary feminist and queer theorizing.

Two examples here provide useful counters. In a film from 1996 and a video work from 1976, Solanas becomes central not to questions of feminist historical narrative but to feminism's timing, and particularly to questions of feminism's reproducibility into the future. The first is the film *I Shot Andy Warhol*, which stars Lili Taylor as Solanas.[42] The film professes to tell Solanas' side of the story, depicting her in Greenwich Village, writing her manifesto and plays, and struggling to make it on the streets. The film is focused in particular on the relationship between Solanas and Warhol (Jared Harris), representing Solanas as a frustrated outsider who becomes a momentary object of kitsch for Warhol. The film is consumed with comparing and contrasting the two characters and their worlds – all the while critiquing the value system of Warhol's world as it excludes the fiery but drab and crude Solanas. This is typified in one of the most memorable scenes of the film in which Warhol and Solanas are shown sitting beside each other in the midst of a party on The Factory's infamous red sofa. Warhol holds a tape recorder up to Solanas and asks her to give a monologue on the spot. Solanas is unable to perform in the way Warhol demands, awkwardly refusing and offering to read to him from *SCUM Manifesto* instead. Warhol humours Solanas but it is clear that her manifesto is out of place at The Factory and not something that Warhol cares to document. Solanas' politics seemingly act as a 'big drag' on Warhol's queer party, as Elizabeth Freeman explains lesbian feminism is often seen as exerting on queer.[43] This emphasis on Solanas not quite living up to the aesthetics of The Factory contributes to the film's critique of Warhol's revolutionary avant-garde, with Solanas' determined political stance and gritty substance again and again contrasted with the fluff of The Factory.

In Dana Heller's reading of the film, she highlights how the intensity of the contrast between the two figures works to separate them at the level of cultural reproducibility. She argues that Harron aligns Warhol with the technology of film and Solanas with the technology of writing, contrasting these two technologies alongside her representation of Solanas and Warhol. Heller suggests that the film is fascinated 'with the possibility that Solanas' derangement was owed to the failure of writing itself, or to shifting technologies of cultural memory'.[44] In the film, the image, represented by Warhol, takes over from writing. The emphasis on Solanas as an undocumented figure, obsessed with the only two copies of her script in the context of the obsessively filming Factory, creates Solanas as 'unreproducible': 'Solanas' memory, writings, and image had all simply vanished, as ephemeral as print itself.'[45] This comparison at the level of reproduction aligns Solanas with the medium of print and the "short life" of radical feminism which is set up against 'the virtual body of a queer capital that traffics merrily, self-consciously, and subversively in the enduring logic of commodity'.[46] Heller argues that the film emphasizes the contrast between Warhol and Solanas:

> By isolating and revisioning a moment wherein the mutually productive sites of pop art and lesbian feminist heroics collide, *I Shot Andy Warhol* stages a "clash of reproductive systems" and refocuses pop art's anxieties about the reproducibility of art on to anxieties related to radical feminism's failure to reproduce itself, carry forth and multiply.[47]

As Solanas explains in *I Shot Andy Warhol* in reference to her manuscript: 'I only have one other copy.' For Heller, this clash of Solanas' 'radical lesbian thought' with the queer aesthetic of Warhol is problematic insofar as 'feminist radicalism, of the sort that Solanas is positioned with, is represented as irrelevant, receding, and unable to proliferate or be reproduced'.[48] Heller thus shows how the film mythologizes Solanas as a means of releasing anxieties about the irreproducibility of a particular kind of woman and a particular kind of feminist politics.

Solanas is linked again to the question of reproduction by a video art piece that was made by Carole Roussopoulos and Delphine Seyrig in 1976. In this

27-minute-long piece, titled *S.C.U.M. Manifesto*, Roussopoulos and Seyrig face each other across a table in what looks to be a domestic setting.[49] Seyrig begins reading from Solanas' manifesto and Roussopoulos transcribes the manifesto on her typewriter. On the table in between the two women is a television, tuned in to a news station. At various points in the video, the pair take breaks from their transcribing to watch news reporting of protests and war from around the world. A loop is created that encompasses the two women, Solanas, and violent protest. While there are resonances being made in the video between Solanas' manifesto's criticism of male power and the images of war, the video also engages with the question of reproduction. They perform the labour of transcription on camera and their labour slows down the reading of the text (as Seyrig must stop while Roussopoulos catches up to her). Moreover, the news on the television stops the two women from their project, interrupting their transcription with news of war and protest. This video, I suggest, invites us to reflect on the process of reproducing feminism – both its necessity (in the face of war) and its difficulties (the labour involved). In their aim to transcribe the entirety of the manifesto, the women ultimately give up after Roussopoulos declares that she is tired. At the end of the video, the impetus behind the project is revealed. Typescript on the screen explains that the pair wanted to transcribe the manifesto because it has gone out of print. In a performative staging of the act of reproducing Solanas' manifesto, the video raises questions about the reproducibility of Solanas' text. Importantly, Solanas again is a central figure in questioning what it means for feminism to be reproduced.

I Shot Andy Warhol and Seyrig and Roussopoulos' video both move beyond questioning Solanas' place in radical feminist history to position Solanas at the centre of larger questions about the timing of feminism. In Harron's film, Solanas is cast as holding the weight of questions of feminism's ability to reproduce itself into the future, where *I Shot Andy Warhol* laments how Solanas, and radical feminism, cannot find a future in the cultural imaginary. While Heller worries that such a depiction of radical feminism is limiting, I insist instead on holding on to the difficulties of futurity attached to Solanas. Both Harron's film and Seyrig and Roussopoulos' video refuse to settle Solanas and instead focus on modes of unsettling – the difficulties of futurity, the blockage that Solanas might represent. These two examples represent counter-points to debates which are framed as either claiming or dismissing Solanas. Instead, they engage with the concept of futurity through Solanas as a figure, perhaps even explore the ways in which Solanas cannot seem to represent futurity. It is this difficulty in representing futurity that interests me. Solanas, in these examples, asks us to reflect on what it takes to represent or move into the future. In *I Shot Andy Warhol* this seems to require a leaving behind of her politics and an ascension into the realm of pure aesthetics. In Seyrig and Roussopoulos' video, the injustices and the labours of the present are just too exhausting. This, to me, is not just asking us to consider how Solanas fails to represent the future, but instead opening up a critique of a mode of futurity that would, and indeed could, leave behind the present. Solanas, in these examples, in her inability to leap wholesale into the future, becomes a figure through which we might critique this version of futurity – a future that demands leaving the past behind. In the following section I draw out this reading through extending the comparison in *I Shot Andy Warhol* between Solanas' version of lesbian feminism and a queer aesthetics.

The lesbian and futurity

In her introduction to *SCUM Manifesto*, Ronell refers to Solanas as 'butch-dykey', touching on one important way that Solanas circulates in the cultural imaginary, namely through a relationship to the figure of the lesbian feminist.[50] Solanas herself never claimed a lesbian identity, and in Fahs' reading of *SCUM Manifesto*, 'espoused the supremacy of asexuality'.[51] However, her shooting of Warhol and her angry insistence on the elimination of all men makes Solanas the 'stereotypical figure of the man-hating, crazed lesbian'.[52] The militant, man-hating Solanas who eschewed heterosexuality and men may thus be the archetype of the figure that Victoria Hesford has termed the 'feminist-as-lesbian'.[53] Hesford describes this figure as having a 'hypervisible presence in both popular and feminist cultural memory'; '[s]he's a monster, she's ridiculous, she's laughable, contemptuous, shameful, or she's joyful and full of proud anger'.[54] Even though Solanas' manifesto does not argue for lesbianism and Solanas never identified as a lesbian, the emphasis on her angry man-hating circulates as the "bad" kind of feminism – the unpopular and the dykey. Solanas as cultural figure seems to embody the ugliness, the gender ambiguity, the man-hating, and the verging-on-lesbian that haunts iterations of feminist identity. She is the figure that seemingly represents the detestable "feminist" in the all too common phrase: "I'm not a feminist, but … ".

If Solanas in some sense becomes the archetypal or stereotypical lesbian feminist, this is a figure who is overwhelmingly understood through concepts of anachronism. In other words, the lesbian is not predominantly thought of as a figure of futurity. Referencing this well-worn characterization of the lesbian, Noreen Giffney, Michelle M. Sauer, and Diane Watt ask in their introduction to *The Lesbian Premodern*, 'when has using the term "lesbian" *not* been considered an anachronistic gesture?'[55] In other words, the lesbian all too frequently is understood as a figure that is outdated, or as in *I Shot Andy Warhol*, terribly out of fashion. In Terry Castle's work, this becomes translated as a kind of ghosting that the lesbian performs on patriarchal culture. Castle argues that the invisibility of lesbian subjectivity within patriarchal culture characterizes the lesbian as ghostly, producing the 'spectral lesbian subject'.[56] In this ghostly form, the lesbian is that which remains on the margins, which is unspeakable, and indeed which cannot find representational status in the present, never mind the future. The difficulty of the lesbian's representational status has also been understood through a logic of sexual sequence. Annamarie Jagose explains that a logic of sequence is central to the organization of modern categories of sexual identification, where hetero-sexuality legitimizes itself as a natural logic of sequence where it poses itself as original and first and homosexuality as secondary and thus derivative. She describes the lesbian's invisibility in part through its impossibility of being known on its own terms, 'as a figure whose particularity rests on the fact that she occupies the definitional center of neither femininity nor homosexuality, the two categories of whose additive logic is presumed to describe her most fully'.[57] In this, the lesbian is imagined as derivative, or, temporally behind.

The lesbian is primarily a figure which threatens the field of the representable, particularly through being somehow "behind". That the lesbian is most frequently imagined as a backward kind of figure, makes her a particularly ripe figure for considering the failures of generational moves forward through time. Perhaps nowhere is this more apparent than in the relationship between the lesbian and the queer. As I have explored in previous chapters, Freeman considers how the lesbian seems to exert a certain pull on the forward motion of queer. Freeman argues that frequently 'the point of queer' is imagined as being 'ahead of actually existing social possibilities' so that 'truly queer queers would dissolve forms, disintegrate identities, level taxonomies, scorn the social, and even repudiate politics altogether'.[58] In this version of queer, the lesbian becomes precisely that which the truly queer would be positioned against. Freeman argues that in the face of this forward-moving queer, and particularly its deconstructionist impulses, the lesbian feminist 'seems to somehow inexorably harken back to essentialized bodies, normative visions of women's sexuality, and single-issue identity politics that exclude people of color, the working class, and the transgendered'.[59] In other words, lesbian feminism and those who are attached to it are often characterized as a 'big drag'.[60] Pulling back on the queer's attempt to move past identity categories, the lesbian is imagined as the opposite of the queer future. Yet, it is precisely in iterations of this backward, anachronistic figure, that Freeman finds queer potential. This potential comes from the figure's insistence on pulling back on notions of progress, on insisting that the past has a hold on the present, and in disrupting our ability to "move on".

The lesbian becomes then a figure that disrupts a linearity which would not only privilege the future, but which would see us in the present as having moved on from a so-called settled past. This point is similarly made by Hesford, who suggests not that the lesbian drags on the queer, but that she haunts feminism. As Hesford argues, the figure of the 'feminist-as-lesbian' ghosts feminism.[61] Hesford argues that haunting is a part of every social and poli-tical order as 'a sign of what has been forcibly expunged or evacuated from that order: the other that threatened to disrupt the emergent hegemony'.[62] In suggesting that the lesbian haunts feminism, Hesford argues that her sig-nificance exceeds the dominant accounts of the second wave movement. The feminist-as-lesbian is a popular figure 'through which perceptions of second wave feminism have been organized as memory in academic feminism', yet

Hesford reads this hypervisibility as actually keeping her quite separate from us.[63] In other words, her already-known-ness makes it impossible to explore her production and also our interest in her. As a figure then, the feminist-as-lesbian represents a tangled site of affect, a reminder, for Hesford, of the complexities of the second wave. She is the excess that points us toward what is unsettled, what exceeds dominant historical narratives. These theorizations of the lesbian imagine her as a profound challenge to notions of time that move linearly forward. Indeed, they enable a reading of Solanas that is not just a "failed" future, but instead perhaps troubles a version of futurity that moves coherently "on".

If the lesbian is characterized as being belated, anachronistic, and derivative, the figure of the queer is described by José Esteban Muñoz primarily through its relationship to the future. In *Cruising Utopia*, he argues that there is something inherently future-oriented about queerness in that it 'lets us feel that this world is not enough, that indeed something is missing'.[64] For Muñoz, queer is always a reaching forward, a 'longing that propels us onward'.[65] To make his case, Muñoz draws on an archive of cultural production from New York in the 1950s and 1960s – a context which he argues produced a particularly rich artistic arena for sentiments of queer utopianism. In this turn back, Muñoz argues that this cultural and artistic moment in New York provides a kind of enrichment to contemporary queer politics. Charmed by artists such as Warhol, Muñoz reads this work and this cultural moment as insisting on queerness as a kind of future opening in the present. For Muñoz, Warhol is a figure exemplary of utopian feeling and a queer utopianism understood as 'a great refusal of an overarching here and now'.[66] Muñoz reads Warhol's work and many other members of the New York avant-garde through this lens of queer potentiality.

While Solanas does not figure in this queer community, to say that Muñoz has forgotten Solanas would be untrue – she makes a brief and telling appearance. In a book full of loving readings of queer artistic figures and practices, perhaps it is unfair for me to pick at the one reference that Muñoz makes to Solanas, but it is precisely this appearance that reveals that the futurity that Muñoz sees as queer cannot be figured by Solanas. Muñoz describes her simply and only once as a disruption to Warhol's practice. In the context of Warhol's project of documenting the dancer Fred Herko, Muñoz writes the following:

> If one recalls early Warhol's interest in cinematically capturing the downtown demimonde and its weirdest denizens, *at least before Valerie Solanas made her indelible mark in his life*, the desire to preserve more of Herko's flickering incandescence strangely makes sense.[67]

In this abrupt and sole reference to Solanas, her presence is one that interrupts Warhol's project – literally shooting through it. Grammatically, Muñoz contains Solanas as a clause that interrupts Warhol's desires. She interrupts the connection between the first half of the sentence and the second, between Warhol and Herko. Solanas appears to disrupt this queer community, getting in the way of its documentation and desire, and perhaps even maiming it. By getting in the way of Warhol's documentation of Herko, Solanas threatens the ability of Warhol to reproduce Herko's aesthetic for the future. She bursts into Warhol's life and quickly recedes, having accomplished in this reference nothing more than a blockade of queer desires. I do not find it surprising that Solanas does not make it into Muñoz's circle of queer avant-garde – a circle that includes Warhol, Herko, and Frank O'Hara. In fact, aside from Elizabeth Bishop, not many women seem able to figure the kind of queer futurity that Muñoz is after. Muñoz's futurity involves an ability to 'see and feel beyond the quagmire of the present'.[68] It is this demand that the future somehow lift us out of the present that Solanas cannot seemingly achieve.

Perhaps Solanas is simply too "dykey" to represent the queer future – too stuck to identity politics, to lesbian feminism, and to anger. Indeed, Solanas' angry manifesto represents a negativity that Muñoz distances his project from. In Muñoz's archive of queer utopianism, he turns away from the negativity of the antirelational thesis, epitomized by Leo Bersani in *Homos* and Lee Edelman in *No Future*.[69] Muñoz turns away from this strand of queer theory, what he deems 'romances of the negative' and charges with turning away from queerness as collectivity.[70] In response to queer negativity that would turn away from futurity, Muñoz argues that 'queerness is primarily about futurity and hope'.[71] In his opposition to Edelman in particular, Muñoz argues for both the importance of futurity to queerness and the integral role that positive affects of hope have to queerness as collectivity. Precisely because Muñoz insists on hope and futurity in opposition to negativity, his understanding of queer collectivity becomes limited to positive affect. His turn away from negativity can thus not consider the potentially world-building qualities of anger, for instance. This has quite clear implications, particularly for feminism. As Halberstam argues in *The Queer Art of Failure*, this turn from negativity has resulted in Muñoz's erasure of histories of feminist thought which draws its strength from negativity. Halberstam terms this 'shadow feminism', a genealogy of feminist thought that works to undo the subject of "woman".[72] Halberstam closely aligns herself to Muñoz's argument that '[q]ueer feminist and queer of color critiques are the powerful counterweight to the antirelational', but does not turn to optimism to counter queer negativity.[73] Instead, she considers how an expansion of the queer archive of negativity challenges negativity as only self-shattering. In this list of the occluded, Halberstam includes Valerie Solanas alongside others such as Jamaica Kincaid, Lesbians on Ecstasy, and Patti Smith. Halberstam argues that this expansion contributes occluded forms of negativity to Muñoz's queer archive such as 'rage, rudeness, anger, spite, impatience, brutal honesty, and disappointment' that is found in '[d]yke anger, anticolonial despair, racial rage, counterhegemonic violence, punk pugilism'.[74]

Drawing on Halberstam's corrective to Muñoz's archive, Solanas' negativity, anger, and despair might be read as generative of a future horizon. To be sure, this is a very different futurity from the one that Muñoz imagines. Yet it is tempting to consider how Solanas' use of the language of the threat does indeed display an aesthetics of open futurity – of imagining, without pro-scribing, a possible future. In her history of American feminism, Castro explains that Solanas' text is a parody and that her proposal to eliminate men should not be 'taken seriously', belonging as it does to the 'realm of political fiction, or even science fiction, written in a desperate effort to arouse public consciousness'.[75] Dismissed as parody, Solanas' text becomes nothing more than an exposition, an effort to arouse consciousness. However, consider Solanas' threat: 'If SCUM ever strikes, it will be in the dark with a six-inch blade' (*SM* 28). While this sentence from *SCUM Manifesto* is frequently cited or quoted as the extreme that is indicative of Solanas' text, it is not usually dissected beyond the violence that it threatens. In Lyon, for example, this sentence is quoted as indicative of the fact that *SCUM Manifesto* offers 'a recipe for more literal violence and less orderly rage' than most political manifestos.[76] Yet, this sentence is nothing as straightforward as a recipe. In fact, everything about this sentence removes it from any certainty or stable relationship between words and deeds. First of all, it begins with "if"; there is no guarantee that SCUM will ever strike. Solanas is not calling for SCUM to strike in this instance – she is positing a hypothetical situation. Secondly, "SCUM" as Solanas describes it is itself an imaginary group, 'a state of mind'.[77] In other words, SCUM is nothing visceral enough to be able to even hold a six-inch blade, never mind wield it at an intended target. Which brings us to yet another uncertainty – who or what is the target? Of course, the supposition is that it might be men, that it might be patriarchy (a slippery target to hit with a blade) – but this is nowhere clear here in this most famous of lines. Finally, this maybe attack by an imagined state of mind is further elusive in the where of the attack: the dark.

The threat of *SCUM Manifesto* goes beyond the male body and targets society as a whole. Solanas threatens not just the male but capitalism more generally and the value systems that come packaged with patriarchal capital-ist states – including higher education, "Great Art", and censorship. She also aims to eliminate distrust, ugliness, hatred, violence, disease, and death. While Solanas explains that SCUM will 'become members of the unwork force, the fuck-up force' as a means to destroy capitalism, the elimination of the male is surely the most infamous of all her threats.[78] Halberstam argues that there is an uncertain relationship to "actual" violence inherent in all representations of violence – the connection between 'imagined violence and "real" violence is unclear, contested, negotiable, unstable, and radically unpredictable; and yet, imagined and real violence is not simply a binary formulation'.[79] In the realm of popular culture and representations of vio-lence, Halberstam locates power in representing violence that targets the majority. Representations of violence perpetrated on women and other minorities at the hands of white men are so commonplace in popular culture that they seemingly go unnoticed. Reversing this logic, Halberstam argues, is thus powerful. Drawing on films such as *Thelma and Louise* and work by artist David Wojnarowicz, Halberstam argues that it is important that we 'imagine the possibility of fighting violence with violence'.[80] In part because any reversal is not simply a reversal as:

> The depiction of women committing acts of violence against men does not simply use 'male' tactics of aggression for other ends; in fact, female violence transforms the symbolic function of the feminine within popular narratives and it simultaneously challenges the hegemonic insistence upon the linking of might and right under the sign of masculinity.[81]

The threat is conceptualized as "enough" – there is no need to transform the threat into action because the potential for action is contained in the words. It is through imagined violence that fantasy can be transformed into productive fear.[82] Halberstam explains that such violent representations demand to be heard: '*My* resistance may cost you *your* life; my answer may silence your question; my entry into representation may erase your control over how I am represented.'[83] Through this reading, Solanas' threat becomes not a parody but an action in and of itself. Rather than a seeming failure to enact her future society, Solanas' threat might be read as a kind of horizon that imagines the possibility of futurity in the present. Similar to Muñoz's description of queerness as a 'forward-dawning futurity', Solanas' threat might similarly be imagined as consumed with a 'kind of potentiality that is open, indeterminate, like the affective contours of hope itself'.[84]

While the temporality of the threat enables a way to imagine Solanas' manifesto as containing an aesthetics of desiring futurity, there are limitations to this reading. Halberstam's work offers a reading of Solanas that is able to "read" rage as a kind of desiring, even future-oriented aesthetic. However, as Dana Luciano has remarked, there is a tendency for work such as Halberstam's, however pointed, to revel in the alternative affects of negativity.[85] In other words, the subcultural lesbian anger comes to be fetishized for its outsider status or its absolute opposition. Rather than insist on Solanas' inclusion into Muñoz's archive of future-oriented queerness, I insist that Solanas cannot make this leap forward. Despite her threatening language and her calls for new forms of sociality and a reorganization of society, Solanas is profoundly anxious about her ability to bring this future into being. This anxiety is legible in her manifesto and an effect of the genre itself. If so far I have been tracing through the difficulties of Solanas representing futurity through her association with the figure of the lesbian, I turn finally to build this argument through a reading of the manifesto genre and her *SCUM Manifesto*. In this section, I consider the manifesto as a genre that has a difficult relationship to futurity, despite its frequent designation as a performative genre. Solanas' manifesto in particular is an anxious and compromised text – a text which aims towards the future but is inevitably haunted by its inability to make this move.

Manifesto time

Manifestos have historically been important forms of textuality in particular for radical feminists, with manifestos such as the 1970 'The Woman Identi-fied-Woman' being definitive texts in radical feminist movements. Rhodes explains that in the 1960s and 1970s radical feminists produced an excess of what she terms 'temporary texts' – 'manifestos, statements of purpose, guides to consciousness raising and other political actions'.[86] These kinds of texts were a primary means through which feminism was disseminated. As Rhodes points out, they created a particular rhetoric and this rhetoric created a more coherent feminist network. Through the creation and sharing of manifestos and statements of purpose, second wave feminism spread and become more coherent as a movement so that the 'emphasis on public, purposeful textuality was a hallmark of the women's liberation movement'.[87] Rhodes argues that the particular kind of public circulation implied by the manifesto makes it an important part of creating feminist community. Felicity Colman echoes this point and argues that the feminist manifesto 'in its many guises is one of the primary means through which feminist knowledge is and has been dis-seminated'.[88] Feminist manifestos have been integral means by which the movement has been shaped and defined.

While manifestos might traditionally be understood as primarily concerned with the future tense – with calling into being a new future in the present – their temporality is not only or simply future-oriented. In their attempts to break with the linear narrative of history, manifestos are imagined as consumed with, in Lyon's words, their 'own versions of "the possible," "the imaginable," and "the necessary"'.[89] Colman explains that the manifesto 'wants to take action, to intervene, to re-imagine and re-remember different forms of exis-tence'.[90] Manifestos have a tendency to be rapidly produced from urgency felt in the present as a way to shift what is considered an imaginable or possible future. In other words, as Colman suggests, '[p]redestined options for the future are often reconfigured' by these texts.[91] Yet, the temporality of the genre is more complicated than this. Manifestos do not only attempt to bring into being a new future, they also construct a particular version of the past. As Martin Puchner argues, the manifesto is a 'construction of a history of rup-ture … a cut in the historical process, an act that attempts to change suddenly the course of history'.[92] Targeting historical continuity with rupture, the manifesto is not only focused on the future, but is equally concerned with narratives of the past. Puchner explains that the manifesto 'does not merely describe a history of rupture, but produces such a history, seeking to create this rupture actively through its own intervention'.[93] Moreover, manifestos are also decidedly discourses of particular moments. The manifesto aims to take action but has to use, in Colman's words, 'existing platforms in order to position a recognisable expression'.[94] In other words, manifestos are always linked to the present in which they are written. The manifesto then does not have an uncomplicated relationship to futurity, as its version of futurity always attempts to rewrite narratives of history from a situated present.

Even the performative nature of manifestos might be read as not only forward-facing but as necessarily attached to the past. That manifestos attempt to turn language into action brings the genre into close contact with performative language. For instance, Morgan, in the introduction to one of the most famous texts of second wave feminism, *Sisterhood Is Powerful*, proclaims that the book itself is an action.[95] As J. L. Austin describes it, uttering performative sentences does more than describe or state that something is being done, 'it is to do it'.[96] His most famous example is the "I do" of the marriage ceremony, where the utterance is not merely descriptive but enacts the marriage itself. As Eve Sedgwick summarizes: 'Austinian performativity is about how language constructs or affects reality rather than merely describing it.'[97] Moreover, as Butler points out, performative speeches are authoritative in nature so that they not only perform an action but also enact a binding power. Butler argues that the performative 'is thus one domain in which power acts *as* discourse'.[98] In Butler's work, the citationality of performativity is integral to the work that it does, so that performative language draws on a citational history. She gives the example of a judge's decision coming from the citation of the law so that it is this citation that 'gives the performative its binding or conferring power'; 'it is *through* the citation of the law that the figure of the judge's "will" is produced and that the "priority" of textual authority is established'.[99]

This drawing on a citational history is part of the force of manifestos. In other words, the manifesto's ability to perform depends on a history of past utterances. Lyon points out that the manifesto's generic form, noted for its 'repeating structure and locutions', is precisely the means through which manifestos are linked to a history of struggle and revolutionary dreaming.[100] To write a manifesto is in some sense to align one's cause with past revolutions, making the manifesto an ideological sign of political combat. Manifestos, according to Lyon, activate 'the symbolic force of the form's role in earlier political confrontations: to write a manifesto is to announce one's participation, however discursive, in a history of struggle against oppressive forces'.[101] A manifesto always refers back to a genealogy of manifesto writing – never quite leaving this past behind but requiring this history. Thus, manifestos contain the same 'temporal complexity' that Sedgwick points out is integral to both Butler and Derrida's usage of performative utterances.[102] Sedgwick describes the performative's 'iteration, citationality, [and] the "always already"' as a 'valuable repertoire of conceptual shuttle movements that endlessly weave between the future and the past'.[103] Dependent on the force of the genre's history and its ideological power, the manifesto draws on the past to enact the future that its utterance is meant to perform. These temporal qualities make it difficult to see the manifesto as entirely future-oriented. Its reliance on histories of utterances and its investment in not only the future but narratives of the past and present might be said to weigh it down.

Solanas, in her manifesto, is completely dissatisfied with the present tense and in this she is keen for women to 'wheel on to something far beyond what [society] has to offer' (*SM* 70). However, at the same moment as her manifesto attempts to rewrite the possibilities for the future, she remains profoundly anxious about the future tense. Throughout the manifesto, Solanas expresses the desire to move into a future beyond the present, yet she struggles to imagine how this move will be enacted. Solanas opens her manifesto with an impatient sentence, describing life 'in this society' as 'at best, an utter bore' (*SM* 35). That she is dissatisfied with the present tense is reiterated in the repetition of 'utter bore', which returns twice more in the manifesto to describe the situation of women in contemporary society (*SM* 36; 62). This leads Solanas to conclude that the only reasonable option for women is to 'overthrow the government, eliminate the money system, institute complete automation and destroy the male sex' (*SM* 35). Yet this is imagined as a change not in the future but in the present. Solanas does not want to hedge her bets on the future: 'Why should there be future generations? What is their purpose? [...] Why should we care what happens when we're dead? Why should we care that there is no younger generation to succeed us?' (*SM* 69). Indeed, the future is not the time when the revolution will happen – the future is not the tense that Solanas cares for. Solanas turns away from the future because she is intent on the change being imminent – 'SCUM is impatient; SCUM is not consoled by the thought that future generations will thrive; SCUM wants to grab some thrilling living for itself' (*SM* 69). Unsatisfied with waiting for progress, Solanas makes demands on the present. Refusing to be satisfied with the progress of future generations, Solanas is emphatic that the future needs to be enacted now.

This rejection of the future is further evident in her consistent insistence on the speed with which her utopia could be imagined in the present, should there be enough support from women. Solanas writes: 'Even without leaving men, women who are aware of the extent of their superiority to and power over men, could acquire complete control over everything *within a few weeks*' (*SM* 70, emphasis added). SCUM is 'too impatient' and why should SCUM wait, asks Solanas, when '[a] small handful of SCUM can take over the country within a year by systematically fucking up the system, selectively destroying property, and murder' (*SM* 71). Solanas reiterates again and again, almost obsessively, the great speed at which SCUM could take over. All SCUM needs is the spark, for '[w]hen SCUM gets hot on their asses it'll shape up fast' (*SM* 75). Solanas' revolution will be 'accomplished very simply and quickly once there is a public demand for it' (*SM* 77); 'its construction will take only a few weeks with millions of people working on it' (*SM* 78). This rush, this impatient demand for an alternative society, does not imagine the future as a distant temporality but instead attempts to reach it in the present. In this, it is an attempt to bring the future into being imminently – to imagine that the present is an easily unsettled political moment. It is a hopeful mode of dreaming that imagines the present could easily be something else – Solanas aims to bring the future into the present by suggesting that the future is "now".

However, despite her attempts to collapse the present into the future, Solanas is profoundly anxious about the failure of this future. Her version of futurity in the present is tangled with an anxiety about her inability to create this futurity. As much as she continues to insist that the future is within reach, these repetitive claims work to reveal an anxiety about the possibilities of leaving behind the present. The urgency with which Solanas demands change thinly veils the fear that her manifesto will not accomplish the change she demands. Ronell argues that Solanas, in some ways, 'shows up as a victim of the failed performative'.[104] This anxiety, I suggest, ghosts the manifesto genre and makes visible the difficulties of a futurity that is imagined as a leap outside of the present. Solanas herself has become weighed down with anxieties around reproducibility and futurity. Obsessed with the potential speed with which her desired changes might be accomplished, Solanas rehearses throughout the manifesto her own inability to bring this new future into being. To return to Muñoz, he argues that it is queerness which enables us, 'in the face of the here and now's totalizing rendering of reality, to think and feel a *then and there*'.[105] In Solanas' iterations of the possibilities of a then and there in the here and now, she ultimately fails to get out of the here and now. Indeed, her anxiousness reveals her inability to "leave behind" this here and now.

Rather than read this as a "failure" of her ability to imagine futurity, perhaps it is this version of futurity that we might want. In other words, perhaps Solanas does not represent an easy or unencumbered or guaranteed feminist futurity – but maybe it is this quality that enables her to represent a critique to a model of time that would leave behind the present. In other words, perhaps she reveals the impossibility of and thus the dangers of imagining futurity as somehow a "move on" from the present. The angry opposition that Solanas espouses cannot, in the end, move past what she is angry about. As Hesford explores in relation to Robin Morgan's manifesto 'Goodbye to All That', anger is a binding emotion that attaches you to that which you are against. 'Goodbye to All That' is a critique of the New Left for its representation of women. As Hesford notes, 'Morgan deploys a mocking, sarcastic tone designed to expose the hypocrisies and contradictions between the New Left's stated political aim of liberation for all people and its rhetorical and symbolic (mis)use of women.'[106] Anger in this manifesto thus binds Morgan in complicated ways to that which she positions herself against. Hesford thus argues that '[t]o react in anger pulls you toward the object of your anger but in a way that is also simultaneously a rejection, a turning away from it'.[107] In Morgan's manifesto, this is a turn away from men, the New Left, and a particular treatment of women; yet, the performative aspect of Morgan's anger is that her reading, 'inevitably, generates a particular view of feminism and of women's liberation – a view that is bound to, but not determined by, what she is rejecting'.[108] In other words, Morgan's anger gains articulation by being opposed to white men in the New Left, and in consequence, this limits what kinds of politics this anger might produce. As Hesford states:

> To put it simply: Morgan can only be a (New Left, white middle-class) woman angry at how she has been belittled and dismissed as a sexual plaything and movement domestic and never an angry brown or black man or woman, and this has consequences for how that anger is read and what it is capable of enacting politically.[109]

This might not be a shortcoming but might instead be a way to theorize feminist futurity as entangled with the very terms that produce it. In Hesford's work, this helps explain some of the limitations in the way in which women's liberation was produced and is remembered as a white, middle-class movement.

Finally then, Solanas' inability to leap into the future tense draws our attention to the difficulties of moving past histories of injury. Rather than suggest we find ways to make her represent a utopian future tense or an outsider rage, perhaps what she offers in the end is a feminist model of futurity that asks us not to leave behind the present in our desires for the future. On the one hand, it is precisely our dissatisfaction with the present that enables hope for a different future. As Claire Colebrook argues, hope 'splits the present' both in its ability to enable us to think beyond the present, and in its potential to hold us back from action in the present.[110] If feminism is in part structured by hope for a different future, this split present is not something we might escape but instead an ongoing negotiation that must occur. Moreover, it is precisely by remaining dissatisfied in the present that the desire for an alternative future is possible. In this, the present cannot be left behind. As Sara Ahmed argues, a critical politics can never be in a simple relationship of 'anti' to what it opposes and thus 'what feminism is against cannot be seen as "exterior" to feminism'.[111] In this view, a politics such as feminism 'cannot simply "overcome" through the detachment the affects of the histories of violence, justice and inequality that structure the demand or hope for transformation'.[112] An emotion such as anger can be read for the way in which it both makes feminist politics possible and also reveals why 'transformations are so difficult (we remain invested in what we critique)'.[113] A feminist futurity is not one then that leaves behind its objects of critique – that successfully leaps into the future – but instead one that turns 'towards those very objects, *as signs of the persistence of that which we are against in the present'*.[114] Futurity, in Ahmed's work, is not guaranteed by letting go of the past but by engaging more closely with it. The manifesto then might not be read as a failed performative so much as reveal the difficulties of futurities that are untied to the present.

Conclusion

This chapter began with the anonymous stencil that insists 'Valerie was right'. As a simple, three-word sentence with a seemingly clear message, the stencil is evocative. However, it is even more evocative when, upon second, third, or fourth glance, its meaning becomes less clear. As an almost epitaph-like marking, it references historical injury. It marks the present yet is oriented toward a past wrong – a wrong perhaps that Valerie might have righted. It is also, I think, imbued with hope for a future. Voiced in a public space it makes reference to someone who remembers, binding those who want to recognize or read the epitaph as belonging to a like-minded community. Perhaps offering a possible alternative future. However, this future is attached to the past and, in particular, to past loss or past wrong. If Solanas is predominantly discussed in relation to her either being part of or outside of her contemporary feminist moment, what is missed in these readings is the opportunity to consider the way in which her relationship to temporality is much more complicated than a presence in her historical feminist moment. This chapter has instead explored how such attempts to settle her meaning miss out on an oppor- tunity to engage with Solanas in relation to questions of futurity in both feminist and queer thought. Solanas, finally, may not be most interesting for what she tells us about radical feminist history, but for what she alerts us to about the future tense. Solanas' feminist timing is far more complicated than the dominant narratives we tell. Indeed, by turning to the temporality of the manifesto, Solanas becomes yet another opportunity to reflect on the non- linearity of feminism's timing, where the future might be conceptualized not as a move forward, but as inevitably tied to and haunted by the desires of the present tense.

Notes

1 Laura Mulvey, 'Visual Pleasure and Narrative Cinema', *Screen*, 16.3 (1975), 6–18.
2 Ibid., p. 6.
3 Ibid., p. 11.
4 Ibid.
5 Mandy Merck, 'Mulvey's Manifesto', *Camera Obscura*, 22.3 (2007), 1–23 (p. 10).
6 Ibid., p. 7.
7 Ibid., p. 13.
8 Ibid., p. 18.
9 Ibid., p. 7.
10 Heller, 'Shooting Solanas: Radical Feminist History and the Technology of Failure', *Feminist Studies*, 27 (2001), 167–89 (p. 168).
11 Quoted in Heller, p. 168 (original citation: Howard Smith and Brian van der Horst, 'Valerie Solanas Interview', *Village Voice*, 25 July 1977, p. 32).
12 Suzanne Moore, 'The Bag Lady of Feminism', *New Statesman*, 28 June 2004.
13 Rowan Gaither, 'Andy Warhol's Feminist Nightmare', *New York Magazine*, 14 January 1991, p. 35.
14 Alice Echols, *Daring to Be Bad: Radical Feminism in America 1967–1975* (Minneapolis and London: University of Minnesota Press, 1989), p. 105.
15 It is tempting to read the stencil as somehow connected to the political uproar that occurred in Sweden, which closely following the publication of Solanas' manifesto into Swedish. For a full exploration of this, see Katherine Harrison, '"Sometimes the Meaning of the Text is Unclear": Making Sense of the *SCUM*

Manifesto in a Contemporary Swedish Context', *Journal of International Women's Studies*, 10.3 (2009), 33–47.

16 Catherine Lord, 'Wonder Waif Meets Super Neuter', *October*, 132 (2010), 135–63, p. 136.

17 Clare Hemmings, *Why Stories Matter: The Political Grammar of Feminist Theory* (Durham, NC and London: Duke University Press), p. 20.

18 Ginette Castro, *American Feminism: A Contemporary History*, trans. Elizabeth Loverde-Bagwell (New York and London: New York University Press, 1990), p. 93; Jacqueline Rhodes, *Radical Feminism, Writing, and Critical Agency: From Manifesto to Modern* (Albany: State University of New York Press, 2005), p. 25; Valerie Solanas, 'SCUM (Society for Cutting Up Men) Manifesto', in *Radical Feminism: A Documentary Reader*, ed. Barbara A. Crow (New York and London: New York University Press, 2000), pp. 201–22; Valerie Solanas, 'SCUM Manifesto (1967)', in *Public Women, Public Words: A Documentary History of American Feminism*, vol. 3, ed. Dawn Keetley and John Pettegrew (Madison, WI: Madison House, 2003), pp. 172–78.

19 Valerie Solanas, 'Excerpts from the SCUM (Society for Cutting Up Men) Manifesto', in *Sisterhood Is Powerful: An Anthology of Writings from the Women's Liberation Movement*, ed. Robin Morgan (New York: Random House, 1970), pp. 514–19; Joanna Russ, 'The New Misandry', *Radical Feminism: A Documentary Reader*, ed. Barbara A. Crow (New York and London: New York University Press, 2000), pp. 167–70.

20 Russ, 'The New Misandry', p. 168.

21 Jill Johnston, *Lesbian Nation: The Feminist Solution* (New York: Touchstone, 1973), p. 353.

22 Heller, p. 180.

23 Sara Evans, *Personal Politics: The Roots of Women's Liberation in the Civil Rights Movement and the New Left* (New York: Vintage Books, 1980), p. 209.

24 Echols, p. 105.

25 Ibid.

26 Quoted in Heller, p. 169 (original citation: Jennifer Baumgardner, 'Who Shot Andy Warhol?', *Ms.*, May–June 1996, p. 74).

27 Rhodes, *Radical Feminism*, p. 47.

28 Ibid., p. 48.

29 Ibid., p. 47.

30 Ibid.

31 Melissa D. Deem, 'From Bobbitt to SCUM: Re-memberment, Scatological Rhetorics, and Feminist Strategies in the Contemporary United States', *Public Culture*, 8 (1996), 511–37 (p. 522).

32 Ibid.

33 Ibid., p. 513.

34 Breanne Fahs, 'Radical Refusals: On the Anarchist Politics of Women Choosing Asexuality', *Sexualities*, 13.4 (2010), 445–61 (p. 446).

35 Ibid.

36 Janet Lyon, *Manifestos: Provocations of the Modern* (Ithaca, NY and London: Cornell University Press, 1999), p. 172

37 Ibid.

38 Ibid., p. 175.

39 Ibid.

40 Avital Ronell, 'The Deviant Payback: The Aims of Valerie Solanas', Introduction to *SCUM Manifesto* (London and New York: Verso, 2004), pp. 1–34 (p. 2).

41 Ibid., p. 17.

42 *I Shot Andy Warhol*, dir. by Mary Harron (BBC Arena, 1996).

43 Elizabeth Freeman, *Time Binds: Queer Temporalities, Queer Histories* (Durham, NC and London: Duke University Press, 2010), p. 62.
44 Heller, p. 170.
45 Ibid., p. 171.
46 Ibid., p. 171.
47 Ibid., p. 181.
48 Ibid., pp. 183–84.
49 *S.C.U.M. Manifesto*, dir. by Carole Roussopoulos and Delphine Seyrig (1976).
50 Ronell, p. 17.
51 Fahs, p. 451.
52 Amanda Third, '"Shooting from the Hip": Valerie Solanas, SCUM and the Apocalyptic Politics of Radical Feminism', *Hecate*, 32.2 (2006), 104–32 (p. 106).
53 Victoria Hesford, 'Feminism and Its Ghosts: The Spectre of the Feminist-as-Lesbian', *Feminist Theory*, 6 (2005), 227–50 (p. 228).
54 Ibid., p. 230.
55 Noreen Giffney, Michelle M. Sauer, and Diane Watt, 'Introduction: The Lesbian Premodern', in *The Lesbian Premodern*, ed. Noreen Giffney, Michelle M. Sauer, and Diane Watt (Basingstoke and New York: Palgrave Macmillan, 2011), pp. 1–20 (p. 1, emphasis in original).
56 Terry Castle, *The Apparitional Lesbian: Female Homosexuality and Modern Culture* (New York: Columbia University Press, 1993), p. 8.
57 Annamarie Jagose, *Inconsequence: Lesbian Representation and the Logic of Sexual Sequence* (Ithaca, NY and London: Cornell University Press, 2002), p. 3.
58 Freeman, *Time Binds*, p. xiii.
59 Ibid., p. 62.
60 Ibid.
61 Hesford, 'Feminism and Its Ghosts', p. 228.
62 Ibid., p. 229. Hesford draws on the methodological insights in Avery F. Gordon, *Ghostly Matters: Haunting and the Sociological Imagination* (Minneapolis and London: University of Minnesota Press, 1997).
63 Hesford, 'Feminism and Its Ghosts', p. 228.
64 José Esteban Muñoz, *Cruising Utopia: The Then and There of Queer Futurity* (New York and London: New York University Press, 2009), p. 1.
65 Ibid.
66 Ibid., p. 133.
67 Ibid., p. 157 (emphasis added).
68 Ibid., p. 1.
69 Ibid., p. 11.
70 Ibid.
71 Ibid.
72 Judith Halberstam, *The Queer Art of Failure* (Durham, NC and London: Duke University Press, 2011), p. 124.
73 Muñoz, p. 17.
74 Ibid., p. 110.
75 Castro, p. 74.
76 Lyon, p. 173.
77 Quoted in Heller, p. 183 (original citation: Howard Smith, 'Valerie Solanas Replies', *Village Voice*, 1 August 1977, p. 28).
78 Valerie Solanas, *SCUM Manifesto* (London and New York: Verso, 2004), p. 71. Hereafter referred to in the text as *SM*.
79 Judith Halberstam, 'Imagined Violence/Queer Violence: Representation, Rage, and Resistance', *Social Text*, 37 (1993), 187–201 (p. 187).
80 Ibid., p. 191.
81 Ibid.

82 Ibid., p. 195.
83 Ibid., p. 195 (emphasis in original).
84 Muñoz, p. 7.
85 Dana Luciano, 'Nostalgia for an Age Yet to Come: *Velvet Goldmine*'s Queer Archive', in *Queer Times, Queer Becomings*, ed. E. L. McCallum and Mikko Tuhkanen (Albany, NY: SUNY Press, 2011) pp. 121–55, p. 145.
86 Jacqueline Rhodes, '"Substantive and Feminist Girlie Action": Women Online', *College Composition and Communication*, 54.1 (2002), 116–42 (p. 116).
87 Rhodes, '"Substantive and Feminist Girlie Action"', p. 117.
88 Felicity Colman, 'Notes on the Feminist Manifesto: The Strategic Use of Hope', *Journal for Cultural Research*, 14.4 (2010), 375–92 (p. 379).
89 Lyon, p. 16.
90 Colman, p. 380.
91 Ibid., p. 378.
92 Martin Puchner, 'Manifesto = Theatre', *Theatre Journal*, 54.3 (2002), 449–65 (p. 451).
93 Ibid.
94 Colman, p. 380.
95 Robin Morgan, *Sisterhood Is Powerful: An Anthology of Writings from the Women's Liberation Movement* (New York: Random House, 1970), p. xiii.
96 J. L. Austin, *How to Do Things With Words*, ed. J. O. Urmson (New York: Oxford University Press, 1970), p. 6.
97 Eve Sedgwick, *Touching Feeling: Affect, Pedagogy, Performativity* (Durham, NC and London: Duke University Press, 2003), p. 5.
98 Judith Butler, 'Critically Queer', *GLQ: A Journal of Lesbian and Gay Studies*, 1.1 (1993), 17–32 (p. 17, emphasis in original).
99 Ibid., p. 17 (emphasis in original).
100 Lyon, p. 29.
101 Ibid., p. 10.
102 Sedgwick, *Touching Feeling*, p. 68.
103 Ibid.
104 Ronell, p. 4.
105 Muñoz, p. 1 (emphasis in original).
106 Victoria Hesford, *Feeling Women's Liberation* (Durham, NC: Duke University Press, 2013), p. 97.
107 Ibid.
108 Ibid., p. 98.
109 Ibid., p. 99.
110 Claire Colebrook, 'Toxic Feminism: Hope and Hopelessness after Feminism', *Journal for Cultural Research*, 14.4 (2010), 323–35 (p. 324).
111 Sara Ahmed, *The Cultural Politics of Emotion* (Edinburgh: Edinburgh University Press, 2004), p. 172.
112 Ibid.
113 Ibid.
114 Ibid., p. 187 (emphasis in original).

5 Learning to see

Alison Bechdel's *Fun Home*

Debates are constantly had (both in academic contexts as well as more informally) over whether particular texts might be claimed as belonging to or evidencing a specific politics, theoretical framework, or community (such as whether something might be feminist or queer; or, whether it might be read through a feminist or queer lens). For example, while certain literary authors, such as Margaret Atwood, have overwhelmingly claimed the title of "feminist", not all of her books have been received as feminist cultural products. Notably, there has been much debate over whether *Oryx and Crake*, Atwood's first book to not feature a female narrator, can be seen to be concerned with, or interesting to, feminism.[1] As I have argued elsewhere in relation to Atwood, presumptions about what is or is not a feminist literary concern have profound effects in terms of the field of feminist literary criticism.[2] In other words, to decide that the novel is uninteresting to feminism because it does not have a female narrator is to define the borders of feminist literary criticism as interested primarily in female self-narration. Not limited to the realm of literature, debates over the feminist credentials of a particular cultural product persist in numerous forms. For example, the HBO series *Girls* has on the one hand been popularly designated as a feminist text in its exploration of female friendship, female sexuality, and embodiment, yet the show has been simultaneously critiqued for its class and race politics, begging questions about how feminist the show might be seen to be.[3] Partly what is at stake in relation to designating objects as feminist or queer has to do with policing the boundaries of these two communities, political approaches, and/or theoretical disciplines.[4]

In this chapter, I consider some of what is at stake in the more recent critical popularity of Alison Bechdel's *Fun Home* and, particularly, its relationship to queer. While previous chapters have turned to literary and cultural texts more generally recognizable as "feminist", this chapter turns to consider how this graphic narrative has been embraced for its resonances with queer work on history and the archive.[5] Throughout this book, I have been considering models of time in feminism's archive that might speak to contemporary feminist and queer theoretical concerns. Part of my insistence has been that generational models of progression make it difficult to approach archives of literary and cultural production as having something to say to contemporary feminist and queer theory. However, it has also been about uncovering histories of so-called "queer time" in feminism's archive. *Fun Home* and the graphic narrative, have both been embraced for their queer potential. While not wanting to disagree with these claims, I consider instead the work that such designation has for the relationship between feminism and queer. In other words, through exploring how the medium's temporal possibilities and contingent construction of narrative have been claimed as having particular resonances with queer projects, feminism and feminism's explorations of similarly contingent knowledge-projects and temporalities become erased. As I outlined in the introduction to this book, there has been contestation over the boundaries between feminism and queer since the inception of queer. Feminism and queer theory are not analogous, and historically, feminism preceded queer theory. Yet what this historical precedence means for both feminism and queer is anything but simple. As Annamarie Jagose puts it, that feminism historically preceded queer frequently results in a 'temporal disciplining of feminist from queer thought that stages them as the before and after of some narrative of critical advancement'.[6] While previous chapters have attempted to counteract this disciplining of feminism through insisting on feminism's own queer temporalities, this chapter considers how a theoretical frame of "queer time" is used to read Bechdel's *Fun Home*. I explore claims to *Fun Home*'s queer temporalities and, building on an insistence throughout this book that feminism itself might challenge linearity and generationality, I argue that the graphic narrative's queerness is produced through its relationship to feminism.

Fun Home weaves together Bechdel's coming out story with her family's history, particularly her father's sexual relationships with young boys and his later suspected suicide. Bechdel's narrative is a remarkable exploration of family history, queer desires, and the struggle to make her father present and knowable posthumously. It has been overwhelmingly embraced by academics concerned with queer history and culture. As Ann Cvetkovich designates it, the graphic narrative has a 'queer sensibility', 'embraces a queer temporality', is an example of 'queer witnessing', which can be productively read alongside queer theorizing of trauma, history, and temporality.[7] Valerie Rohy similarly argues that *Fun Home* 'engages some of queer theory's most timely issues: teleology, historicism, fantasy, and the retroactivity of identity'.[8] As well as engaging with many of queer theory's concerns, the graphic narrative formally experiments with both genre and the canon, leading theorists to claim that Bechdel 'cheerfully queers the canon'[9] as well as 'rewrite[s] queer generational histories'.[10] Indeed, throughout the narrative, Bechdel experiments with the relationship between comics and high modernism, leading Ariela Freedman to argue that Bechdel makes a case for graphic narratives as high literature, putting 'the graphic narrative in irreverent, iconoclastic dialogue with literary modernism'.[11] Moreover, Cvetkovich explores the links that Bechdel makes between lesbian feminism and modernist literature, describing these literary references as both the claiming of a paternal legacy for lesbian feminism and an 'unapologetic relation to the lesbian feminist culture within which Alison came out'.[12]

These claims to a queering of familial, historical, and literary genealogy are integral to *Fun Home*. Yet, I find it surprising, given Bechdel's interest in genealogies throughout the narrative, that claims to *Fun Home*'s queerness are frequently made with minimal reflection on what this designation accomplishes. In other words, if one of Bechdel's concerns is a queering of inheritance, perhaps it might be important then to question the predominance of claims to *Fun Home* as a queer narrative, for the potential erasures and foreclosures that this designation might enact.

As Victoria Hesford points out, the book's appeal to a variety of audiences produces it as 'a cultural object that cuts across the "false purity" of the distinctions between subcultures and national public cultures, as well as those between queer and feminist history'.[13] An analysis of *Fun Home* concludes Hesford's book *Feeling Women's Liberation*, concerned throughout with how it is that women's liberation was and continues to be produced in popular and academic memory. Having the last word in Hesford's book, *Fun Home* is a narrative for Hesford to explore the relationship between queer and feminist histories. Alison, in *Fun Home*, continually explores the resonances between her father's literary and cultural archive and her own lesbian feminist inheritance. Toward the beginning of her book, Hesford rightly notes, 'a feminist concern with its own history and the queer desire for history have left each untouched and often unnoticed by the other'.[14] By the end, it is *Fun Home* that Hesford proposes might be a 'remembering of women's liberation that is also a queer desire for history'.[15] Hesford offers a rich reading of the way in which lesbian feminism is unsettled in *Fun Home*, intersecting for instance with Alison's butch identity and her identifications with her father's queerness. In this, Bechdel produces a narrative in which the situated nature of Alison's history also opens up an archive of lesbian feminism to other kinds of affects.

Similar to Hesford, I place *Fun Home* central to questions about the relationship between feminism and queer. However, rather than suggest that the book might open up more complex ways of bridging the divide between feminist and queer histories, as Hesford suggests, I consider the ways in which a history of feminist thinking about vision and sexuality is potentially erased in claims to *Fun Home*'s queerness. I explore the relationship between feminism and queer not in the graphic narrative itself, but in responses to it. In other words, I do not designate *Fun Home* as a "feminist" book (in opposition to claims to its queerness), but instead I explore how feminist theoretical insights have been all but erased in engagements with the book's queerness. Beginning by considering *Fun Home*'s resonances with recent queer historiography, I explore how graphic narrative is a unique form particularly suited to complicating univocal, linear time. The remainder of the chapter contains a reading of *Fun Home* that maps its exploration of technologies of vision, family gazes, queer recognition, and visuality as an embodied practice.

Bechdel fights off any understanding of the eye as that which has instant or innocent access to the field of the visual – narrating instead the slow process of how it is she comes to see what she sees. This 'slowed-down reading and looking', as Hillary Chute terms it, is an integral aspect of the formal structure of comics, and positions it as 'apposite to feminist cultural production'.[16] Through a reading of *Fun Home* I draw out the temporal complexities of the text and emphasize in particular the way that it casts vision as slow and situated. As I will show in this chapter, the often erasure of the field of vision as absolutely integral to the project as a whole is simultaneously an elision of what histories of feminist theorizing of the visual add to not only graphic scholarship but the production of queerness. This chapter maps how Bechdel uses images to explore the field of the visual – from the family album, to the family gaze, to looking queer – asking how we learn to see what we see. While *Fun Home* can be read in relation to histories of graphic narratives or queer historiography, I argue for *Fun Home* as enabling a relationship between queer historical knowledge projects, graphic narrative, and feminist notions of embodied vision.

Graphic time and *Fun Home*'s queer history

The graphic narrative, in its play with the connection between text and image, requires new 'interpretive skills', new modes of literary critique as it simultaneously creates new ways of doing literary, historical and cultural critique.[17] As a form, it incorporates multiple voices into single frames – the narrative voice, the speaking characters, as well as the visual representation. The interplay between image and text means graphic narrative always speaks in at least two registers – sometimes image and text are entirely disconnected, sometimes they work together to create a fuller picture of the scene, and sometimes the connection between the two is unclear. In Scott McCloud's influential *Understanding Comics*, he argues that reading comics is similar to putting together pieces of a puzzle, so that through pulling together the panels or fragments of the narrative, the reader actively creates meaning.[18] McCloud describes comics as 'a medium where the audience is a willing and conscious *collaborator* and closure is the agent of *change, time,* and *motion*'.[19]

Through creating breaks in time and space, comics represent time as fractured and discontinuous. McCloud argues that the panel is comics' most important icon, explaining that the panel 'acts as a sort of general indicator that time or space is being divided'.[20] Will Eisner describes the visual language of the panels – their size, their spacing, their shape, their relation to each other, and the duration of the activity within the panel – as comprising the 'grammar' of comics.[21] As Chute rightly suggests, it is necessary to see panels as 'boxes of time'.[22] Each box contains a certain amount of time, but this time could be a moment or a much longer duration. As readers move across these unconnected moments they create closure, smoothing out the fractured representation of time. Comic language works in part in the rhythm of the construction of reality – '[i]n our daily lives we often commit closure, mentally completing that which is *incomplete*'.[23] Comic language both represents the impossibility of closure at the same time that it plays with the inevitable means through which readers construct narrative closure. The narrative closure that McCloud identifies as part of the visual language of comics becomes an essential insecurity of the form itself. The spaces between panels both insist on and resist closure, demanding that any closure the reader might create for herself be recognized as an unstable creation. In their ability to represent narrative as irreconcilable, multiple, and constructed, comics, explains Jared Gardner, draw attention to 'the excess that refuses the cause-and-effect argument, the trace that threatens to unsettle the present's narrative of its own past (and thereby of itself)'.[24]

The architecture of the comics page is a place for the configuration of these boxes of time – a space for play with chronology, sequence, and narrative time.[25] The panels shape the time within them but also the spaces between panels – the gutter – could represent minutes, seconds, days, or even years. Furthermore, panels do not necessarily follow a linear trajectory – with the past sitting comfortably next to a panel in the narrative's "present". While the montage effect of graphic narrative has much in common with cinematic narrative, Jason Dittmer points out that there is more play with temporality on a comics page where 'the mechanised and standardised temporality of filmic projection can be replaced with the forward-and-back temporality of plurivectorial reading practices and comics' potential for simultaneity in thought and speech'.[26] This graphic narration of time requires that the viewer always be prepared to move through time in surprising ways, never offering linear temporal coherence. Literature can similarly move through time, explore narrative sequence, and demand the reader be flexible to move back and forth from future to present to past, however, as Chute and DeKoven argue, there is something particular about the visual representation of time alongside text that ensures graphic narratives are always 'cross-discursive' in ways that are never rectified.[27] With each turn of the page, the viewer is presented with a new set of moments simultaneously – each panel on any given page is viewed immediately and all at once, accruing meaning as the viewer's eyes follow the narrative. These turns of the page ensure that the viewer is always confronted with the whole of the page at the same time as the individual panels – there is the possibility of being thrown into multiple times simultaneously. As Bechdel explains in an interview with Chute:

'I don't know how in writing I would be able to do this crazy jumping back and forth in time and space [...] You can write about that but there's something about being able to access in this emotionally vivid way these different moments [...] visually. You're just in the scene, you don't have to read some lengthy, tedious description, you're just there.'[28]

The immediacy with which the viewer is confronted with multiple scenes and panels on a comics page makes graphic narrative a particularly well-suited medium for moving backward and forward through time, juxtaposing different moments side-by-side, and working through relationships between these moments.

Bechdel's use of the graphic narrative's formal, and particularly temporal, possibilities is integral to *Fun Home*'s queerness. Indeed, Heike Bauer explicitly connects queer reading and cultural representation with the graphic narrative, suggesting that the aforementioned formal qualities of comics might be precisely what Eve Sedgwick defines as the 'open mesh of possibilities, gaps, overlaps, dissonances and resonances, lapses and excesses of meaning'.[29] *Fun Home* is frequently read as part of a new wave of graphic narratives that take as their subject historical narrative, memory, and trauma – one of the earliest of these being Art Spiegelman's *Maus: A Survivor's Tale*, which Freedman argues 'redefined the potential scope and claims of the genre of the graphic memoir'.[30] As a narrative that aims to act as witness to Bechdel's father's life and sexuality as well as the trauma of his death, *Fun Home* not only contributes to the exploration of themes of trauma and memory in graphic narrative, it also furthers graphic narrative claims to history through its queer slant. As Cvetkovich suggests, *Fun Home* queers the focus on trauma and history of texts such as *Maus* and Marjane Satrapi's *Persepolis* because it challenges 'the relation between the catastrophic and the everyday' making 'public space for lives whose very ordinariness makes them historically meaningful'.[31] Similar to the way that *Maus* and *Persepolis* focus on second-generation witnessing, *Fun Home*, suggests Cvetkovich, can be read as an attempt by Bechdel to be a 'sympathetic witness' to her father's story – to construct his history in ways that might expand the possibilities of reading his life beyond labelling him a 'pedophile, suicide, or tragic homosexual'.[32] Locating larger historical events, such as Stonewall and Watergate, in the context of her family's history, the narrative not only considers Bechdel's family narrative, it also insists on reading the trauma of a lesbian daughter alongside larger more recognizably historical events.

Part memorialization, part family album, part reading list of modernist fiction, Bechdel's narrative is, as Rohy explains it, a 'textual form of queer archive' in its bringing together of ephemeral and non-traditional historical documentation.[33] Moreover, *Fun Home* refuses to settle on one understanding of the truth about Bechdel's father, his sexuality, and her relationship to him, insisting instead on piecing together the past from a variety of different angles. Key scenes in the narrative, such as Bruce's death and Alison's phone conversation with her mother about her father's sexuality, are revisited multiple times throughout the narrative. Rohy points to the various archives represented in *Fun Home*, from the family library to Alison's diary, and argues that these archives offer 'a way for *Fun Home* to inhabit disparate narratives and temporal modes, learning what each one enables and forecloses'.[34] In this way, Bechdel tests out the many available stories about her family as well as the many different ways of conceiving of an archival project. This jumping back and forth through time results in, as Monica B. Pearl points out, *Fun Home* unfolding 'neither chronologically nor through prolepsis and analepsis, but through a layered telling, adding additional information and impressions over the story as it has already been told'.[35] So while from the beginning Bruce Bechdel's "fall" is already described, the narrative will return multiple times to fill out the details of his death, returning to depict the truck that hit him and the road on which it happened in many different panels. In an interview Bechdel explains that reproducing a newspaper page for one of her comic pages exemplifies her storytelling process:

> 'A newspaper is filled with thousands of stories. Every daily paper, every day is filled with all these little glimpses of people's lives. And so, when I'm telling this story about my family I'm very carefully culling little tidbits of things and putting them in a particular order in order to make a narrative, but it could just as easily be some other order, some other story.'[36]

Her narrative emphasizes the plurality of perspectives contained in her family's history – not content with a final version, she continues to hint at the many different ways to view life growing up in the Bechdel home.

Considering sexuality and queerness in and through time, particularly how she might look backwards to connect her father's sexuality with her own as well as place it within dominant narratives of gay history (Stonewall, AIDS), Bechdel asks similar questions to a number of recent queer historiographers. Recent work by queer theorists such as Carolyn Dinshaw, Elizabeth Freeman, and Heather Love has dealt with what Rohy outlines as the 'ahistorical' offence of making claims to a history of queer sexuality by employing creative methodologies that emphasize contingent connections, temporal multiplicities, and affect as a mode of queer history.[37] Queer history, as Rohy describes it, is always an 'optical illusion' because of the necessary limitations of reading sexual identity in the past through the vantage point of the present.[38] Rather than settling on any narrative truth about her father's identity, Bechdel explores the multiple available historical narratives of gay identity. On one of many contemplative pages, Bechdel ponders her attempt at reading her father's sexuality alongside wider gay and lesbian rights activism of the 1970s, considering the possibility that if her father had been out in the 1970s, he may have been part of the AIDS epidemic of that time. In testing out this alternative history, the sexual space he may have occupied, or that was running alongside the closeted temporality he did occupy, Bechdel does not quite settle on an easy positioning of her father: 'Or maybe I'm trying to render my senseless personal loss meaningful by linking it, however posthumously, to a more coherent narrative.'[39] She continues: 'A narrative of injustice, of sexual shame and fear, of life considered expendable. It's tempting to say that, in fact, this *is* my father's story' (*FH* 196, emphasis in original). While she acknowledges the narrative that one might be tempted to read onto her father's life, Bechdel also complicates the "truth" of this narrative. In the following panel Alison is drawn smoking a cigarette looking over a setting sun: 'There's a certain emotional expedience to claiming him as a tragic victim of homophobia, but that's a problematic line of thought […] For one thing, it makes it harder for me to blame him' (*FH* 196). This page shows Alison testing out a historical narrative for her father, resisting it, and all the while emphasizing her own stakes in the narrative. Cvetkovich points out Bechdel's resistance to aligning her father with either a negative or positive gay narrative: 'She is willing to claim her father for herself and hence for history, insisting that his story be incorporated into a more fully historicized present but also that its unassimilability be acknowledged in order to problematize the present.'[40] It is precisely this kind of tentative, resistant, and self-reflexive narrative of her father, his sexuality, and her family that makes *Fun Home* resound so strongly with contemporary queer historiography.

As well as tracing through a queer history of her family, Bechdel also creates what might be described as other queer genealogies. In considering how history and fiction are closely intertwined, Bechdel also refuses to read history in only its traditional places – instead reading family history as it runs alongside larger historical events, notably Stonewall, as well as turning to so-called private sites such as the diary of a young girl, the family photo album, or the family library. These moves between fact and fiction, perhaps best emphasized through her identification with her father through literary figures such as Proust and Fitzgerald, lead Rohy to posit that this is what a queer genealogy looks like – not the blood relationships between father and daughter but the 'strands of identification and disidentification – gendered, literary, aesthetic, archival – that engage the two in an endless conversation'.[41] *Fun Home* is undoubtedly not only a historical project but also about the process of doing history. From the way she insists she knows her family best through literary figures, to her continued telling of her father's story through the fictional characters he loved, Bechdel resists separating fact from fiction, contributing to contemporary literary historical turns in queer theory.

Concepts such as the queer archive, queer temporalities, and queer historiography have become attached to *Fun Home* through these theoretical encounters. Yet, my concern is with the way in which this reading of *Fun Home* insists on its resonances with queer theory at the expense of perhaps a more feminist inflected genealogy. This is not just to suggest that there are other ways to read the narrative. Instead, I posit more forcefully that the queerness of *Fun Home* – the queer reading of history, family, and sexuality – is made possible through an unspoken relationship to feminist thought. Integral to the queerness of *Fun Home* is the way Bechdel's contingent, circular, and inconclusive family history is played out through the embodiment of vision. In the rest of this chapter I argue for a more sustained exploration of the visual field and particularly how vision is integral to her narration of her relationship with her father and her sexuality. This focus on the visual brings the graphic narrative into closer contact with a history of feminist theory, suggesting that perhaps the *Fun Homes*'s queerness is actually contained in its feminist "views".

How the lesbian daughter sees

It is the discovery of the photograph of Roy, the Bechdel family babysitter, that Bechdel credits with being the catalyst for the creation of *Fun Home*.[42] The photo, taken by her father during a family vacation (where her mother was notably absent), is an erotic snapshot of Roy as he lounges in his underwear. She describes the photo as 'a stunning glimpse into [her] father's hidden life, this life that was apparently running parallel to [her family's] regular every-day existence'.[43] Bechdel narrates the discovery of the photo of Roy as glimpsing a part of her father that she had never seen before – that up until now had been hidden from view. From this first glimpse Bechdel traces through growing up in her family home, considering how one grows up seeing in the family. In seeking to understand the visual evidence of the Roy photograph, Bechdel undertakes the project in *Fun Home* of exploring how it is she learns to see what she sees. This mimics the act of finding the photo of Roy – the photo does not speak on its own. If *Fun Home* came about because of Bechdel's discovery of the photo of Roy, then *Fun Home* must be seen as taking the reader on a long journey in order to understand how it is that Bechdel sees the photo. This places Bechdel's narrative not only in a lineage of queer historiographers, but also of visual culture theorists. As John Berger explains, seeing is a process, so that '[t]he way we see things is affected by what we know or believe', and Bechdel traces through her family history, unpacking how she sees what she sees.[44]

Alison's childhood is explored throughout the narrative as a struggle with her father at the level of the visual. *Fun Home* depicts Bruce Bechdel as being obsessed with the visual – from the family home, to Alison's appearance, to his own stylized masculinity. The first chapter of *Fun Home* details the obsessive way Bruce restores the family home and maintains its image. His obsession with design draws Bechdel to write: 'He used his skilful artifice not to make things, but to make things appear to be what they were not' (*FH* 16). Bruce is not only consumed with the surface of things, or with artifice, but with a particular "look". Bruce's obsession with restoring the family home can be read as the desire to create the world to a particular visual image. This extends to his stylizing of himself, his family, and Alison in feminine dress. Moreover, it is precisely this kind of look that Alison first resists. In a panel that depicts Alison dusting the family home, Bechdel writes: 'My own decided preference for the unadorned and purely functional emerged early' (*FH* 14). Just under that panel a young Alison explains, 'When I grow up, my house is going to be all metal, like a submarine' (*FH* 14). Alison's aesthetic develops in opposition to her father's preference for embellishment and adornment – her desire is to surround herself in a visual landscape that is completely other to the family home her father so painstakingly restores. Opposite the panel depicting Bruce taking a family photo with the family posed in front of the restored home, Bechdel includes her own image of the family watching television, eating popcorn, and playing inside the house – her own portrait of them 'really living' (*FH* 17). Placed side by side in the narrative, the images represent Bruce and Alison's competing visions of the family. It is this resistance to her father's vision that similarly plays out in relation to young Alison's gendered presentation. In many of the childhood and young adult scenes, Alison is drawn struggling against the femininity her father is intent on dressing her up in. There is a particular fight over a barrette that extends over seven panels, followed by a struggle with a pearl necklace. From the barrettes to pearls to skirts, Bruce's aesthetic is represented as being forced onto Alison's body.

A poignant scene considers the gendering of the field of the visual and has thus far gone unmentioned in critical engagements. A friend of Bruce's hands him a rolled up document that Bruce tells Alison not to open because it is 'dirty' (Fig. 5.1, *FH* 111). In the last panel on the bottom of the page, Alison is shown disobeying her father's wishes and unrolling the paper. As Alison gains visual access to the image in the act of unrolling the sheet, the viewer turns the page in a similar act of "unfurling" to reveal the image – a calendar page containing an image of a naked woman (Fig. 5.2, *FH* 112). This visual memory is thus replayed in the graphic narrative to have the viewer participate in the act of looking with Alison – the reader not only turns the page as Alison unrolls the paper, she also is positioned above her shoulder, looking with her at the image of the naked woman: 'I felt as if I'd been stripped naked myself, inexplicably ashamed, like Adam and Eve' (*FH* 112). A later panel shows Alison looking as her brothers discover the calendar. Positioned above them sitting in a tree, she watches their excitement as they view the image of the naked woman (Fig. 5.3, *FH* 112). That same afternoon, Alison, her brothers and Bruce arrive at the mine for a visit, where Alison sees yet another calendar depicting a naked woman hung in the miners' office. After this panel, Bechdel writes, '[a]s the man showed us around, it seemed imperative that he not know I was a girl' (*FH* 113). Alison tells her brother to call her 'Albert' instead of 'Alison' (*FH* 113).

These pages show Alison learning a gendered lesson about the visual field – namely the lesson that women are to be looked at, displayed, and sexualized. As Laura Mulvey famously explains, '[i]n their traditional exhibitionist role women are simultaneously looked at and displayed, with their appearance coded for

Figure 5.1 Alison discovers the pinup, *Fun Home*. Figures 5.1–5.5 are from *Fun Home: A Family Tragicomic* by Alison Bechdel. Copyright © 2006 Alison Bechdel. Published by Houghton Mifflin Harcourt and Jonathan Cape. Reprinted by permission of Houghton Mifflin Harcourt Publishing Company and by arrangement with Random House Children's Publishers UK, a division of The Random House Group Limited. All rights reserved.

Figure 5.2 Alison unrolls the pinup, *Fun Home*

Figure 5.3 Alison watches her brothers, *Fun Home.*

strong visual and erotic impact so that they can be said to connote *to-be-looked-at-ness*.[45] Through her experience with the calendar pin-ups, Alison learns something about gender and the visual field – woman as sexual object 'holds the look, plays to and signifies male desire'.[46] Alison's desire to resist this gaze leads her to hide the fact that she is a girl. She disidentifies with woman as object by hiding the fact of her female body and thus dodging the gaze. *Fun*

Home narrates visual learning as an integral part of Alison's childhood, where she is confronted with normative femininity by her father and by the wider world. However, it is precisely the field of the visual which Bechdel retains a commitment to – finding not only normative scripts, but pleasure as well.

Indeed, it is not by turning away from the visual that Alison is able to carve out a queer identity, but precisely by cleaving to it. During a trip to Philadelphia, Bruce and Alison eat at a local diner and Alison spots her first bulldyke (*FH* 118). Alison's wide eyes emphasize the text box: 'I didn't know there were women who wore men's clothes and had men's haircuts' (*FH* 118). The top panel on this page depicts Alison and her father spotting the masculine woman and the bottom panel shows Bruce and Alison shifting their gazes to each other. Asking Alison, 'Is *that* what you want to look like?', her father schools her in her visual appearance (*FH* 118, emphasis in original). Alison knows that the response her father desires is a "no", and Bechdel writes: 'What else could I say?' (*FH* 119). Similar to the way that he tells her she better 'damn well identify' (*FH* 201) with Joyce's *Portrait of an Artist as a Young Man*, Bruce uses this moment to instruct Alison on what it is she should look like. He does not ask her if that is what she wants to "be" – he asks her if she wants to "look like" the bulldyke. Despite her father's stern warnings about looking a certain way, that glimpse of female masculinity is described as a sustaining force for young Alison. The 'surge of joy' that Alison feels when she sees the bulldyke articulates a visual connection – 'someone they've never spoken to but know by sight' (*FH* 118). Bechdel emphasizes that there is a certain knowledge that is transmitted from the sight of the bulldyke – a connection that she feels through the butch's appearance. Moreover, there is a lasting effect that this sight has for Alison, despite her father's shaming: 'But the vision of the truck-driving bulldyke sustained me through the years … ' (*FH* 119). The field of the visual is both a place where her father exerts a certain control over Alison and also where Alison is able to articulate a particular kind of resistance.

Jacqueline Rose's canonical feminist reading of the connection between sexuality and the field of vision emphasizes that the field of the visual reveals sexual difference as an imperfect construction.[47] Rose explores how, in Freud, ruptures at the site of sexual difference are intricately bound with the visual field, so that '[a] confusion at the level of sexuality brings with it a disturbance of the visual field'.[48] If the image reflects a contingency at the level of sexual difference, the image and more generally "looking" become key sites of feminist analysis. As Rose argues, a 'feminism concerned with the question of looking' might exploit the potential ruptures at the site of vision.[49] Jennifer Lemberg argues, pointing to Bechdel's connection of her first orgasm with drawing, that drawing functions as an outlet for queer desires that 'under her father's vigilant maintenance of her femininity and oppressive social norms, are continually held at bay'.[50] I suggest then that Bechdel's narrative demonstrates that the field of the visual not only constrains her through the "image" of femininity, but also ruptures at the site of these gender and sexual norms to open up visual pleasures for her emerging lesbian identity.

Alison navigates the visual in order to resist dominant ways of seeing, while also constructing alternative visual pleasures. At fourteen when Alison's friend Beth attempts to get her to go to a high school football match, Alison explains, 'I don't wanna go to the game. I hate football' (*FH* 181). Her friend flips through *GQ*, a men's magazine (which Alison managed to get a copy of by explaining she was thinking of becoming a fashion designer), commenting on the attractiveness of the men and Alison is looking at her. In response to Alison's lack of interest in attending the football game, her friend responds, 'So don't watch it. The point is to see people' (*FH* 181–82). Alison misses the point of attending the football match precisely because she does not "see" correctly. This is emphasized by her focus on her friend who "correctly" turns her desiring gaze to the *GQ* magazine – a magazine which Alison reads with a desire for masculinity not as object but subjectively for herself. Instead of going to the football game, Alison and Beth stay home and rummage through Alison's father's closet, dressing each other in men's suits, admiring their appearances in a mirror. Bechdel narrates the play as feeling 'too good to actually be good' (*FH* 182). Alison's play in these panels is contrasted to the watching of the football game and the reading of the *GQ* magazine – her looking at herself in the mirror in her father's clothes is a different kind of looking than going to the football game to see people. These pages describe an alternative visual field of gender and sexual play that Alison creates for herself. Resisting watching the football game and the people there, Alison instead sees herself dressed in her father's clothes in the mirror. From her cross-dressing to the image of the bulldyke, Alison is able to fashion alternative visual narratives, resisting what she is supposed to see and instead fashioning other kinds of visual knowledge for herself – finding what she wants to see and know for herself in bulldykes at truck stops and in *GQ* magazines.

Family photos and family recognition

Fun Home draws heavily on the family photo as imaging technology to consider how to see and make sense of family history. This focus on photography, and particularly the genre of the family photo, signals *Fun Home*'s concern with technologies of visualization as well as the possibilities of cultivating alternative views. Alongside the primacy given to the photo of Roy, Bechdel fills *Fun Home* with dozens of replicated photos. From passport photos, to family album photos, to drawn film stills, to school photos, Bechdel utilizes a variety of reproduced photos to aid her narrative. Each chapter heading contains a family photograph, making the book itself appear as a family album. She even reproduces family photos that are not her own – as with the snapshots of Fitzgerald's and Joyce's families. The centrality of the family photograph is not surprising given the importance this photograph has in terms of a visualizing technology of the family. Marianne Hirsch argues that the photograph is the 'family's primary instrument of self-knowledge and representation – the means by which family memory would be continued and perpetuated, by which the family's story would henceforth be told'.[51] In other words, family photography is a site where the family represents itself as it wishes it appeared – and this idealized version of family is both shaped by and shapes dominant family ideology. In turning to the family album to ask questions after her father's death and sexuality, Bechdel searches the visual archive of her family for both what was seen and also to see again, differently. In the same way that she resists the construction of her body by the male gaze, Bechdel explores the function of the family photo as a heteronormative visualizing technology. She challenges this normalizing technology through showing how it can not only contain but enable queer looks. Bechdel opens up the visual sphere of the heteronormative family to accommodate other kinds of vision – namely queer desires.

Rather than the discovery of the photo of Roy somehow destroying the image of Bechdel's family through its apparent revelation of her father's homosexual desires, the photo becomes a way for Bechdel to expand upon the kinds of visual evidence that are contained in family albums. In the negative reel from her family holiday, Bechdel describes how the 'murky' photo of Roy follows the 'bright shots' of her and her brother on the beach – her family vacation photos seemingly interrupted by the sexual photo of her babysitter taken by her father (*FH* 102). The photo of Roy might be said to puncture the family reel as well as wounding Bechdel upon its discovery, acting as the painful 'prick' that Roland Barthes describes photos can inflict.[52] However, just below this panel where the photo of Roy is linearly arranged following photos of Alison and her brothers playing on the beach, we are shown a panel which depicts Bechdel's hands as she compiles the photos of herself and her brothers playing on the beach with the photo displaying her father's stylized masculinity. In this panel, Bechdel's hands become a literal coming to grips, a gripping of her family in her hands, holding them together and interrupting the spatiality of the negative reel, complicating the linear story that the negatives seemingly tell. This page also highlights the way that photographs are formally very similar to comic panels – where re-arranging photos looks a lot like formatting panels.

Bechdel brings together the various aspects of her father and her family that seem incompatible – her and her brothers' play with her father's secret young male lover; a family vacation and a lovers' tryst. She opens up space to see her family vacation as both a family vacation and a lovers' tryst. She does not write over the family vacation with the knowledge of it also being a lovers' getaway. She writes in the following panel that 'the two ways are revealed to converge – to have always converged – through a vast network of transversals' (*FH* 102). In other words, what first appear as opposites indeed coexisted. The family vacation does not become artifice with the knowledge of the sexual relationship between her father and Roy. Bechdel reads the family album – a normative visualizing apparatus for family ideology – as containing other kinds of knowledge, particularly visual evidence of a queer kind. Bechdel suggests that even in the family album, there are multiple ways to see and multiple perspectives. The family vacation that she experienced as a child can coexist with the vision of Roy that she discovers later in life.

This careful negotiation of vision in the family continues in relation to Bechdel's attempts throughout *Fun Home* to retroactively connect with her father through their "shared" queer sexualities. The family photo album contains the possibility of different kinds of visual knowledge, and so too does the visual field of the family itself. Bechdel seems to make possible seeing her father's sexuality as not separate from her family but enmeshed within it, seeing the family album and family photography as encasing queer desires. She brings a similar queering to the 'familial look'.[53] Hirsch argues for the importance of considering how familial looks 'create and consolidate the familial relations among the individuals involved, fostering an unmistakable sense of mutual recognition'.[54] In other words, she draws attention to the importance of identity confirmation through a familial economy of looking – where, for example, looks exchanged between mother and son create and solidify the relationship and identities of the two. Perhaps the most famous example of theorizing this familial look of recognition that Hirsch describes can be found in *Camera Lucida*, where Barthes turns to his family album after his mother's death. He turns to the album in search of an image of his mother that expresses her truth, an image where he can find her as she really is. He finds a photo depicting her as a little girl posing in a winter garden – the Winter Garden Photo – and describes this image as truly capturing her, her 'unique being'.[55]

Bechdel makes a similar journey to that of Barthes, looking through old family photos in the wake of her father's death. However, in Bechdel's search for answers about her father – to discover whether his death was a suicide or accident and to understand her relationship to him – the photo that she finds is not an image of her father, but the image of Roy. In the same way that the Winter Garden Photo contains for Barthes the "truth" of his mother, the photo of Roy is situated at the centre of Bechdel's search for the "truth" of her father. In this photo of Roy, Bechdel finds the kind of answer that Barthes finds in the Winter Garden Photo. The photograph structures *Fun Home* and her relationship to her father – as a centrefold it is given privileged space, and as the narrative's catalyst it becomes a touchstone in her connection to her father and her exploration of her father's hidden life. In the Winter Garden Photo, Barthes finds not only his mother, but himself – or the part of himself that was embedded in their relationship.[56] He finds in this image a quality of their relationship that brings not only recognition of her as his mother, but also recognition of himself as her son. The mutuality of this recognition is an important aspect of the kind of familial looking that Hirsch theorizes. Bechdel finds her father and the qualities of her relationship to her father in the image of Roy, describing how the photo caused her to experience a 'posthumous bond' with her father, 'like [they] were comrades'.[57] She thus accesses a sense of recognition in the image of Roy – recognition of her own sexuality in an image of her father's desired object. However, while Barthes' discovery of the Winter Garden Photo acts as a finally realized conclusion in his search for his mother, the photograph of Roy is the beginning of the project of *Fun Home*, not so much an endpoint but the murky and ambiguous place from which her connection to her father begins but also can never be concluded.

Despite the temptation to only read the connection between father and daughter in *Fun Home* as a connection on the literary plane, I suggest that the field of the visual joins Bruce and Alison just as much, if not more than the many books they share, discuss, and argue over. Pearl argues that '[o]ne of the narrative threads in *Fun Home* is that the family, especially father and daughter, communicates better by way of literature than through actual direct verbal discourse'.[58] A reviewer makes a similar pronouncement, concluding his review with the statement: 'What ultimately brought her and her father together, in fact, were books.'[59] However, over-emphasizing the role of literature and books in the text overlooks and impoverishes the medium in which Bechdel chooses to tell this story, negating the many ways that Bechdel visually negotiates a relationship to her father. Bechdel uses the multiple ways

Figure 5.4 Alison and Bruce in front of the mirror, *Fun Home*.

of formatting graphic narrative panels to represent the connections between Alison and Bruce. In other words, the panel is configured by Bechdel as a space where multiple looks intersect, from Alison to her father to Bechdel and the reader; the panel holds multiple possibilities in terms of looks. Bechdel thus reconceptualizes Chute's description of panels as "boxes of time" instead perhaps as "boxes of looks", where the graphic narrative not only permits play with narrative time, but also can incorporate numerous, competing looks. Bechdel uses these possibilities to depict the connection between Alison and her father as an intersecting gaze, the crossing of their gender and sexual desires.

Alison and her father are not only both attracted to a particular gender crossing – with Alison desiring masculinity and her father showing a certain desire for feminine ornamentalism – but this crossing also occurs on the visual field where their looks intersect. In one panel Bechdel depicts their gazes reflected in the mirror assessing each other's appearances as they prepare to go to a wedding (Fig. 5.4, *FH* 98). In this panel Bruce dresses Alison up in the femininity he himself wants to embody, and she, in turn, finds an outlet for her desired masculinity in and through her father: 'While I was trying to compensate for something unmanly in him … He was attempting to express something feminine through me' (*FH* 98). Note the many crossings that the graphic panel is able to contain. Alison and Bruce's gazes cross as they look at each other in the mirror and as readers our gaze can be positioned behind Alison or behind Bruce, moving our perspective between the two. Their crossing gazes are emphasized by the crossing lines of the speech bubbles, so that Alison's words are positioned above her father's head reflected in the mirror and her father's words float above her appearance in the mirror. The narration in the panel also moves from one side to the other, ensuring the reader crosses back and forth as she proceeds to make sense of the panel, following the long-standing argument over Alison's appearance that Bechdel describes as 'a war of cross-purposes' (*FH* 98). Above the panel, Bechdel writes: 'Not only were we inverts. We were inversions of one another' (*FH* 98). A similar intersection of gazes occurs on page 99 in a panel where Alison is depicted perusing fashion magazines and recommending items to her father (*FH* 99). Positioned over her shoulder, looking at the male fashion model along with her, the two of them are again drawn in a way to have their gazes meet – but meet in a complicated middle: 'But I wanted the muscles and tweed like my father wanted the velvet and pearls – subjectively, for myself', writes Bechdel (*FH* 99).

Bruce's translation of his desires through Alison's body and Alison's play with masculinity through Bruce's body demonstrates the kind of crossing that Sedgwick argues is intrinsic to queer. It also emphasizes the visual crossing that is necessary to understand not only Alison's desires or her father's desires, but the tentative relationship between a closeted father and a "not-yet" lesbian daughter. Sedgwick reads "queer" as a particular kind of 'crossing': 'The word "queer" itself means *across* – it comes from the Indo-European root–*twerkw*, which also yields the German *quer* (transverse), Latin *torquere* (to twist), and English *athwart*.'[60] In *Tendencies*, Sedgwick investigates how queer crosses the

Figure 5.5 Photo comparison, *Fun Home.*

lines of gender and sexuality, resisting a model of 'homosexuality-as-gender inversion'.[61] Sedgwick defines queer as something more than a reversal of gender and instead considers 'passionate queer things that happen across the lines that divide genders, discourses, and "perversions"'.[62] The way that these crossings bring father and daughter close to each other is emphasized in a panel where Bechdel's hand holds two pictures – one of her father and one of herself, at similar ages (Fig. 5.5, *FH* 120). Aside from finding what she sees as physical similarities between the images of father and daughter, she enquires into the erotics behind them asking if the boy who took her father's photo was his lover as the girl who took her photo was hers. In this panel Bechdel positions herself in the place of both one of her own lovers as well as possibly her father's. These moments of crossing gazes starkly contrast with the scene between Alison and Bruce in the car (*FH* 220–21). In this scene Bruce and Alison verbally acknowledge their cross-gendered desires, with Bruce admitting, 'When I was little, I really wanted to be a girl […] I'd dress up in girls' clothes', and Alison responding, 'I wanted to be a boy! I dressed up in boys' clothes!' (*FH* 220–21). However, their gazes never meet in this scene – Bruce stares straight ahead the entire time, and Alison looks away dejectedly at the end of the conversation, a failed emotional and visual connection.

Bechdel's story connects Alison and her father through moments of erotic looking – recognizing in each other something of which they desire for themselves. Reading these moments alongside Barthes' text, it becomes possible to see these instances as being about not only the interconnectedness Cvetkovich reads between 'perverse and normal sexuality, obsession and art, or preliberated closeted queers and out and proud lesbians and gays', but the familial and the queer.[63] The familial look in this case I would argue becomes entwined with and inextricable from a queerer look – they not only look at each other as father and daughter, their gazes at each other are bound up with their queerly gendered and sexual desires. In the same way that Barthes searches for recognition in photographs of his mother, Bechdel searches for a queer recognition in the family album. Similar to how the image of Roy is inseparable from the family photo album, the relationship between Alison and her father is a complicated mix of familial and queer recognition. The meeting of their gaze on the bulldyke, their intersecting gaze in the mirror, and their shared gaze of the man in the magazine – these cross-gender, inverted, and queer desiring gazes are, in Bechdel's narrative, the instances where Alison and her father's looking is not contained by the dominant family economy of looking but also where they come closest to mutual recognition.

Embodied vision

Fun Home explores the different ways vision is a learned process as well as a field of power to be navigated. It approaches the visual field and the image not only through content, but through experience; as Rose explains, it matters 'not just what we see but how we see'.[64] While *Fun Home* can be read in relation to histories of graphic narratives or queer historiography, it also creates a relationship between queer historical knowledge projects, feminist vision, and graphic narrative. Bechdel explores dominant visualizing technologies such as photography and narrates how Alison cultivates alternative ways of navigating the visual field. In this, *Fun Home*'s conception of vision resonates in particular with aspects of the work of Donna Haraway, who emphasizes partial perspective and seeing as a feminist mode of knowing. In 'Situated Knowledges', Haraway responds to what she perceives as a 'much maligned sensory system in feminist discourse: vision' and argues that '[v]ision can be good for avoiding binary oppositions'.[65] She commits to the field of the visual despite the way historically the eyes have been used, and conceived, in a 'perverse capacity – honed to perfection in the history of science tied to militarism, capitalism, colonialism, and male supremacy – to distance the knowing subject from everybody and everything in the interests of unfettered power'.[66] Haraway maps how vision is intrinsically connected to the body, so that a feminist vision would emphasize not unfettered access or visual control, but instead an accountable, situated, and embodied practice that is always partial. It is this interest in embodied partial perspective that I locate as integral to *Fun Home*'s production of queerness. *Fun Home* succeeds in considering how vision is a complicated field of possibilities, and despite Bechdel's careful depiction of how Alison navigates the visual field, she also emphasizes that, as graphic artist, the entirety of *Fun Home* as visual evidence is complicated by her own partial perspective. So while I outlined in the beginning of the chapter that *Fun Home* is often read for the way its narrative spirals non-linearly around the truth rather than providing any conclusion, Bechdel's insistence on her own embodied vision is essential to the contingency of her knowledge about her family and her father.

This partiality of vision is emphasized through another crossing, namely the crossing of the graphic artist's vision with that of the reader. Bechdel crosses the reader's look with her own through positioning the reader over Alison's shoulder in the many panels where her and Bruce's visions cross. In the panel where she looks at a picture of stylized masculinity desiring it for herself, her own subject, and her father looks over her shoulder seemingly desiring it for himself as object, the reader is positioned over his shoulder observing the crossing of looks (*FH* 99). This positioning acts as a reminder that we, as readers, see what she shows us – we see with her, or over her shoulder. To return to my comparison between Alison finding the photo of Roy and Barthes finding the Winter Garden Photo, Barthes refuses to reproduce the Winter Garden Photo explaining that for us it would only be ordinary.[67] Hirsch argues that 'he cannot *show* us the photograph because we stand outside the familial network of looks and thus cannot *see* the picture in the way that Barthes must'.[68] While Barthes denies his reader such looks, Bechdel ensures that our experience of photos is mediated by our knowledge of her looking. Her hand in part is a means of making the reader complicit as witness to her story – we do not just read the narrative, we participate in witnessing Bechdel's handling of her family's archive. She shows us the photographs, insisting that there is something for us to see, but in reproducing them through her own hand with her own bias, she emphasizes that what we see is always going to be mediated by her body, which as I have outlined, has its own limitations and history of vision. This extra layer of reproduction provided through graphic narrative provides a means for Bechdel to include the photo of Roy in a way that Barthes cannot – her re-drawing of the photo keeps the original hidden yet arguably attempts to show us as readers how she "sees".

Along with placing the reader over Alison's shoulder in many scenes to position the viewer as witness to Alison's vision, another way Bechdel emphasizes her situated, embodied vision is through the reproduction of her hand in *Fun Home*. Particularly in the two-page centrefold of Roy, Bechdel's hand is drawn precisely where the reader's hand is ostensibly holding the page of the book (*FH* 100–1). The hand invites the reader to see as she sees, to witness her own witnessing of the photographs. As her father presumably touched Roy, enacting his desire, Bechdel too touches Roy – touches his photograph and a material manifestation of her father's desire for him. And as readers, we place our thumb overtop Bechdel's thumb, touching her touching Roy. From the Roy photo where Bechdel's hand is life-sized, to the photos of her family beach holiday, to the photos where Bechdel reads so much similarity into Alison and her father, Bechdel's hand is a persistent presence (*FH* 102; 120). It is the hand that does the work in Bechdel's graphic narrative – drawing, re-drawing, tracing, and inking her story. The hand emphasizes Bechdel's particular viewpoint – it constantly connects *Fun Home* to a specific viewing body while also connecting vision to a certain kind of labouring body – the labours of her hands are intimately tied to her vision.

Martin Jay argues that the French feminist concern with a unique woman's language was intrinsically connected to a critique of vision, 'often pitting the temporal rhythms of the body against the mortifying spacialization of the eye'.[69] Jay explains that French feminists insisted 'on a language of proximity rather than distance, a language closer to the sense of touch and taste than sight'.[70] For Luce Irigaray, the denigration of female sexuality in psychoanalysis goes hand in hand with oculocentrism, where in contrast to the male penis, '[t]he little girl, the woman, supposedly has *nothing* you can see. She exposes, exhibits the possibility of a *nothing* to see. Or at any rate she shows nothing that is penis-shaped or could substitute for a penis.'[71] Irigaray connects the privileging of male sexuality to the privileging of sight and argues that women's sexuality, which cannot be mastered in 'the twinkling of an eye', is better understood in nonvisual terms through the sense of touch.[72] This emphasis on female sex through the sense of touch over vision is articulated in 'When Our Lips Speak Together' through metaphors of touching labial lips.[73] In response to this privileging of sight that Irigaray designates as a privileging of male sexuality, the graphic narrative opens up the possibility for representations of embodied vision; in particular the slow and laborious work of vision.

Bechdel's hand connects vision to the body, emphasizing the way that the artist's hands translate her vision. Bechdel's artistic production is a labour of her hands. The presence of Bechdel's hand holding the photos references her hand as the reproducer of the photographs – drawn in rather than directly inserted into the narrative as photos – reminding us as readers that we are not seeing the photos, but instead Bechdel's careful and intricate reproductions. Bechdel emphasizes not only the bodily aspect of vision but also brings the hand back into the process of vision – as readers our access to her images depends on her reproducing them. Importantly as well, the labour of this act references the visual project that I have been tracing through *Fun Home*. The labouring hand in Bechdel's work emphasizes not only the slow pace of learning to see, but also an embodied vision – a vision that is grounded in a specific body.

Bechdel's artistic process reflects this concern with technologies of vision and the labour of seeing. Indeed, as a narrative, *Fun Home* considers how long and slow the process of coming to see something can be, where Bruce's sexuality is something Bechdel only sees retrospectively. Bechdel re-draws everything in *Fun Home* in her own hand – whether this be a police report, her father's letters, or her own younger self's diary entries. Discussing the reproduction of her childhood diary and her father's letters, Bechdel explains that it's 'all very carefully traced and redrawn'.[74] The emphasis on reproduction extends to include a particularly strong reliance on photography as not only an important narrative device but as integral to Bechdel's practice. To grasp photography's importance to Bechdel's creative process, one need only consider the pained way in which she draws her panels – posing herself as the characters, photographing herself, and then drawing her comics from the photos.[75] Chute explains:

> For every pose in every panel of the entire book (and there are almost 1,000 panels), Bechdel created a reference shot by posing for her digital camera. In a panel, say, depicting a classroom of children sitting at desks, Bechdel posed for every child in the frame.[76]

Bechdel explains her reliance on photography as such: 'I can't even draw the simplest pose now without a reference shot.'[77] What the reader sees is not just an image that Bechdel draws, but a scene that Bechdel acts out, photographs, and then draws. This process makes *Fun Home* a narrative that is layered with creation and re-creation at the optical level – the book itself is a "fun home" reflecting back at the viewer many different ways of seeing. Bechdel's methodology for creating *Fun Home* thus mimics one of the central concerns of the work itself – namely how to visualize her family and her family's history.

As a final comment on Bechdel's hand and its relationship to temporality and embodied vision, I consider the connection between the hand and vision in American artist Lisa Oppenheim's *The Sun Is Always Setting Somewhere Else* (Fig. 5.6).[78] For this piece, Oppenheim sourced photos on photo-sharing websites such as Flickr taken by American soldiers in Iraq. Each photo she uses – there are fifteen in total – is of a sunset. After printing off these sourced photos, Oppenheim then photographs herself in New York City holding the photos of the Iraqi sunsets overtop of her own sunset view, throughout the course of an entire sunset. When exhibited in galleries, these fifteen images are screened and looped from a 35 mm projector. Oppenheim, similar to Bechdel, deliberately makes her hand visible holding the photograph. In the same way as Bechdel's hand, Oppenheim's hand helps refocus the eye. It is the hand that guides the eye toward what we, as viewers, have access to. Oppenheim's body holding the photograph of Iraq is thus just as much a subject of the image as are the two sunsets themselves. While Bechdel re-draws her photographs, participating in a reproduction of them that highlights her own biases, Oppenheim's hand prints out digital images of the Flickr images, photographs these photos, and then finally screens them through the technology of a 35 mm projector. The hand in both cases references the labour that is not represented – namely the laborious reproduction that is carried out by the artist's hand.

Further, in her title's insistence that the sun is always setting somewhere "else", Oppenheim draws attention to how an image is able to gesture towards

Figure 5.6 Still from Lisa Oppenheim, *The Sun Is Always Setting Somewhere Else.*

not only what is present but also what is absent. She explains, 'I try to make images that point towards the main event as well as in other directions'.[79] Oppenheim's own photograph of the Iraqi sunset over her New York City sunset is a brief moment of chance. If she misses the sunset by a minute or two on either side, the image is less successful – the two sunsets do not link up. Emphasizing that the sun is always setting suggests the never-ending setting of the sun, but the timing of her photos emphasizes the limited perspective any one person has of this constant action. Her hand emphasizes that while her work points in other directions, it also only gives us visual access to her direction – to the direction in which her body is pointed. Her body masters the direction we are given as viewers. Her hand is the hand that scrolled through American soldiers' Flickr accounts, her hand pressed the download button on these images, and her hand holds the image over the sunset that her body is directionally facing. As viewers we see what she constructs and her hand emphasizes this construction. Even while holding up the image of the Iraqi sunset, it is written over her New York City sunset. She does not give us access to both sunsets really – she emphasizes the partial perspective of watching the sun set. That the sun is always setting somewhere else, makes the sunset in its entirety something that we, as located viewers, can never grasp in its entirety.

What Oppenheim's work contributes to thinking about Bechdel's hand is this particular emphasis on location – or on her embodied vision. Oppenheim's hand and her images draw out precisely the kind of work that Bechdel's hand references. Both hands emphasize the artist at work and the mediation of vision through the particular artistic hand. Further, these hands draw attention to vision as work or as something that is created from a particular body. Their hands emphasize that not only their vision, but our vision as viewers, is mediated through their bodies.

Conclusion

To assume that there is something final, complete, or all-knowing about our present is to close off the inevitable and necessary connections in and across time. One strategy to avoid this totalizing view is to insist upon the partiality of the present. The knowing self is, according to Haraway, 'partial in all its guises, never finished, whole, simply there and original; it is always constructed and stitched together imperfectly, and *therefore* able to join with another, to see together without claiming to be another'.[80] Perhaps we might consider this metaphor of being stitched together as a means to think about feminism's timing. Our present is always constructed and stitched together imperfectly – as graphic narratives and archive projects make all too apparent – so that the past and the future are stitched into our imperfect present bodies. This chapter insists that claims to a certain medium or certain text's queerness do field formation work that expands beyond a particular reading of a text. In other words, arguments that *Fun Home* is a queer narrative that speaks to particularly contemporary concerns in queer theory confirm desires for queer to signify non-linear temporalities. Yet, I hope to have shown throughout that *Fun Home*'s queerness might not be so separate from feminist theorizing, and feminist work on the field of vision in knowledge production. This is not to quibble with individual readings, but to suggest that a trend to read queerness without reading its relationship to feminist knowledge production potentially produces a linear, generational narrative where literary and cultural objects that are "queer" need not be considered through feminism. The arguments in this chapter insist that these designations matter for challenging a generational narrative that sees queer transcend feminism.

Bechdel narrates her coming of age on the visual field, her struggles with dominant vision, her connection with Bruce through their queer looks, and her limited embodied perspective. Her hands remind us that vision is always mediated by bodies that have their own histories of vision – bodies that see from particular perspectives and that have learned relationships to the field of vision. To see the photo of Roy in terms of her family's narrative, Bechdel must go back and trace through how it is she comes to see as she sees. This involves considering how her vision developed in opposition to her father's, how she resisted normative gender and sexuality on the visual plane, and how she will forever be constrained by her own partial perspective. In Bechdel's hands, the graphic narrative becomes a medium for thinking through processes of vision and narrating a history not only of her family, her coming out, but also of growing up learning to see. It also becomes a site for exploring the contemporary relationship between feminist and queer theory, a text that challenges the displacement of feminist knowledge by queer through insisting that its queerness might be a product of feminism.

Notes

1 See J. Brooks Bouson, '*Oryx and Crake* Introduction', in *Margaret Atwood: The Robber Bride, The Blind Assassin, Oryx and Crake*, ed. J. Brooks Bouson (London and New York: Continuum, 2010), pp. 125–28; Elaine Showalter, 'The Snowman Cometh', *London Review of Books*, 24 July 2003, p. 35; Fiona Tolan, *Margaret Atwood: Feminism and Fiction* (Amsterdam and New York: Rodopi, 2007).
2 Sam McBean, 'What Stories Make Worlds, What Worlds Make Stories: Margaret Atwood's *Oryx and Crake*', in *The SAGE Handbook of Feminist Theory*, ed. Mary Evans and others (London: Sage Publications Ltd, 2014), pp. 149–62.
3 For a number of feminist responses to *Girls*, see Kumarini Silva and Kaitlynn Mendes (eds), 'Commentary and Criticism: HBO's *Girls*', *Feminist Media Studies*, 13.2 (2013), pp. 355–74.
4 The mechanics of this boundary policing has been explored in relation to narratives of feminism's "passing" in Lisa Adkins, 'Passing on Feminism: From Consciousness to Reflexivity', *European Journal of Women's Studies*, 11.4 (2004), 427–44. The relationship that feminist and queer theory have to the object "gender" has been explored in Robyn Wiegman, 'Interchanges: Heteronormativity and the Desire for Gender', *Feminist Theory*, 7.89 (2006), 89–103.
5 I take "graphic narrative" here, following on from Hillary Chute, to both link this form to comics and to move from the more limited "graphic novel". Hillary Chute, *Graphic Women: Life Narrative and Contemporary Comics* (New York: Columbia University Press, 2010), p. 2.
6 Annamarie Jagose, 'Feminism's Queer Theory', *Feminism & Psychology*, 19 (2009), 157–74 (p. 160).
7 Ann Cvetkovich, 'Drawing the Archive in Alison Bechdel's *Fun Home*', *WSQ: Women's Studies Quarterly*, 36.1–2 (2008), 111–28 (pp. 112, 124, 126).
8 Valerie Rohy, 'In the Queer Archive', *GLQ: A Journal of Lesbian and Gay Studies*, 16.3 (2010), 340–61 (p. 357).
9 Jane Tolmie, 'Modernism, Memory and Desire: Queer Cultural Production in Alison Bechdel's *Fun Home*', *Topia: Canadian Journal of Cultural Studies*, 22.77 (2009), 77–95 (p. 87).
10 Cvetkovich, 'Drawing the Archive', p. 124.
11 Ariela Freedman, 'Drawing on Modernism in Alison Bechdel's *Fun Home*', *Journal of Modern Literature*, 32 (2009), 125–40 (p. 126).
12 Cvetkovich, 'Drawing the Archive', p. 124.
13 Victoria Hesford, *Feeling Women's Liberation* (Durham, NC and London: Duke University Press, 2013), p. 261.
14 Ibid., p. 6.
15 Ibid., p. 260.
16 Chute, *Graphic Women*, p. 9.
17 Gillian Whitlock, 'Autographics: The Seeing "I" of the Comics', *MFS: Modern Fiction Studies*, 52.4 (2006), 965–79 (p. 968).
18 Scott McCloud, *Understanding Comics: The Invisible Art* (New York: Harper-Perennial, 1994), p. 62.
19 Ibid., p. 65 (emphasis in original).
20 Ibid., p. 99.

21 Will Eisner, *Comics and Sequential Art: Principles and Practice of the World's Most Popular Art Form* (Tamarac, FL: Poorhouse, 2004), p. 39.
22 Chute, *Graphic Women*, p. 6.
23 McCloud, p. 63 (emphasis in original).
24 Jared Gardner, 'Archives, Collectors, and the New Media Work of Comics', *MFS: Modern Fiction Studies*, 52.4 (2006), 787–806 (p. 801).
25 Thomas A. Bredehoft, 'Comics Architecture, Multidimenstionality, and Time: Chris Ware's *Jimmy Corrigan: The Smartest Kid on Earth*', *MFS: Modern Fiction Studies*, 52.4 (2006), 869–90.
26 Jason Dittmer, 'Comic Book Visualities: A Methodological Manifesto on Geography, Montage and Narration', *Transactions of the Institute of British Geographers*, 35.2 (2010), 222–36 (p. 235).
27 Hillary L. Chute and Marianne DeKoven, 'Introduction: Graphic Narrative', *MFS: Modern Fiction Studies*, 52.4 (2006), 767–82 (p. 769).
28 Hillary L. Chute, *Hillary Chute Interviews Alison Bechdel* (Critical Inquiry Online Feature, 2011). <http://criticalinquiry.uchicago.edu/hillary_chute_interviews_alison_bechdel> (accessed 20 October 2014).
29 Eve Sedgwick, Tendencies (New York and London: Routledge, 1993), p. 7; Heike Bauer, 'Vital Lines Drawn from Books: Difficult Feelings in Alison Bechdel's *Fun Home* and *Are You My Mother?*', *Journal of Lesbian Studies*, 18.3 (2014), 266–81 (p. 269).
30 Freedman, p.126.
31 Cvetkovich, 'Drawing the Archive', p. 111.
32 Ibid., p. 113.
33 Rohy, 'In the Queer Archive', p. 341.
34 Ibid., p. 344.
35 Monica B. Pearl, 'Graphic Language: Redrawing the Family (Romance) in Alison Bechdel's *Fun Home*', *Prose Studies*, 30.3 (2008), 286–304 (p. 289).
36 Chute, *Hillary Chute Interviews Alison Bechdel*.
37 Valerie Rohy, *Anachronism and Its Others: Sexuality, Race, Temporality* (Albany: State University of New York, 2009), p. 67. See Carolyn Dinshaw, *Getting Medieval: Sexualities and Communities, Pre- and Postmodern* (Durham, NC: Duke University Press, 1999); Elizabeth Freeman, *Time Binds: Queer Temporalities, Queer Histories* (Durham, NC: Duke University Press, 2010); Heather Love, *Feeling Backward: Loss and the Politics of Queer History* (Cambridge, MA: Harvard University Press, 2007).
38 Rohy, *Anachronism and Its Others*, p. 123.
39 Alison Bechdel, *Fun Home: A Family Tragicomic* (London: Jonathan Cape, 2006), p. 196. Hereafter referred to in the main text as *FH*.
40 Cvetkovich, 'Drawing the Archive', p. 124.
41 Rohy, 'In the Queer Archive', p. 349.
42 Hillary L. Chute, 'An Interview with Alison Bechdel', *MFS: Modern Fiction Studies*, 52.4 (2006), 1004–13 (p. 1005).
43 Chute, 'An Interview with Alison Bechdel', p. 1006.
44 John Berger, *Ways of Seeing* (London: Penguin, 1972), p. 8.
45 Laura Mulvey, 'Visual Pleasure and Narrative Cinema', *Screen*, 16.3 (1975), 6–18 (p. 11, emphasis in original).
46 Ibid.
47 Jacqueline Rose, *Sexuality in the Field of Vision* (London and New York: Verso, 1986). See in particular Chapter 10, 'Sexuality in the Field of Vision'.
48 Ibid., p. 226.
49 Ibid., p. 232.
50 Jennifer Lemberg, 'Closing the Gap in Alison Bechdel's *Fun Home*', *WSQ: Women's Studies Quarterly*, 36.1–2 (2008), 129–40 (p. 134).

51 Marianne Hirsch, *Family Frames: Photography, Narrative, and Postmemory* (Cambridge, MA: Harvard University Press, 1997), pp. 6–7.
52 Roland Barthes, *Camera Lucida: Reflections on Photography*, trans. Richard Howard (London: Vintage Books, 1980), p. 47.
53 Hirsch, p. 2.
54 Ibid.
55 Barthes, p. 71.
56 Hirsch, p. 1.
57 Chute, 'An Interview with Alison Bechdel', p. 1006.
58 Pearl, p. 287.
59 Douglas Wolf, 'Fun Home', *Salon*, 6 June 2006. <www.salon.com/2006/06/05/bechdel> (accessed 20 October 2012).
60 Sedgwick, *Tendencies*, p. xii.
61 Ibid., p. xiii.
62 Ibid.
63 Cvetkovich, 'Drawing the Archive', p. 119.
64 Rose, p. 231.
65 Donna Haraway, 'Situated Knowledges: The Science Question in Feminism and the Privilege of Partial Perspective', *Feminist Studies*, 14.3 (1988), 575–99 (p. 581).
66 Ibid.
67 Barthes, p. 73.
68 Hirsch, p. 2 (emphasis in original).
69 Martin Jay, *Downcast Eyes: The Denigration of Vision in Twentieth-Century French Thought* (Berkeley: University of California Press, 1993), p. 528.
70 Ibid., p. 529.
71 Luce Irigaray, *Speculum of the Other Woman*, trans. Gillian C. Gill (Ithaca, NY: Cornell University Press, 1985), p. 47 (emphasis in original).
72 Irigaray, *Speculum of the Other Woman*, p. 48.
73 Luce Irigaray, 'When Our Lips Speak Together', trans. Carolyn Burke, *Signs: Journal of Women in Culture and Society*, 6.1 (1980), 69–79.
74 Chute, 'An Interview with Alison Bechdel', p. 1007.
75 Ibid., p. 1009.
76 Hillary L. Chute, 'Gothic Revival', *The Village Voice*, 4 July 2006. <www.villagevoice.com/2006-07-04/books/gothic-revival/> (accessed 20 October 2014), 1–3, (p. 2).
77 Chute, 'An Interview with Alison Bechdel', p. 1010.
78 Lisa Oppenheim, *The Sun Is Always Setting Somewhere Else*, looped slide projection of fifteen slides, 35 mm Kodak Ektagraphic Slide Projector (2006). Online version available in *Art & Research: A Journal of Ideas, Contexts and Methods*, 1.2 (2007). <www.artandresearch.org.uk/v1n2/sunsets.html> (accessed 20 October 2014).
79 Quoted in Laurie Cluitmans, 'Lisa Oppenheim Reanimates the Past', *Metropolis M*, 5 (2010). <http://metropolism.com/magazine/2010-no5/tijdrekken/english> (accessed 20 October 2014).
80 Haraway, p. 681 (emphasis in original).

Conclusion

In 1972, Faith Wilding performed *Waiting* at Womanhouse in Los Angeles.[1] Wilding's performance consisted of her seated in a rocking chair, hunched over, reciting a poem about the connection between womanhood and the temporality of waiting: 'Waiting to be a pretty girl [...] Waiting to menstruate [...] Waiting to be a woman.'[2] As she recites her poem, Wilding rocks back and forth continuously, using her body, as Amelia Jones explains, 'performatively to engage the spectator in a metaphorically rhythmic and repetitive narration of a woman's life experience'.[3] In Wilding's piece, waiting is the mode in which normative femininity is enacted; from waiting for puberty to waiting to get married, Wilding describes women's lives as being a passive existence through time. I am interested in this piece not only because it theorizes temporality from a feminist perspective, but also because Wilding revisits this piece in her 2007 performance, *Wait With*.[4] Similar to this book's interest in exploring feminism's recent archive with the aim of considering how it might speak to contemporary desires to move beyond generational models of feminism's timing, Wilding turns back to revisit her past work and the potential contained within it for the present.

Wilding explains in a 2008 performance of *Wait With* that her impetus for the reinterpretation was to 'revisit and comment on an early work, which had become iconic and frozen in time'.[5] The performance involves a screening of the original work and then the delivery of a new monologue, followed by a discussion with audience members. Wilding's monologue proclaims that her aim is to 'undo and redo waiting/*Waiting*'. In *Wait With*, Wilding conceptualizes waiting less as a solitary act of repetition but instead as a collective space of potential: 'I want to perform a body with bodies. Becoming body in common. Undoing the singular fiction of Wilding.' Waiting is transformed in the second performance from a passive act into an active doing: 'Wait with, an act of political love. Wait with, an action. Wait with, a meditation. Wait with, a space of resistance.' In *Wait With*, Wilding considers the potential for solidarity contained in waiting as political protest. Further, she extends this reading of waiting as community-building through inviting the audience to dialogue with her. Through dialogue, the "singular fiction of Wilding" is undone by the audience's contributions.

While in some sense *Wait With* challenges the original, its ultimate effect is not an undoing of the original. First, by screening the original and revisiting the temporality of waiting, *Wait With* cannot and does not finally move on in any simple way from *Waiting*. It neither gives new life to *Waiting* nor completely writes over this past performance with its present translation. Second, any easy move on is denied similarly by the audience, whose own desires, at least in the 2008 Berlin performance, resist letting Wilding move away from the original, with one audience member explicitly explaining that she is 'waiting for 1970s feminism ... waiting for Faith to reperform waiting ... waiting for re-faith in feminism'. Moreover, the audience contributions both build on Wilding's idea of the hope contained in the time of waiting as well as challenge this conception with their own experiences. The performance does not revise or undo the original *Waiting*. Instead, through the audience's participation and the multiple interpretations of waiting, Wilding's *Wait With* becomes a site of feminist feeling, conflict, and disagreement in and about time.

This book was compelled by a millennial moment in which the dominance of a singular model of feminism in time seemed overwhelming, despite an archive of rich feminist explorations of time's contours. Despite the numerous critiques of generational models, it seemed to me that few people were turning to explore alternatives from within feminism's own late twentieth- and early twenty-first-century literary and cultural archive. This project was driven as well by a recent turn to claims of non-linearity and anti-generationality as queer modes of temporality. My aim throughout has been, on the one hand, the perhaps almost benign assertion that despite the dominance of certain modes of telling feminism's time, feminism's literary and cultural archive contains explorations of time otherwise conceived. I have attempted to enfold numerous popular feminist figures, texts, and genres into queer temporality theory, drawing on this theory as methodology through which to approach my case studies yet also suggesting that my case studies be read as theories of their own. I have suggested that texts which canonically are imagined as representing a particular historical moment in feminism (such as riot grrrl or second wave feminism) might actually be read for the way in which they resist dominant models of time. In turning to the popular in feminism and to more popular generic forms, this book has also attempted to expand the remit of what kinds of texts might be seen to signify queerly and thus to intervene into queer temporality theory with a history of feminist literary and cultural production. Finally, in the previous chapter, I considered how the designation of contemporary texts as resonant with queer temporality theory has the potential to erase genealogies of feminist thinking, or the queerness of feminism's temporalities.

Starting from the collective experience of waiting that Wilding produces, I want to reflect in this conclusion on what this book's persistent privileging of asynchrony and interruption in time might mean for belonging. Early readers of this work raised questions about whether I was celebrating temporal disruption for the sake of temporal disruption and simultaneously turning away from history in the process. I hope, at this point, that it is clear that this book aims not so much to celebrate non-linearity for the sake of non-linearity. Instead, I have argued that approaches to feminist literary and cultural texts which presume that they belong to a particular period of feminism miss out on the alternative models of temporality that these very texts contain. Indeed, at its worst such approaches refuse to let these texts have currency in contemporary feminist thinking. Yet, in some ways, my approach, and its concern with dislodging texts from their historical moments, seems to deny these texts any historical belonging. It is precisely a sense of historical belonging that is promised by the division of feminism into generations or waves. Not only does the generational or wave model work to organize and make sense of the past – position certain texts as belonging to historically situated concerns in feminism – it also ascribes a specificity to feminism now. Undeniably, there is an attraction to staking claims on a feminist present that is cohesive and different from the feminist past – not least of which is the community in and for the present that it purports to call into being. In the opening to this book, I reflected on an introductory module in feminist theory that I took as an undergraduate. I recalled the anxiety and confusion that this learning experience inspired in me – primarily because the way it engaged with an archive of feminist thinking refused to leave the past settled and thus refused my own desires to locate a coherent present in which I could claim a sense of feminist belonging. Yet, I now want to insist that belonging does not need to be contained by models of linear progress or loss or demarcated generations or waves. In other words, the alternative is not "merely asynchrony".

It is precisely from queer theory that I have attempted to draw on an archive of thinking which considers forms of belonging that do not depend on and actively resist the dictates of both linearity and calls to historicize. This is not to suggest that the feminist explorations of time that I have looked at in this book need queer theory to be read. Rather, it is queer insistences on recognizing this asynchronous timing as offering feelings of belonging that I want to finally draw on. In other words, what seems finally significant here about queer temporality theory is its commitment to exploring the ways in which a sense of community might be felt despite or in the face of the absence of models of generation, inheritance, or futurity. In other words, forms of belonging exist, as Elizabeth Freeman suggests, not only within dominant historical models but might also produce alternative ways of 'living in relation to the indeterminately past, present, and future others: that is, of living historically'.[6] It is this emphasis on the possibilities of other kinds of belonging in time for feminism that I want to end on. Robyn Wiegman suggests that due to feminism's own irreducibility to, yet inseparability from, situated subjects who act in its name, it is difficult 'being in time with feminism'.[7] Models of linear generational time seemingly alleviate the difficulties of being in time with feminism, despite and because of the complexities that they erase. Yet, it is the possibilities of belonging "out of time" that I want to end on. Undeniably, there is an attraction to being in time with feminism. It suggests a proximity, a closeness, and a belonging that is ostensibly denied by being out of time with feminism, but perhaps we might consider how being out of time offers other forms of belonging. I am particularly interested here in the possibilities of inhabiting the dissonances of feminism's time as collective experience.

If I began this book by considering the confusion of not being able to feel like I could get a handle on feminism's present as an undergraduate, could not with any finality position myself in feminism's time, I end by asking how precisely this feeling of loss might be the place to start building belonging. Indeed, it might be important to recognize these desires and also consider what is lost by acceding to the allure of overly simplified narratives of feminism in time. In 2011, I was part of an event at the Showroom Gallery in London, put on by Cinenova, a non-profit distributor of films and videos made by women. The exhibition was called 'Reproductive Labour' and involved a number of screenings and events which invited the public to explore Cinenova's archive. The particular event that I was a part of, 'The Dialectic of Sex: A Reproduction', aimed to transcribe Shulamith Firestone's *The Dialectic of Sex*. It involved a number of readers, myself included, who read *The Dialectic of Sex* aloud while one person attempted to transcribe the text, sitting at a computer whose screen image was projected onto a gallery wall.[8] Along with the aim of transcription, the readers were invited to interrupt the process with questions about the text, or comments on Firestone's ideas. As a durational piece interested in questions of both reproduction and labour, the text became experienced through a focus on time: how long it takes to read aloud, how long it takes to type what is read, and how long it takes to collectively come to terms with what is being read.

As transcribers, we failed miserably. We took on average about twenty minutes to get through two pages of Firestone's text. Needless to say, we came nowhere close in our four hours to transcribing the entire book. We were restless and the process was slow, so much slower than any of our individual reading habits. Rather than skip through or over words, passages, or ideas, we slowed down with them and questioned together Firestone's thoughts and language. We considered the labour of reading her in our present – the work we had to do to make sense of her words and the ways in which we did not have to work that hard. In some ways, we were attempting Carolyn Dinshaw's 'touches across time', exploring what it means to feel the past in the present.[9] Or, in Freeman's terms, perhaps we were seeking out a kind of 'temporal drag' by inhabiting Firestone's text as something that might open up the present to unforeseen future possibilities.[10] Yet, I would suggest that our experiences with the text were also somewhat less loving, less desirable, and the text was not always inviting. Perhaps, as Heather Love describes her archive of negativity, Firestone's text also 'resist[ed] our advances', in its language, its politics, and its desires.[11] Each of us, I believe, in different ways, felt pushed away by the text – the text seemed to push us away even as we attempted to erase our distance from it.

I think now that what was remarkable about this performance was the kind of belonging it produced. This experience of reading together and of reading slowly produced, for me, a belonging in feminism that did not require a complete identification with feminisms' past. Nor did it require that I turned away completely from this past to understand the present as that which is different from what has come before. In other words, to "belong" did not depend on historical identification or dis-identification with Firestone. Instead, belonging became a product of experiencing, discussing, and questioning time. The time of reading, the time of writing, the time of thinking, and the time of feminisms' pasts, presents, and futures. If waves and generations offer a sense of cohesion to feminism's time and enable one to position oneself in relation to this time, this reading offered community not through an acceptance of a shared time but through an exploration of what it felt like to read, to be estranged, and to both feel resistant to and touched by the text.

I still want to belong in and to feminism. The event at the Showroom Gallery allowed me to experience collectively a form of belonging that did not depend on approaching feminism in time as something that might already be known and settled. Instead, the belonging came precisely from the shared experience of dislocation in time, of uncertainty about the past, the present, or the future. It is this sentiment finally that I want to end on. Perhaps a form of belonging that does not presume the past is settled, the present is knowable and shared, or the future is predictable or wholly other, is what I have to offer, is what I hope might provide a counter to generational models of time.

Notes

1 Faith Wilding, *Waiting* (Los Angeles: Womanhouse, 1972).
2 Faith Wilding, 'Waiting: A Poem' (1972), available: <http://faithwilding.refugia.net/waiting.html> (accessed 20 October 2014).
3 Amelia Jones, 'Faith Wilding and the Enfleshing of Painting', *n.paradoxa* 10 (1999), 16–29 (p. 17).
4 Faith Wilding, *Wait With* (Los Angeles: Wack!, 2007; Berlin: re.act.feminism, 2008).
5 All quotes are from the 2008 Berlin performance which can be accessed online: 'Faith Wilding, Wait-With', re.act.feminism: A Performing Archive. <www.reactfeminism.org/nr1/artists/wilding.html> (accessed 20 October 2014).
6 Elizabeth Freeman, *Time Binds: Queer Temporalities, Queer Histories* (Durham, NC and London: Duke University Press, 2010), p. xxii.
7 Robyn Wiegman, 'On Being in Time with Feminism', *Modern Language Quarterly*, 65.1 (1999), 161–76 (p. 163).
8 The event, in its interest in reproduction and transcription, also involved a screening of *Shulie*, dir. by Elisabeth Subrin (Video Data Bank, 1997), and *S.C.U.M. Manifesto*, dir. by Carole Roussopoulos and Delphine Seyrig (1976).
9 Carolyn Dinshaw, *Getting Medieval: Sexualities and Communities, Pre- and Postmodern* (Durham, NC and London: Duke University Press, 1999), p. 50.
10 Freeman, *Time Binds*, p. 62.
11 Heather Love, *Feeling Backward: Loss and the Politics of Queer History* (Cambridge, MA and London: Harvard University Press, 2007), p. 8.

Bibliography

Adkins, Lisa, 'Passing on Feminism: From Consciousness to Reflexivity?', *European Journal of Women's Studies*, 11 (2004), 427–444

Ahmed, Sara, 'This Other and Other Others', *Economy and Society*, 31.4 (2002), 558–572

——, *The Cultural Politics of Emotion* (Edinburgh: Edinburgh University Press, 2004)

——, *Queer Phenomenology: Orientations, Objects, Others* (Durham, NC and London: Duke University Press, 2006)

——, 'Imaginary Prohibitions: Some Preliminary Remarks on the Founding Gestures of the "New Materialism"', *European Journal of Women's Studies*, 15.1 (2008), 23–39

——, *The Promise of Happiness* (Durham, NC and London: Duke University Press, 2010)

Andrew, Barbara, 'The Psychology of Tyranny: Wollstonecraft and Woolf on the Gendered Dimension of War', *Hypatia*, 9.2 (1994), 85–101

Ang, Ien, 'Feminist Desire and Female Pleasure: On Janice Radway's *Reading the Romance: Women, Patriarchy and Popular Literature*', *Camera Obscura*, 6.1_16 (1988), 179–190

Austin, J. L., *How to Do Things with Words*, ed. J. O. Urmson (New York: Oxford University Press, 1970)

Bailey, Cathryn, 'Making Waves and Drawing Lines: The Politics of Defining the Vicissitudes of Feminism', *Hypatia*, 12 (1997), 17–28

Barthes, Roland, *Camera Lucida: Reflections on Photography*, trans. Richard Howard (London: Vintage Books, 1980)

Bauer, Heike, 'Vital Lines Drawn from Books: Difficult Feelings in Alison Bechdel's *Fun Home* and *Are You My Mother?*', *Journal of Lesbian Studies*, 18.3 (2014), 266–281

Bechdel, Alison, *Fun Home: A Family Tragicomic* (London: Jonathan Cape, 2006)

Benhabib, Seyla, 'On Hegel, Women, and Irony', in *Feminist Interpretations of G.W.F. Hegel*, ed. Patricia J. Mills (University Park: Pennsylvania State University Press, 1996), pp. 25–43

Berger, John, *Ways of Seeing* (London: Penguin, 1972)

Berlant, Lauren, *The Female Complaint: The Unfinished Business of Sentimentality in American Culture* (Durham, NC: Duke University Press, 2008)

Bersani, Leo, *Homos* (Cambridge, MA: Harvard University Press, 1995)

Booker, M. Keith, 'Woman on the Edge of a Genre: The Feminist Dystopias of Marge Piercy', *Science-Fiction Studies*, 21.3 (1994), 337–350

Booth, Austin and Mary Flanagan, 'Introduction', in *Reload: Rethinking Women + Cyberculture*, ed. Mary Flanagan and Austin Booth (Cambridge, MA and London: MIT Press, 2002), pp. 25–41

Bouson, J. Brooks, '*Oryx and Crake* Introduction', in *Margaret Atwood: The Robber Bride, The Blind Assassin, Oryx and Crake*, ed. J. Brooks Bouson (London and New York: Continuum, 2010), pp. 125–128

Braidotti, Rosi, 'Learning from the Future', *Australian Feminist Studies*, 24.59 (2009), 3–9

Bredehoft, Thomas A., 'Comics Architecture, Multidimensionality, and Time: Chris Ware's *Jimmy Corrigan: The Smartest Kid on Earth*', *MFS: Modern Fiction Studies*, 52.4 (2006), 869–890

Brown, Wendy, 'The Impossibility of Women's Studies', *differences: A Journal of Feminist Cultural Studies*, 9.3 (1997), 79–101

——, *Politics Out of History* (Princeton: Princeton University Press, 2001)

——, 'Women's Studies Unbound: Revolution, Mourning, Politics', *parallax*, 9.2 (2003), 3–16

Bruhm, Steven and Natasha Hurley, 'Introduction', in *Curiouser: On the Queerness of Children*, ed. Steven Bruhm and Natasha Hurley (Minneapolis and London: University of Minnesota Press, 2004)

Burman, Erica and Jackie Stacey, 'Introduction: The Child and Childhood in Feminist Theory', *Feminist Theory*, 11.3 (2010), 227–240

Butler, Judith, *Gender Trouble* (New York and London: Routledge, 1990)

——, *Bodies That Matter: On the Discursive Limits of "Sex"* (New York and London: Routledge, 1993)

——, 'Critically Queer', *GLQ: A Journal of Lesbian and Gay Studies*, 1.1 (1993), 17–32

——, 'Against Proper Objects', *differences: A Journal of Feminist Cultural Studies*, 6.2–3 (1994), 1–26

——, *The Psychic Life of Power: Theories in Subjection* (Stanford, CA: Stanford University Press, 1997)

——, *Antigone's Claim: Kinship Between Life and Death* (New York: Columbia University Press, 2000)

——, *Precarious Life: The Powers of Mourning and Violence* (London and New York: Verso, 2004)

——, 'Sexual Politics, Torture, and Secular Time', *The British Journal of Sociology*, 59.1 (2008), 1–23

Callé, Sophie, *Take Care of Yourself* (London: Whitechapel Gallery, 2009)

Carter, Angela, *The Magic Toyshop* (London: Virago, 1981)

——, *The Passion of New Eve* (London: Virago, 1982)

Caserio, Robert L. and others, 'The Antisocial Thesis in Queer Theory', *PMLA*, 121.3 (2006), 819–828

Castañeda, Claudia, *Figurations: Child, Bodies, Worlds* (Durham, NC and London: Duke University Press, 2002)

Castle, Terry, *The Apparitional Lesbian: Female Homosexuality and Modern Culture* (New York: Columbia University Press, 1993)

Castro, Ginette, *American Feminism: A Contemporary History*, trans. Elizabeth Loverde-Bagwell (New York and London: New York University Press, 1990)

Chute, Hillary, 'An Interview with Alison Bechdel', *MFS: Modern Fiction Studies*, 52.4 (2006), 1004–1013

——, 'Gothic Revival', *The Village Voice*, 4 July 2006. <www.villagevoice.com/2006-07-04/books/gothic-revival/> (accessed 20 October 2014), 1–3

——, *Graphic Women: Life Narrative and Contemporary Comics* (New York: Columbia University Press, 2010)

——, *Hillary Chute Interviews Alison Bechdel* (Critical Inquiry Online Feature, 2011). <http://criticalinquiry.uchicago.edu/hillary_chute_interviews_alison_bechdel> (accessed 20 October 2014)

Chute, Hillary L. and Marianne DeKoven, 'Introduction: Graphic Narrative', *MFS: Modern Fiction Studies*, 52.4 (2006), 767–782

Cluitmans, Laurie, 'Lisa Oppenheim Reanimates the Past', *Metropolis M*, 5 (2010). <http://metropolism.com/magazine/2010-no5/> (accessed 20 October 2014)

Colebrook, Claire, 'Stratigraphic Time, Women's Time', *Australian Feminist Studies*, 24.59 (2009), 11–16

——, 'Toxic Feminism: Hope and Hopelessness after Feminism', *Journal for Cultural Research*, 14.4 (2010), 323–335

Coleman, Rebecca, '"Things That Stay": Feminist Theory, Duration and the Future', *Time & Society*, 17.1 (2008), 85–102

Coleman, Rebecca and Debra Ferreday, eds, Special Issue: Hope and Feminist Theory, *Journal for Cultural Research*, 14.4 (2010)

Colman, Felicity, 'Notes on the Feminist Manifesto: The Strategic Use of Hope', *Journal for Cultural Research*, 14.4 (2010), 375–392

Cramer, Patricia, '"Loving in the War Years": The War of Images in *The Years*', in *Virginia Woolf and War: Fiction, Reality and Myth*, ed. Mark Hussey (Syracuse, NY: Syracuse University Press, 1991), pp. 203–224

Cvetkovich, Ann, *An Archive of Feelings: Trauma, Sexuality and Public Cultures* (Durham, NC and London: Duke University Press, 2003)

——, 'Drawing the Archive in Alison Bechdel's *Fun Home*', *WSQ: Women's Studies Quarterly*, 36.1–2 (2008), 111–128

Davies, Ben and Jana Funke, eds, *Sex, Gender and Time in Fiction and Culture* (Basingstoke: Palgrave Macmillan, 2011)

Dawkins, Richard, *The Selfish Gene* (Oxford: Oxford University Press, 2006)de Oliveira, Rosiska Darcy, *In Praise of Difference: The Emergence of a Global Feminism* (New Brunswick, NJ: Rutgers University Press, 1991)

Deem, Melissa D., 'From Bobbitt to SCUM: Re-memberment, Scatological Rhetorics, and Feminist Strategies in the Contemporary United States', *Public Culture*, 8 (1996), 511–537

Derrida, Jacques, *Spectres of Marx*, trans. Peggy Kamuf (London and New York: Routledge, 1994)

——, *Archive Fever: A Freudian Impression*, trans. Eric Prenowitz (Chicago and London: University of Chicago Press, 1996)

Detloff, Madelyn, '"Tis Not My Nature to Join in Hating, But in Loving": Toward Survivable Public Mourning', in *Modernism and Mourning*, ed. Patricia Rae (Lewisburg, PA: Bucknell University Press, 2007), pp. 50–68

differences: A Journal of Feminist Cultural Studies, Special Issue: Women's Studies on the Edge, 9.3 (1997)

Dinshaw, Carolyn, *Getting Medieval: Sexualities and Communities, Pre- and Postmodern* (Durham, NC and London: Duke University Press, 1999)

——, 'Temporalities', in Paul Strohm (ed.), *Oxford Twenty-First-Century Approaches to Literature: Middle English* (Oxford: Oxford University Press, 2007), pp. 107–123

Dinshaw, Carolyn and others, 'Theorizing Queer Temporalities: A Roundtable Discussion', *GLQ: A Journal of Lesbian and Gay Studies*, 13.2–3 (2007), 177–195

Dittmer, Jason, 'Comic Book Visualities: A Methodological Manifesto on Geography, Montage and Narration', *Transactions of the Institute of British Geographers*, 35.2 (2010), 222–236

Driscoll, Catherine, *Girls: Feminine Adolescences in Popular Culture and Cultural Theory* (New York: Columbia University Press, 2002)

Duggan, Lisa, *The Twilight of Equality? Neoliberalism, Cultural Politics and the Attack on Democracy* (Boston: Beacon Press, 2003)

Echols, Alice, *Daring to Be Bad: Radical Feminism in America 1967–1975* (Minneapolis and London: University of Minnesota Press, 1989)

Edelman, Lee, *No Future: Queer Theory and the Death Drive* (Durham, NC and London: Duke University Press, 2004)

Elliott, Jane, 'The Currency of Feminist Theory', *PMLA*, 121.5 (2006), 1697–1703

——, *Popular Feminist Fiction as American Allegory: Representing National Time* (Basingstoke and New York: Palgrave Macmillan, 2008)

Elshtain, Jean Bethke, 'Antigone's Daughters Reconsidered: Continuing Reflections on Women, Politics, and Power', in *Life-World and Politics: Between Modernity and Postmodernity*, ed. Stephen K. White (Notre Dame, IN: University of Notre Dame Press, 1989), pp. 222–235

——, 'Antigone's Daughters', in *Feminism and Politics*, ed. Anne Phillips (Oxford: Oxford University Press, 1998), pp. 363–377

Epps, Brad and Jonathan Katz, eds, Special Issue: Monique Wittig: At the Crossroads of Criticism, *GLQ: A Journal of Lesbian and Gay Studies*, 13.4 (2007)

Evans, Sara, *Personal Politics: The Roots of Women's Liberation in the Civil Rights Movement and the New Left* (New York: Vintage Books, 1980)

Fahs, Breanne, 'Radical Refusals: On the Anarchist Politics of Women Choosing Asexuality', *Sexualities*, 13.4 (2010), 445–461

Feigenbaum, Anna, 'Remapping the Resonances of Riot Grrrl: Feminisms, Post-feminisms, and the "Processes" of Punk', in *Interrogating Postfeminism: Gender and the Politics of Popular Culture*, ed. Yvonne Tasker and Diane Negra (Durham, NC and London: Duke University Press, 2007), pp. 132–152

Ferguson, Margaret, Special Issue: Feminism in Time, *Modern Language Quarterly*, 65.1 (2004)

Fire, dir. by Deepa Mehta (Zeitgeist Films, 1996)

Fleming, Katie, 'Fascism on Stage: Jean Anouilh's *Antigone*', in *Laughing with Medusa: Classical Myth and Feminist Thought*, ed. Vanda Zajko and Miriam Leonard (Oxford: Oxford University Press, 2006), pp. 163–186

Freedman, Ariela, 'Drawing on Modernism in Alison Bechdel's *Fun Home*', *Journal of Modern Literature*, 32 (2009), 125–140

Freeman, Elizabeth, 'Packing History, Count(er)ing Generations', *New Literary History*, 31.4 (2000), 727–744

——, 'Time Binds, or, Erotohistoriography', *Social Text*, 23.3–4 (2005), 57–68

——, 'Introduction', *GLQ: A Journal of Lesbian and Gay Studies*, 13.2–3 (2007), 159–176

——, ed., Special Issue: Queer Temporalities, *GLQ: A Journal of Lesbian and Gay Studies*, 13.2–3 (2007)

——, 'Still After', *South Atlantic Quarterly*, 106.3 (2007), 495–500

——, *Time Binds: Queer Temporalities, Queer Histories* (Durham, NC and London: Duke University Press, 2010)

Freud, Sigmund, 'Mourning and Melancholia', in *The Standard Edition of the Complete Psychological Works of Sigmund Freud*, vol. XIV (1914–1916), trans. James Strachey (London: Hogarth Press, 1957), pp. 243–258

——, *The Ego and the Id*, in *The Standard Edition of the Complete Psychological Works of Sigmund Freud*, vol. XIX (1923–1925), trans. James Strachey (London: Hogarth Press, 1961), pp. 3–68

——, *On Sexuality: Three Essays on the Theory of Sexuality and Other Works*, ed. Angela Richards, trans. James Strachey (London: Penguin Books, 1977)

Gaither, Rowan, 'Andy Warhol's Feminist Nightmare', *New York Magazine*, 14 January 1991, p. 35

Gardner, Jared, 'Archives, Collectors, and the New Media Work of Comics', *MFS: Modern Fiction Studies*, 52.4 (2006), 787–806

Gearhart, Sally Miller, *The Wanderground: Stories of the Hill Women* (Watertown, MA: Persephone Press, 1979)

——, 'Future Visions: Today's Politics: Feminist Utopias in Review', in *Women in Search of Utopia*, ed. Ruby Rohrlich and Elaine Hoffman Baruch (New York: Schocken, 1984), pp. 296–310

Giffney, Noreen, Michelle M. Sauer, and Diane Watt, 'Introduction: The Lesbian Premodern', in *The Lesbian Premodern*, ed. Noreen Giffney, Michelle M. Sauer, and Diane Watt (Basingstoke and New York: Palgrave Macmillan, 2011), pp. 1–20

Gordon, Angus, 'Turning Back: Adolescence, Narrative, and Queer Theory', *GLQ: A Journal of Lesbian and Gay Studies*, 5.1 (1999), 1–24

Gordon, Avery F., *Ghostly Matters: Haunting and the Sociological Imagination* (Minneapolis and London: University of Minnesota Press, 1997)

Gottlieb, Joanne and Gayle Wald, 'Smells Like Teen Spirit: Riot Grrrls, Revolution and Women in Independent Rock', in *Microphone Fiends: Youth Music and Youth Culture*, ed. Andrew Ross and Tricia Rose (London: Routledge, 1994), pp. 250–274

Grewal, Inderpal and Caren Kaplan, eds, *Scattered Hegemonies: Postmodernity and Transnational Feminist Practices* (Minneapolis and London: University of Minnesota Press, 1994)

Grosz, Elizabeth, *Becomings: Explorations in Time, Memory, and Futures* (Ithaca, NY: Cornell University Press, 1999)

——, 'Feminist Futures?', *Tulsa Studies in Women's Literature*, 21.1 (2002), 13–20

——, *The Nick of Time: Politics, Evolution, and the Untimely* (Durham, NC: Duke University Press, 2004)

——, *Time Travels: Feminism, Nature, Power* (Durham, NC and London: Duke University Press, 2005)

Gubar, Susan, 'What Ails Feminist Criticism?', *Critical Inquiry*, 24.4 (1998), 878–902

——, 'Notations *in Media Res*', *Critical Inquiry*, 25.2 (1999), 380–396

Halberstam, Judith, 'Imagined Violence/Queer Violence: Representation, Rage, and Resistance', *Social Text*, 37 (1993), 187–201

——, *In a Queer Time and Place: Transgender Bodies, Subcultural Lives* (New York and London: New York University Press, 2005)

——, 'Keeping Time with Lesbians on Ecstasy', *Women and Music: A Journal of Gender and Culture*, 11 (2007), 51–58

——, *The Queer Art of Failure* (Durham, NC and London: Duke University Press, 2011)

Hall, Sarah, *The Carhullan Army* (London: Faber and Faber, 2007)

Halperin, David M., *Saint Foucault: Towards a Gay Hagiography* (Oxford: Oxford University Press, 1995)

Haran, Joan, '(Re)Productive Fictions: Reproduction, Embodiment and Feminist Science in Marge Piercy's Science Fiction', in *Science Fiction, Critical Frontiers*, ed. Karen Sayer and John Moore (Basingstoke: Macmillan, 2000), pp. 154–168

Haraway, Donna, 'Situated Knowledges: The Science Question in Feminism and the Privilege of Partial Perspective', *Feminist Studies*, 14.3 (1988), 575–599

Haritaworn, Jin, 'Loyal Repetitions of the Nation: Gay Assimilation and the "War on Terror"', *DarkMatter*, 3 (2008)

Haritaworn, Jin, Adi Kuntsman, and Silvia Posocco, eds, *Queer Necropolitics* (London: Routledge, 2014)

Harrison, Katherine, '"Sometimes the Meaning of the Text Is Unclear": Making Sense of the *SCUM Manifesto* in a Contemporary Swedish Context', *Journal of International Women's Studies*, 10.3 (2009), 33–47

Hegel, G. W. F., *The Phenomenology of Spirit*, trans. A. V. Miller (Oxford, Clarendon Press, 1977)

Heller, Dana, 'Shooting Solanas: Radical Feminist History and the Technology of Failure', *Feminist Studies*, 27 (2001), 167–189

Hemmings, Clare, *Why Stories Matter: The Political Grammar of Feminist Theory* (Durham, NC and London: Duke University Press, 2011)

Henry, Astrid, *Not My Mother's Sister: Generational Conflict and Third-Wave Feminism* (Bloomington: Indiana University Press, 2004)

Hesford, Victoria, 'Feminism and Its Ghosts: The Spectre of the Feminist-as-Lesbian', *Feminist Theory*, 6 (2005), 227–250

——, *Feeling Women's Liberation* (Durham, NC: Duke University Press, 2013)

Hesford, Victoria and Lisa Diedrich, eds, *Feminist Time Against Nation Time: Gender, Politics, and the Nation-State in an Age of Permanent War* (Lanham, MD and Plymouth: Lexington Books, 2008)

Hicks, Heather, 'Striking Cyborgs: Reworking the "Human" in Marge Piercy's *He, She and It*', in *Reload: Rethinking Women + Cyberculture*, ed. Mary Flanagan and Austin Booth (Cambridge, MA and London: MIT Press, 2002), pp. 85–106

Hirsch, Marianne, *Family Frames: Photography, Narrative, and Postmemory* (Cambridge, MA: Harvard University Press, 1997)

Hoffman Baruch, Elaine and Lucienne J. Serrano, eds, *Women Analyze Women: In France, England and the United States* (New York: New York University Press, 1988)

Hogeland, Lisa Marie, 'Against Generational Thinking', *Women's Studies in Communication*, 24.1 (2001), 107–121

Holland, Catharine A., 'After Antigone: Women, the Past, and the Future of Feminist Political Thought', *American Journal of Political Science*, 42.4 (1998), 1108–1132

Honig, Bonnie, *Antigone, Interrupted* (Cambridge: Cambridge University Press, 2013)

Hopkins, David and Tom Kurzanski, *Antigone* (Silent Devil, 2006)

Hutchings, Kimberly, *Hegel and Feminist Philosophy* (Oxford: Blackwell Publishing Ltd, 2003)

I Shot Andy Warhol, dir. by Mary Harron (BBC Arena, 1996)

Irigaray, Luce, 'When Our Lips Speak Together', trans. Carolyn Burke, *Signs*, 6.1 (1980), 69–79

——, *Speculum of the Other Woman*, trans. Gillian C. Gill (Ithaca, NY: Cornell University Press, 1985)

——, *Thinking the Difference: For a Peaceful Revolution*, trans. Karin Montin (London: Athlone Press, 1994)

Jacobs, Amber, *On Matricide: Myth, Psychoanalysis, and the Law of the Mother* (New York: Columbia University Press, 2007)

Jagose, Annamarie, *Inconsequence: Lesbian Representation and the Logic of Sexual Sequence* (Ithaca, NY and London: Cornell University Press, 2002)

——, 'Feminism's Queer Theory', *Feminism & Psychology*, 19 (2009), 157–174

Jameson, Fredric, 'Marx's Purloined Letter', in *Ghostly Demarcations: A Symposium on Jacques Derrida's Spectres of Marx*, ed. Michael Sprinkler (London and New York: Verso, 1995), pp. 26–67

——, *Archaeologies of the Future: The Desire Called Utopia and Other Science Fictions* (London and New York: Verso, 2005)

Jay, Martin, *Downcast Eyes: The Denigration of Vision in Twentieth-Century French Thought* (Berkeley: University of California Press, 1993)

Johnston, Jill, *Lesbian Nation: The Feminist Solution* (New York: Touchstone, 1973)

Jones, Amelia, 'Faith Wilding and the Enfleshing of Painting', *n.paradoxa*, 10 (1999), 16–29

Jones, Libby Falk, 'Gilman, Bradley, Piercy, and the Evolving Rhetoric of Feminist Utopias', in *Feminism, Utopia, and Narrative*, ed. Libby Falk Jones and Sarah Webster Goodwin (Knoxville: University of Tennessee Press, 1990), pp. 116–129

Joseph, Betty, 'Gendering Time in Globalization: The Belatedness of the Other Woman and Jamaica Kincaid's *Lucy*', *Tulsa Studies in Women's Literature*, 21.1 (2002), 67–83

Kearney, Mary Celeste, 'The Missing Links: Riot Grrrl – Feminism – Lesbian Culture', in *Sexing the Groove: Popular Music and Gender*, ed. Sheila Whiteley (New York and London: Routledge, 1997), pp. 207–229

King, Katie, 'The Situation of Lesbianism as Feminism's Magical Sign: Contests for Meaning and the U.S. Women's Movement, 1986–1972', *Communications*, 9 (1986), 65–91

Kristeva, Julia, 'Women's Time', *Signs: Journal of Women in Culture and Society*, 7.1 (1981), 13–35

Lacan, Jacques, 'The Essence of Tragedy: A Commentary on Sophocles' *Antigone*', in *The Ethics of Psychoanalysis 1959–1960*, vol. VII, ed. Jacques-Alain Miller, trans. Dennis Porter (London: Tavistock/Routledge, 1992), pp. 243–290.

Laderman, David, *Punk Slash! Musicals: Tracking Slip-Sync on Film* (Austin: University of Texas Press, 2010)

Ladies and Gentlemen: The Fabulous Stains, dir. by Lou Adler (Paramount Pictures, 1981)

Laird, Holly, ed., Special Issue: Feminism and Time, *Tulsa Studies in Women's Literature*, 21.1 (2002)

Lemberg, Jennifer, 'Closing the Gap in Alison Bechdel's Fun Home', *WSQ: Women's Studies Quarterly*, 36.1–2 (2008), 129–140

Leonard, Marion, '"Rebel Girl, You Are the Queen of My World": Feminism, "Subculture", and Grrrl Power', in *Sexing the Groove: Popular Music and Gender*, ed. Sheila Whiteley (New York and London: Routledge, 1997), pp. 230–255

——, *Gender in the Music Industry: Rock, Discourse, and Girl Power* (Aldershot: Ashgate: 2007)

Leonard, Miriam, 'Lacan, Irigaray, and Beyond: Antigones and the Politics of Psychoanalysis' in *Laughing with Medusa: Classical Myth and Feminist Thought*, ed. Vanda Zajko and Miriam Leonard (Oxford: Oxford University Press, 2006), pp. 121–140

Lévi-Strauss, Claude, *Myth and Meaning* (London: Routledge, 2001)

Lloyd, Moya, 'Butler, Antigone and the State', *Contemporary Political Theory*, 4 (2005), 451–468

Looser, Devoney and E. Ann Kaplan, eds, *Generations: Academic Feminists in Dialogue* (Minneapolis: University of Minnesota Press, 1997)

Lord, Catherine, 'Wonder Waif Meets Super Neuter', *October*, 132 (2010), 135–163

Lost and Delirious, dir. by Léa Pool (Greg Dummett Films, 2001)

Love, Heather, *Feeling Backward: Loss and the Politics of Queer History* (Cambridge, MA and London: Harvard University Press, 2007)Luciano, Dana, 'Nostalgia for an Age Yet to Come: *Velvet Goldmine*'s Queer Archive', in *Queer Times, Queer Becomings*, ed. E. L. McCallum and Mikko Tuhkanen (Albany, NY: SUNY Press, 2011) pp. 121–155

Lyon, Janet, *Manifestos: Provocations of the Modern* (Ithaca, NY and London: Cornell University Press, 1999)

Making of Ladies and Gentlemen: The Fabulous Stains, dir. by Sarah Jacobson. <www.youtube.com/watch?v=lNYR_XlwEx0> (accessed 20 October 2014)

Magarey, Susan, 'Dreams and Desires: Four 1970s Feminist Visions of Utopia', *Australian Feminist Studies*, 22.53 (2007), 325–341

Martin, Biddy, 'Sexualities Without Genders and Other Queer Utopias', *Diacritics*, 24.2–3 (1994), 104–121

Martinson, Anna M., 'Ecofeminist Perspectives on Technology in the Science Fiction of Marge Piercy', *Extrapolation*, 44.1 (2003), 50–68

McBean, Sam, 'Review Article: Queer Temporalities', *Feminist Theory*, 14.1 (2013), 123–128

——, 'What Stories Make Worlds, What Worlds Make Stories: Margaret Atwood's *Oryx and Crake*', in *The SAGE Handbook of Feminist Theory*, ed. Mary Evans and others (London: Sage Publications Ltd, 2014), pp. 149–162

McClintock, Anne, *Imperial Leather: Race, Gender, and Sexuality in the Colonial Contest* (New York and London: Routledge, 1995)

McCloud, Scott, *Understanding Comics: The Invisible Art* (New York: HarperPerennial, 1994)

McRobbie, Angela, *The Aftermath of Feminism: Gender, Culture and Social Change* (London: Sage Publications, 2009)

Meaney, Gerardine, *(Un)Like Subjects: Women, Theory, Fiction* (New York: Routledge, 1993)

Merck, Mandy, 'Mulvey's Manifesto', *Camera Obscura*, 22.3 (2007), 1–23

Mills, Patricia J., 'Hegel's Antigone', in *Feminist Interpretations of G. W. F. Hegel*, ed. Patricia J. Mills (University Park: Pennsylvania State University Press, 1996), pp. 59–88

Modleski, Tania, *Loving With a Vengeance: Mass-Produced Fantasies for Women* (Hamden, CT: Archon Books, 1982)

Mohanty, Chandra Talpade, *Feminism Without Borders: Decolonizing Theory, Practicing Solidarity* (Durham, NC and London: Duke University Press, 2003)

Moore, Suzanne, 'The Bag Lady of Feminism', *New Statesman*, 28 June 2004

Morgan, Robin, *Sisterhood Is Powerful: An Anthology of Writings from the Women's Liberation Movement* (New York: Random House, 1970)

Morris, Gary, 'Punk Girls on Film: Ladies and Gentlemen: The Fabulous Stains', *Bright Lights Film Journal*, 28 (2000). <www.brightlightsfilm.com/28/fabulousstains.php> (accessed 20 October 2014)

Moylan, Tom, *Demand the Impossible: Science Fiction and the Utopian Imagination* (New York: Methuen, 1986)

Mulvey, Laura, 'Visual Pleasure and Narrative Cinema', *Screen*, 16.3 (1975), 6–18

Muñoz, José Esteban, *Cruising Utopia: The Then and There of Queer Futurity* (New York and London: New York University Press, 2009)

Nealon, Christopher, *Foundlings: Lesbian and Gay Historical Emotion Before Stonewall* (Durham, NC: Duke University Press, 2002)

Ngai, Sianne, *Ugly Feelings* (Cambridge, MA: Harvard University Press, 2005)

Nguyen, Mimi Thi, 'Riot Grrrl, Race, and Revival', *Women & Performance: a journal of feminist theory*, 22.2–3 (2012), 173–196

Nussbaum, Martha, 'The Professor of Parody: The Hip Defeatism of Judith Butler', *The New Republic*, 22 February 1999, pp. 37–45

Oldfield, Sybil, 'Virginia Woolf and Antigone: Thinking Against the Current', *South Carolina Review*, 29 (1996), 45–57

Oppenheim, Lisa, *The Sun Is Always Setting Somewhere Else*, looped slide projection of fifteen slides, 35 mm Kodak Ektagraphic Slide Projector (2006). Online version available in *Art & Research: A Journal of Ideas, Contexts and Methods*, 1.2 (2007). <www.artandresearch.org.uk/v1n2/sunsets.html> (accessed 30 January 2012)

Pearl, Monica B., 'Graphic Language: Redrawing the Family (Romance) in Alison Bechdel's *Fun Home*', *Prose Studies*, 30.3 (2008), 286–304

Pearson, Carol, 'Women's Fantasies and Feminist Utopias', *Frontiers: A Journal of Women's Studies*, 2.3 (1977), 50–61

Pfaelzer, Jean, 'The Changing of the Avant Garde: The Feminist Utopia', *Science-Fiction Studies*, 15.3 (1988), 282–294

——, 'Response: What Happened to History?', in *Feminism, Utopia, and Narrative*, ed. Libby Falk Jones and Sarah Webster Goodwin (Knoxville: University of Tennessee Press, 1990), pp. 191–200.

Phelan, Peggy, *Mourning Sex: Performing Public Memories* (New York and London: Routledge, 1997)

Piercy, Marge, *Woman on the Edge of Time* (London: Women's Press, 1979)

Puar, Jasbir K., 'Queer Times, Queer Assemblages', *Social Text*, 23.3–4 (2005), 121–139

——, *Terrorist Assemblages: Homonationalism in Queer Times* (Durham, NC: Duke University Press, 2007)

Puchner, Martin, 'Manifesto = Theatre', *Theatre Journal*, 54.3 (2002), 449–465

Radway, Janice, *Reading the Romance: Women, Patriarchy and Popular Literature* (London: Verso, 1987)

RhinoMedia. <http://rhinomedia.com/store/ProductDetail.lasso?Number=511847> (accessed 7 June 2012)

Rhodes, Jacqueline, '"Substantive and Feminist Girlie Action": Women Online', *College Composition and Communication*, 54.1 (2002), 116–142

——, *Radical Feminism, Writing, and Critical Agency: From Manifesto to Modern* (Albany: State University of New York Press, 2005)

Riley, Denise, *'Am I That Name?': Feminism and the Category of 'Women' in History* (Basingstoke: Macmillan, 1988)

The Ring, dir. by Gore Verbinski (DreamWorks, 2003)

Riordan, Ellen, 'Commodified Agents and Empowered Girls: Consuming and Producing Feminism', *Journal of Communication Inquiry*, 25.3 (2001), 279–297

Robinson, Iain, "'You Just Know When the World Is About to Break Apart": Utopia, Dystopia and New Global Uncertainties in Sarah Hall's *The Carhullan Army*', in *Twenty-First Century Fiction: What Happens Now*, ed. Siân Adiseshiah and Rupert Hildyard (Basingstoke: Palgrave Macmillan, 2013), pp. 197–211

Rohy, Valerie, 'Ahistorical', *GLQ: A Journal of Lesbian and Gay Studies*, 12.1 (2006), 61–83

——, *Anachronism and Its Others: Sexuality, Race, Temporality* (Albany: State University of New York Press, 2009)

——, 'In the Queer Archive: *Fun Home*', *GLQ: A Journal of Lesbian and Gay Studies*, 16.3 (2010), 341–361

——, 'On Homosexual Reproduction', *differences: A Journal of Feminist Cultural Studies*, 25.1 (2012), 102–130

Ronell, Avital, 'The Deviant Payback: The Aims of Valerie Solanas', Introduction to *SCUM Manifesto* (London and New York: Verso, 2004), pp. 1–34

Roof, Judith, *Come As You Are: Sexuality and Narrative* (New York and Chichester: Columbia University Press, 1996)

——, 'Generational Difficulties; or, The Fear of a Barren History', in *Generations: Academic Feminists in Dialogue*, ed. Devoney Looser and E. Ann Kaplan (Minneapolis and London: University of Minnesota Press, 1997), pp. 69–87

——, 'Antagone: A Play in Three Acts', *CR: The New Centennial Review*, 2.1 (2002), 259–266

Rose, Jacqueline, *Sexuality in the Field of Vision* (London and New York, Verso, 1986)

——, 'Julia Kristeva – Take Two', in *Ethics, Politics, and Difference in Julia Kristeva's Writing*, ed. Kelly Oliver (New York: Routledge, 1993)

Rosenberg, Jessica and Gitana Garofalo, 'Riot Grrrl: Revolutions from Within', *Signs: Journal of Women in Culture and Society*, 23.3 (1998), 809–841

Rubin, Gayle, 'Thinking Sex: Notes for a Radical Theory of the Politics of Sexuality', in *Pleasure and Danger: Exploring Female Sexuality*, ed. Carole Vance (Boston: Routledge & Kegan Paul, 1984), pp. 267–319

Russ, Joanna, 'Recent Feminist Utopias', in *Future Females: A Critical Anthology*, ed. Marleen S. Barr (Bowling Green, OH: Bowling Green State University Popular Press, 1981), pp. 71–85

——, 'The New Misandry', *Radical Feminism: A Documentary Reader*, ed. Barbara A. Crow (New York and London: New York University Press, 2000), pp. 167–170

Sargisson, Lucy, *Contemporary Feminist Utopianism* (London and New York: Routledge, 1996)Schilt, Kristen, "'Riot Grrrl Is … ": The Constestation over Meaning', in *Music Scenes: Local, Translocal, and Virtual*, ed. Andy Bennett and Richard A. Peterson (Nashville, TN: Vanderbilt University Press, 2004), pp. 115–130

Scott, Joan W., 'Fantasy Echo: History and the Construction of Identity', *Critical Inquiry*, 27.2 (2001), 284–304

S.C.U.M. Manifesto, dir. by Carole Roussopoulos and Delphine Seyrig (1976)

Sedgwick, Eve, 'Queer Performativity: Henry James's *The Art of the Novel*', *GLQ: A Journal of Lesbian and Gay Studies*, 1.1 (1993), 1–16

——, *Tendencies* (Durham, NC and London: Duke University Press, 1993)

——, *Touching, Feeling: Affect, Pedagogy, Performativity* (Durham, NC and London: Duke University Press, 2003)

Segal, Lynne, 'Only Contradictions on Offer', *Women: A Cultural Review*, 11.1–2 (2000), 19–36

Shih, Shu-Mei, 'Towards an Ethics of Transnational Encounter, or "When" Does a "Chinese" Woman Become a "Feminist"?', *differences: A Journal of Feminist Cultural Studies*, 13.2 (2002), 90–126

Showalter, Elaine, 'The Snowman Cometh', *London Review of Books*, 24 July 2003

Shulie, dir. by Elisabeth Subrin (Video Data Bank, 1997)

Silva, Kumarini and Kaitlynn Mendes (eds), 'Commentary and Criticism: HBO's *Girls*', *Feminist Media Studies*, 13.2 (2013), pp. 355–374

Sjöholm, Cecilia, *The Antigone Complex: Ethics and the Invention of Feminine Desire* (Stanford, CA: Stanford University Press, 2004)

Söderbäck, Fanny, 'Introduction: Why Antigone Today', in *Feminist Readings of Antigone*, ed. Fanny Söderbäck (Albany: SUNY Press, 2010), pp. 1–14

Solanas, Valerie, 'Excerpts from the SCUM (Society for Cutting Up Men) Manifesto', in *Sisterhood Is Powerful: An Anthology of Writings from the Women's Liberation Movement*, ed. Robin Morgan (New York: Random House, 1970), pp. 514–519

——, 'SCUM (Society for Cutting Up Men) Manifesto', in *Radical Feminism: A Documentary Reader*, ed. Barbara A. Crow (New York and London: New York University Press, 2000), pp. 201–222

——, 'SCUM Manifesto (1967)', in *Public Women, Public Words: A Documentary History of American Feminism*, vol. 3, ed. Dawn Keetley and John Pettegrew (Madison, WI: Madison House, 2003), pp. 172–178

——, *SCUM Manifesto* (London and New York: Verso, 2004)

Sophocles, *The Oedipus Cycle*, trans. Dudley Fitts and Robert Fitzgerald (Harcourt Brace & Company, 2002)

Springer, Kimberly, 'Third Wave Black Feminism?', *Signs: Journal of Women in Culture and Society*, 27.4 (2002), 1059–1082

Steiner, George, *Antigones* (Somerset: Messrs. Cox, Sons & Co. Ltd., 1979)

——, *Antigones* (Oxford: Clarendon, 1984)

Stockton, Kathryn Bond, *The Queer Child, or Growing Sideways in the Twentieth Century* (Durham, NC and London: Duke University Press, 2009)

Swanson, Diana L., 'An Antigone Complex? Psychology and Politics in *The Years* and *Three Guineas*', in *Virginia Woolf Texts and Contexts*, ed. Beth Rigel Daugherty and Eileen Barrett (New York: Pace University Press, no date), pp. 35–39

Tasker, Yvonne and Diane Negra, *Interrogating Postfeminism: Gender and the Politics of Popular Culture* (Durham, NC: Duke University Press, 2007)

Teslenko, Tatiana, *Feminist Utopian Novels of the 1970s: Joanna Russ and Dorothy Bryant* (New York and London: Routledge, 2003)

Third, Amanda, '"Shooting from the Hip": Valerie Solanas, SCUM and the Apocalyptic Politics of Radical Feminism', *Hecate*, 32.2 (2006), 104–132

Tolan, Fiona, *Margaret Atwood: Feminism and Fiction* (Amsterdam and New York: Rodopi, 2007)

Tolmie, Jane, 'Modernism, Memory and Desire: Queer Cultural Production in Alison Bechdel's *Fun Home*', *Topia: Canadian Journal of Cultural Studies*, 22.77 (2009), 77–95

Trainor, Kim, '"What Her Soul Could Imagine": Envisioning Human Flourishing in Marge Piercy's *Woman on the Edge of Time*', *Contemporary Justice Review*, 8.1 (2005), 25–38

Traub, Valerie, 'The Present Future of Lesbian Historiography', in *A Companion to Lesbian, Gay, Bisexual, Transgender, and Queer Studies*, ed. George E. Haggerty and Molly McGarry (Oxford: Blackwell Publishing, Ltd, 2007), pp. 124–145

Tripp, Aili Mari, 'The Evolution of Transnational Feminisms: Consensus, Conflict, and New Dynamics', in *Global Feminism: Transnational Women's Activism, Organizing, and Human Rights*, ed. Myra Marx Ferree and Aili Mari Tripp (New York and London: New York University Press, 2006), pp. 51–75

van der Tuin, Iris, '"Jumping Generations": On Second- and Third-Wave Feminist Epistemology', *Australian Feminist Studies*, 24.59 (2009), 17–31

Wald, Gayle, 'Just a Girl? Rock Music, Feminism and the Cultural Constructions of Female Youth', *Signs*, 23.3 (1998), 585–610

Whitlock, Gillian, 'Autographics: The Seeing "I" of the Comics', *MFS: Modern Fiction Studies*, 52.4 (2006), 965–979

Wiegman, Robyn, 'What Ails Feminist Criticism? A Second Opinion', *Critical Inquiry*, 25.2 (1999), 107–136

——, 'Feminism, Institutionalism and the Idiom of Failure', *differences: A Journal of Feminist Cultural Studies*, 11.3 (1999/2000), 107–136

——, 'Feminism's Apocalyptic Futures', *National Women's Studies Association Journal*, 14.2 (2000), 805–825

——, 'Academic Feminism Against Itself,' *NWSA Journal*, 14.2 (2002), 18–37

——, *Women's Studies on Its Own: A Next Wave Reader in Institutional Change* (Durham, NC: Duke University Press, 2003)

——, 'On Being in Time with Feminism', *Modern Language Quarterly*, 65.1 (2004), 161–176

——, 'Interchanges: Heteronormativity and the Desire for Gender', *Feminist Theory*, 7.89 (2006), 89–103

——, 'Un-Remembering Monique Wittig', *GLQ: A Journal of Lesbian and Gay* Studies, 13.4 (2007), 505–518

——, 'The Intimacy of Critique: Ruminations on Feminism as a Living Thing', *Feminist Theory*, 11.1 (2010), 79–84

——, *Object Lessons* (Durham, NC and London: Duke University Press, 2012)

Wilding, Faith, *Waiting* (Los Angeles: Womanhouse, 1972)

——, 'Waiting: A Poem' (1972), available: <http://faithwilding.refugia.net/waiting.html> (accessed 20 October 2014)

——, *Wait With* (Los Angeles: Wack!, 2007; Berlin: re.act.feminism, 2008). Berlin performance available: 'Faith Wilding, Wait-With', Re.Act.Feminism: A Performing Archive. <www.reactfeminism.org/entry.php?l=lb&id=166&e=a> (accessed 20 October 2014)

Wittig, Monique, *Les Guérillères*, trans. David Le Vay (London: Women's Press, 1979)

Wolf, Douglas, 'Fun Home', *Salon*, 6 June 2006. <www.salon.com/2006/06/05/bechdel> (accessed 20 October 2014)

Woolf, Virginia, *A Room of One's Own and Three Guineas* (London: Vintage, 2001)

——, *The Years* (London: Vintage Books, 2004)

Zajko, Vanda and Miriam Leonard, 'Introduction', in *Laughing with Medusa: Classical Myth and Feminist Thought*, ed. Vanda Zajko and Miriam Leonard (Oxford: Oxford University Press, 2006), pp. 1–20

Index